Leadership in Social Care

RESEARCH HIGHLIGHTS **51**

Research Highlights in Social Work

This topical series examines areas of particular interest to those in social and community work and related fields. Each book draws together different aspects of the subject, highlighting relevant research and drawing out implications for policy and practice. The project is under the editorial direction of Professor Joyce Lishman, Head of the School of Applied Social Studies at the Robert Gordon University in Aberdeen, Scotland.

Other titles in this series

Substance Misuse
The Implications of Research, Policy and Practice
Edited by Joy Barlow
ISBN: 978 1 84310 696 8
Research Highlights in Social Work 53

Youth Offending and Youth Justice
Edited by Monica Barry and Fergus McNeill
ISBN: 978 1 84310 689 0
Research Highlights in Social Work 52

Public Services Inspection in the UK
Edited by Howard Davis and Steve Martin
ISBN: 978 1 84310 527 5
Research Highlights in Social Work 50

Co-Production and Personalisation in Social Care
Changing Relationships in the Provision of Social Care
Edited by Susan Hunter and Pete Ritchie
ISBN: 978 1 84310 558 9
Research Highlights in Social Work 49

Developments in Social Work with Offenders
Edited by Gill McIvor and Peter Raynor
ISBN: 978 1 84310 538 1
Research Highlights in Social Work 48

Residential Child Care
Prospects and Challenges
Edited by Andrew Kendrick
ISBN: 978 1 84310 526 8
Research Highlights in Social Work 47

Managing Sex Offender Risk
Edited by Hazel Kemshall and Gill McIvor
ISBN: 978 1 84310 197 0
Research Highlights in Social Work 46

Leadership in Social Care

Edited by
Zoë van Zwanenberg

RESEARCH HIGHLIGHTS **51**

Jessica Kingsley Publishers
London and Philadelphia

Robert Gordon University
School of Applied Social Studies
Faculty of Health and Social Care
Garthdee Road Aberdeen AB10 7QG

First published in 2010 by
Jessica Kingsley Publishers
116 Pentonville Road
London N1 9JB, UK
and
400 Market Street, Suite 400
Philadelphia, PA 19106, USA

www.jkp.com

Library of Congress Cataloging in Publication Data

Leadership in social care / edited by Zo? van Zwanenberg.
    p. cm. -- (Research highlights in social work ; 51)
  Includes bibliographical references and index.
  ISBN 978-1-84310-969-3 (pb : alk. paper) 1. Social work administration. 2. Social case work--Management. 3. Social service. 4. Leadership. I. Van Zwanenberg, Zoë.
  HV41.L354 2010
  361.3068'4--dc22
                                   2009017874

British Library Cataloguing in Publication Data
A CIP catalogue record for this book is available from the British Library

ISBN 978 1 84310 969 3

Printed and bound in Great Britain by
MPG Books Group, Cornwall

Contents

Part III Leadership Development

Figures and Tables

FIGURES

TABLES

Editor's Acknowledgements

I would like to thank all the contributors for their work and their patience as we have pulled this together. I would also like to thank Professor Joyce Lishman, of Robert Gordon University, and the Research Highlights group for their support in commissioning this work and seeing it through to its conclusion.

I would like to give particular thanks to Richard Bolden of Exeter University who undertook a major literature review which informed the development of the leadership model for *Changing Lives*.

I would also like to thank Ashleigh Dunn, who was then Head of Research and Development at the Scottish Leadership Foundation, for all her work in developing the model and approach.

I would also like to thank Linda Ann Smith, who has continued to work with the leadership model to develop the newly launched leadership framework for social services in Scotland.

My final thanks are to Stephen Jones and Melanie Wilson at Jessica Kingsley Publishers for their support, help and guidance throughout the process of editing this selection of work.

Preface

Zoë van Zwanenberg

I am really delighted to be able to bring you this selection of chapters on some of the new areas of research in the area of leadership for social work services.

Much of the work reflected in this selection has come from Scotland. This focus on one relatively small place might be seen to be limited, but the issues that are being addressed in Scotland are the same as those across the UK and beyond. These issues include tightening of resources set against greater public expectations, recognition of the need to work with the whole system and not just its separate parts and recognition that change and development are inherently leadership issues.

In the past few years we have seen a series of major reports in the UK on perceived service failures which have resulted in tragedy, from Victoria Climbié to Baby P, and in every case the issue of leadership has been raised. Service leaders at senior levels have felt constrained to resign in acknowledgement of their corporate responsibility for service issues and at service delivery level leaders and managers have faced inquiry teams, the press and their colleagues in both social work and other disciplines and have accepted the leadership responsibility for shortcomings in service delivery.

In all of this, the cry has been for more and better leadership but, without a deep understanding of what that leadership needs to be, how it is grounded, trained and supported and how in our multi-disciplinary and multi-organisational partnership world it needs to develop and grow, we are likely to continue as we always have and we know that is not good enough.

This selection of chapters includes the views of two senior social work practitioners. They come from very different angles, the one talking out of his deep experience of his own practice, using himself as his own research material, and the other using the disciplines of positive psychology to reflect on the experience of practitioners and the need to not just change our approach but to believe that such a change is both possible and will yield positive results.

The work that is reflected in the other contributions to the book comes from a wide range of academics and independent researchers. Part I is concerned with the growing focus on leadership of the social work profession, which is moving beyond the leadership of any organisation or part of an organisation to the wider issues of the profession as a whole. Within this section there is also some focus on the new work that looks at the leadership role of service users, carers and citizens and the impact that this will have on the leaders of the profession as they take person-centred care forward on the basis of a partnership with users and carers.

Part II develops the partnership thinking further and brings together some of the exciting new thinking about collaboratives and what the leadership role or roles look like in this context. This work also brings together some different approaches to the research itself and recognises that we may have to shift our views about research and evidence when we are working in these complex areas of collaboration, coalitions and place-based cooperatives.

Part III takes us into the critical area of leadership development. If we are to both develop and sustain leaders for these new and complex roles, and for this we mean leaders at every level of the organisation and in the community, then what is required from us to support learning and what can we learn from other related professional groups who are on the same journey?

I hope that you will find the contributions to this book stimulating and intriguing and that they will lead you to wish to know more and to do more yourself about developing, sustaining and researching leadership for the benefit of social care services and their users.

PART I
Leadership
of the Profession

CHAPTER 1

Leadership for 21st Century Social Work

Zoë van Zwanenberg

Introduction

The 21st Century Review of Social Work carried out in Scotland published its findings in the document *Changing Lives* in 2006 (Scottish Executive 2006). This document reflected the wide range of research and enquiry that the Review team had engaged in and highlighted the centrality of the concept of leadership to the future of not just the profession but of the successful development of services by all types of providers, whether professionally qualified or not.

One of the critical groups that input to and influenced the final shape of the report was the User and Carer Panel and it was their focus on the leadership role of users and carers that started to move the thinking about leadership beyond the role of the professional and strategic leader.

This shift in the understanding of where leadership sits, and the challenge this presents for traditional notions of power and control, is fundamental to the new shape of service design and delivery that is being advocated not just by the working groups charged with leading the implementation of the Review's recommendations, but by service providers who are actively engaged in redesign in partnership with users and carers.

Changing Lives

The *Changing Lives* review team devoted time to studying the current state of social work services and the social work profession, gaining an in-depth understanding of the challenges and opportunities facing them. In its final report the review team identified the core drivers of changes as:

- Doing more of the same, however well designed or ICT facilitated, is not sustainable.

- Social work does not operate in isolation and in focusing on change it must work in partnership with other agencies.

- The social work profession needs to develop and adapt its core skills and values to develop better and new ways of working to manage risk and outcomes for individuals.

- Social work needs to take on a leadership role, for the profession, for partnerships and for the development of services.

From these core drivers for change the review team outlined the critical areas of development that would need to be addressed:

- Development of services which have an outcome focus and whole systems approach, thereby developing the capacity for sustainable change, including:
  o commissioning
  o prevention
  o addressing national priorities
  o performance improvement framework
  o service redesign
  o governance.

- Development of the capacity and capability of the profession and the wider workforce through establishing shared approaches and understanding of:
  o leadership
  o role of the chief social work officer
  o role and impact of the Social Work Inspection Agency (SWIA)
  o development of professional practice
  o development of the range of roles

- o university and college engagement in research and development of practice

- o practice governance and performance accountability

- o development of an approach to continuous learning.

- Development of active and effective service user and carer engagement, which actively informs service design and delivery, leading to greater capacity to deliver:

  - o personalisation of services

  - o co-production of service design and delivery approaches

  - o effective citizen leadership

  - o user and carer involvement in research and development

  - o user and carer perspectives incorporated into inspection and review.

- Culture change that enables change to become a dynamic and continuous aspect of professional practice and service delivery, which would utilise these new approaches to:

  - o leadership

  - o risk

  - o governance

  - o partnership

  - o co-production

  - o personalisation.

These demands for dynamic and continuous change can be summarised as a cycle of interconnected concepts that inform the whole approach to the work undertaken by the working groups developing the detailed actions and activities that have resulted from the *Changing Lives* report (see Figure 1.1).

At the base of all this work, the report stressed that the core values of social work should remain unchanged, as they have a continuing value and validity that, whilst tested and stretched through the review process, have shown themselves to have enduring relevance. These core values are:

- respecting the right of the individual to self-determination

- promoting participation

- taking a whole person approach
- understanding each individual in the context of their family and community
- identifying and building on the strengths of the individual.

FIGURE 1.1: THE DEMAND CYCLE

Changing Lives work programme

The work programme that resulted from this review took as its core the need to:

- develop the capacity to deliver personalised services and
- develop a competent and confident workforce.

From these two fundamental requirements the work of the various work groups developed the critical constructs that inform and link the different 'products' which form the major part of the implementation process.

The underpinning constructs

At the base of all the 'products' of the working groups there are six core constructs, which are all informed by and based in the fundamental social work values outlined above. These constructs form the six essential elements that inform the 'products' from each of the work streams and together they ensure coherence between the work streams. These core constructs also form the basis for the dynamic culture that *Changing Lives* seeks to engender across all services and organisations.

These six core constructs are:

1. Personalisation

The fundamental tenets of this construct are that such an approach 'enables the individual alone, or in groups, to find the right solutions for them and to be a participant in the delivery of a service. From being a recipient of the services, citizens become actively involved in selecting and shaping the services they receive' (Service Development Group, Changing Lives 2008).

The principles that underpin this in relation to all individuals are:

- dignity
- privacy
- choice
- safety
- realising potential
- equality and diversity.

Personalisation: A Shared Understanding (Service Development Group, Changing Lives 2008) details this core construct and with its sister paper *Commissioning for Personalisation* (Service Development Group, Changing Lives 2009) looks to provide practical applications for this fundamental construct. The construct focuses on the service and the demand on the workforce to further develop its person centred approach.

2. Citizen leadership

The document on *Principles and Standards of Citizen Leadership* (Changing Lives Users and Carers Forum 2008) details the principles and standards of this core construct. They are fundamental to personalisation but go well beyond service design and delivery and advocacy to legitimise the leadership roles of every citizen for themselves and others in demanding:

- recognition of potential
- provision of opportunities for development
- early involvement in service design and delivery

- opportunity to be person centred in that every citizen should be enabled to show their leadership in the way that suits them best

- provision of information, that is clear and timely

- opportunity for equality and recognition that citizens can and will lead in challenging perceived inequalities

- greater citizen control through partnership working

- expectation that citizens will seek to lead for the benefit of others who use services.

This construct focuses on the role of the citizen and their need to take up an active leadership role and to have this supported and recognised. It is the other side of the personalisation coin, and is critical to the delivery of new service designs that are fit for purpose.

The articulation of this construct in a published document is a major development, giving real legitimacy to a shift in the power balance between service user and provider. It demands a different set of responses from organisational leaders and the development of an approach to parity of esteem which will have profound consequences for the training and professional development of staff.

The construct builds on some of the new notions of leadership such as adaptive leadership as described by Ron Heifetz (1994) whilst also referring back to concepts such as servant leadership (Greenleaf 1991). It pushes leadership away from being the prerogative of those in positional power within organisations, to being about a set of behaviours and responses that focus on issues and outcomes rather than resources and processes.

In terms of the Purpose, People, Process and Performance model the citizen leader has a key role in sharing purpose, being recognised as one of the key people, helping to design and share process and, critically, being a judge of performance.

3. Service improvement

The whole approach to service improvement as a core construct is encapsulated in the Performance Inspection Model developed by the Social Work Inspection Agency 2009. This model asks six fundamental questions:

- What key outcomes have we achieved for people who use our services?

- What impact have we had on people who use our services and other stakeholders?

- How good is our delivery of key processes?
- How good is our management?
- How good is our leadership?
- What is our capacity for improvement?

As a construct this approach to improvement requires evidence that includes 'hard' outputs and outcomes and 'soft' evidence of behaviours, attitudes and organisational culture being combined to provide a continuous and dynamic approach to achieving sustainable change. The construct does not create a fixed desired end state, but pushes towards a cycle of continuous positive improvement that challenges all service providers to be striving for ever better processes and outcomes. It is also a model that is based in notions of co-production rather than producer led and controlled.

By asking about leadership and management separately the model makes it clear that leadership is not just about control but is about partnership and the development of clarity of purpose.

As a construct this improvement model is fundamental to the whole culture of continued change and development that is the basis of the *Changing Lives* report.

4. Leadership – of the profession, of services and organisations and of individual practice

The construct of leadership that has been developed goes beyond the concept of the individual named as 'leader' in any organisation, and looks to the development of an inclusive concept of leadership that involves those individuals, their organisations and the whole profession of social work and social care services. The construct also works across organisational boundaries to actively support partnership working both with service users, carers and other service providers such as the National Health Service (NHS).

This construct of leadership was developed after a major research process including a fundament literature review conducted by Exeter University and an active enquiry process which engaged leaders and academics from across the UK and internationally. It was designed to reflect what good public service leadership should look like (Figure 1.2).

The construct takes the four challenges of Purpose, People, Process and Performance as its base and reconceptualises leadership as being about outcomes achieved rather than just the actions of individuals or groups that may lead to those outcomes. On this basis the construct is designed to embrace citizen leaders as co-authors of the leadership approach.

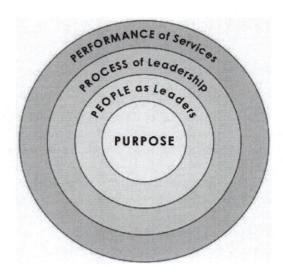

FIGURE 1.2: MODEL OF LEADERSHIP

The basis of this construct is that leadership, whilst founded in core values and behaviours, has to result in purposeful action that is directed at achieving defined and described outcomes that can be measured and judged. In this construction of leadership, individual actions or the development of organisational processes that are not linked to both defined ambitions (Purpose) and outcomes (Performance), and that are not part of a continuous cycle of development and improvement are not seen as relevant for either the development of the individual, the organisation or the profession. As a result leadership is seen as being bigger than the individual, even though the individual leader is central to its achievement in practice.

This notion of leadership links with the recent research on collaborative processes and moves away from the traditional 'heroic' models that have pervaded the populist literature on leadership for the last ten years. It develops a group of leadership practices that mirror the qualities desired in citizen leaders and builds towards the ambition for co-production as a service improvement model.

A description of what this means in very personal terms of leaders is given in Figure 1.3, which describes what a leader does on a day to day basis if they are fulfilling this particular vision of leadership.

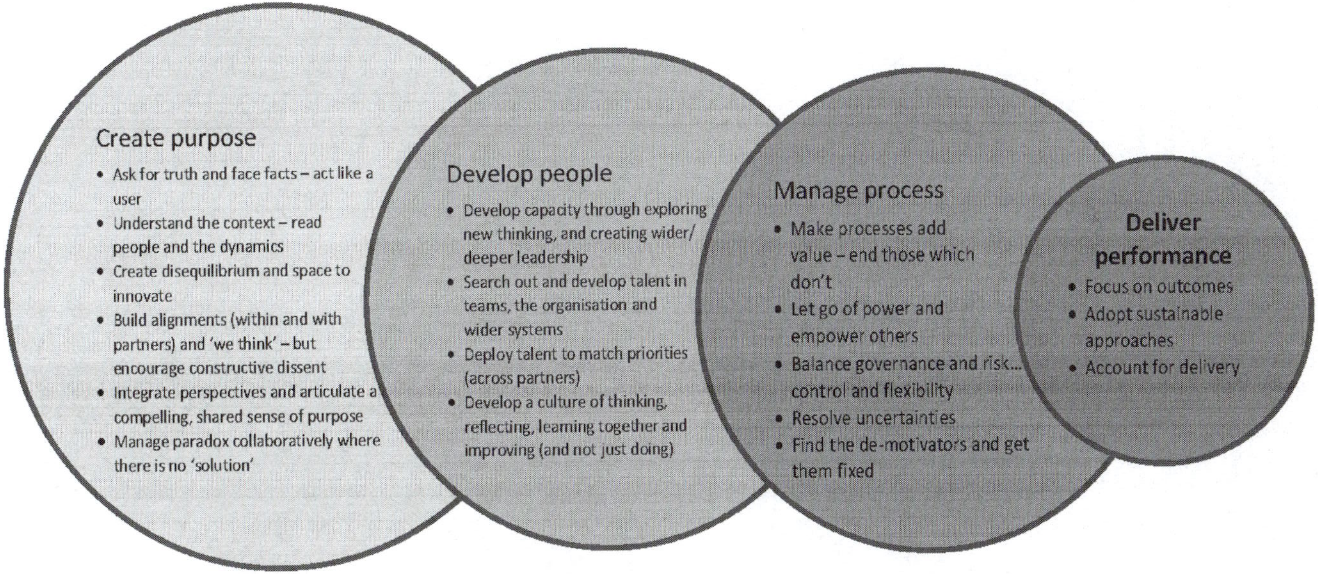

Create purpose

- Ask for truth and face facts – act like a user
- Understand the context – read people and the dynamics
- Create disequilibrium and space to innovate
- Build alignments (within and with partners) and 'we think' – but encourage constructive dissent
- Integrate perspectives and articulate a compelling, shared sense of purpose
- Manage paradox collaboratively where there is no 'solution'

Develop people

- Develop capacity through exploring new thinking, and creating wider/ deeper leadership
- Search out and develop talent in teams, the organisation and wider systems
- Deploy talent to match priorities (across partners)
- Develop a culture of thinking, reflecting, learning together and improving (and not just doing)

Manage process

- Make processes add value – end those which don't
- Let go of power and empower others
- Balance governance and risk... control and flexibility
- Resolve uncertainties
- Find the de-motivators and get them fixed

Deliver performance

- Focus on outcomes
- Adopt sustainable approaches
- Account for delivery

FIGURE 1.3: WHAT DO LEADERS DO?

5. Learning, research and development

Learning, as it appears in all of this work, encompasses more than formal learning and qualifications. It is constructed as fundamental to professional practice at all levels and in all work roles. Learning is also constructed as a continuous process, requiring all people working or engaging with social work services to seek to develop their ability to reflect on current practice, learn from both successes and mistakes and put that learning into practice.

The construct also applies to all working in the field of learning, both formally in terms of educational institutions and through management and supervision processes, and informally through development of reflective practice, curiosity and openness to challenge and review.

Learning as a construct is sister to the construct of improvement, and has embedded within it research and development. These are fundamental parts of learning, and in the way that the notion of learning has been constructed for *Changing Lives*, research and development are also fundamental to the development and continuous improvement of services.

As with leadership, learning, research and development are used in this body of work as core constructs in relation to individual practitioners and also to services and organisations.

6. Governance

Governance, as a core construct, goes beyond sound management in terms of financial and organisational propriety and moves into the area of professional practice and professional development. Good governance in this context brings together notions of corporate governance, professional governance and staff governance, thereby linking together issues of service and organisational design with the management and development of staff and the management of resources.

Good governance is seen to be a comprehensive approach to the planning, design, commissioning and provision of services and is also seen to be the responsibility of all staff and not just those in designated senior positions. This broadening of governance also extends to service users and carers who have a critical governance role in the challenge they bring as leaders and the demands they should make in respect of personalisation.

As a construct, governance incorporates issues of risk assessment and risk management alongside the challenge for continuous innovation and change that will ensure services and service design continue to develop as the needs of individuals change and develop and as research development and learning further inform and challenge current practice and the drive for improvement.

The qualities of citizen leaders

Much has been written about the qualities desired in leaders and one of the questions asked through this review process was whether these are really different for citizen leaders. The team that developed the construct arrived at five core qualities:

- Challenge the process.
- Inspire a shared vision.
- Enable others to act.
- Model the way.
- Encourage the spirit.

These feel very different from the qualities we so often see listed for organisational leaders but on reviewing the work of Robert K. Greenleaf (1991) we can see the thinking that lies behind these qualities.

The servant leader is servant first, as the citizen, service user or carer is, and the drive that leads to taking a leadership role is the drive to serve, to create something better for others and self. Greenleaf characterises the traditional institutional leader as driven by a will to be leader first, a drive that tends to be more about power and material reward than it is about service at its most fundamental level.

The model of leadership developed for *Changing Lives* is close to that of the servant leader, working out of the base of core social work values and an image of the ideal public servant. The personal qualities illustrated in Figure 1.4 could be matched against those described for the citizen leader, again leading to developing a sound base of partnership or collaborative working, where a matching of values can be critical for success, as described in Chapters 5 and 7 in this book.

This makes us really question motivations for leadership and it is interesting that less attention is paid to this issue of motivation at a fundamental level than is given to the manifestations of motivation in terms of behaviour, attitudes and belief. It will also become a major issue if we are to seriously advocate and support the development of citizen leaders without losing the qualities of 'servant leader' that the current document describes.

Future development

In terms of the development of future leaders, the question of how we set about the development of citizen leaders has largely been left open, though the

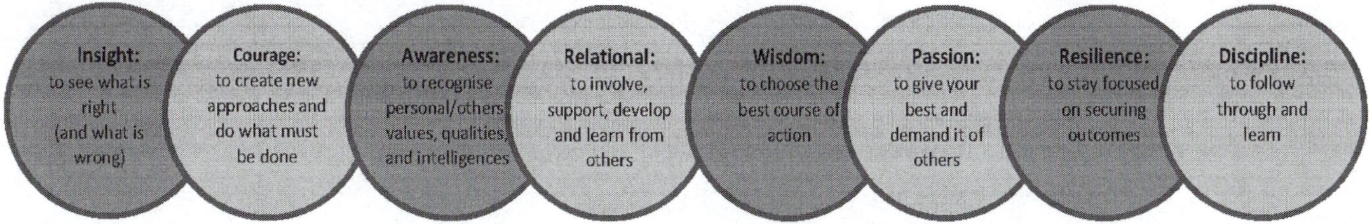

Insight: to see what is right (and what is wrong)

Courage: to create new approaches and do what must be done

Awareness: to recognise personal/others values, qualities, and intelligences

Relational: to involve, support, develop and learn from others

Wisdom: to choose the best course of action

Passion: to give your best and demand it of others

Resilience: to stay focused on securing outcomes

Discipline: to follow through and learn

FIGURE 1.4: QUALITIES OF LEADERS

examples given such as Citizen Advocacy, Community Care Forums and other collective advocacy groups do give models which can be developed further. A plea for training and development has been voiced, but as yet responses have been primarily localised and particular.

If we address the issue of empowering citizens effectively then the second key challenge becomes the development of leaders within social care services so that they are prepared to work in partnership with this growing group of articulate, highly motivated and engaged citizen leaders.

The requirement to work with constructive challenge, to develop skills of empathy and engagement and most critically to share power and control, whilst rooted in the core values of social work, will remain a challenge and require new forms of training and development.

The continuous learning framework also developed as part of this *Changing Lives* implementation process gives a robust way forward. As with the Purpose, People, Process and Performance model for leadership the learning framework is based in a combination of robust research and a return to core service values. There is a sense of the circle having turned and a new phase being entered. Prospective research on the impact of these changes in attitude to the image both of who the leaders are and of how they demonstrate that leadership will be essential if momentum is to build and sustain.

Conclusion

The research, discussion and consultation that made the process of both writing and responding to the 21st Century Review so rich, has also created expectations amongst social care staff, services users and carers. The descriptions of the core leadership roles of service providers and citizens have opened the opportunity for some very new ways of working. The next task for research will be to track the impact of this thinking on practice and to seek to establish whether or not these new models of leadership can really bring about the changes in service that the review identified as critical for the future.

References

Changing Lives Users and Carers Forum (2008) *Citizen Leadership, Principles and Standards of Citizen Leadership.* Available at www.scotland.gov.uk/Publications/2006/02/ 020944 08/0, accessed 5 May 2009.

Greenleaf, R.K. (1991) *The Servant as Leader.* Indianapolis: Robert K. Greenleaf Centre. Originally published 1970.

Heifetz, R. (1994) *Leadership with No Easy Answers.* Cambridge, MA: Harvard University Press.

Scottish Executive (2006) *Changing Lives: Report of the 21st Century Social Work Review.* Edinburgh: Scottish Executive.

Service Development Group, Changing Lives (2008) *Personalisation: A Shared Understanding.* Edinburgh: Scottish Government.

Service Development Group, Changing Lives (2009) *Commissioning for Personalisation: More of the Same Won't Do.* Edinburgh: Scottish Government. Available at www.scotland.gov.uk/ Resource/Doc/269193/0080033.pdf, accessed 6 May 2009.

Social Work Inspection Agency (2009) *Guide to support Self-Evaluation.* Edinburgh: Scottish Government.

Further Reading

Clark, F. and Dunn, J. (2006, 2008) *Continuous Learning Framework.* SSSC and IRISS.

Frick, D.M. and Spear, L.C. (eds) (1996) *On Becoming a Servant Leader.* San Francisco: Jossey-Bass.

Moore, M. (1995) *Creating Public Value.* Cambridge, MA: Harvard University Press.

Van Zwanenberg, Z. (2008) *Changing Lives Analytical Review. Report for Chairs of Change Programmes.*

CHAPTER 2

Practitioner Leadership: How Do We Realise the Potential Within?

Harry Stevenson

There will never be a paradise with people like angels

Walking and swinging through forests of music,

But let us have the decency of a society

That helps those who cannot help themselves

It can be done: it must be done: so do it.

'*Brothers and Keepers*'
Edwin Morgan
(Reprinted with the kind permission of ADSW)

Introduction

At the Association of Directors of Social Work (ADSW) Conference in May 2008, the former international athlete, Kriss Akabusi, spoke in the final session on the theme of leadership. In a motivational and uplifting presentation he highlighted his personal experience of an army sergeant who believed in him and encouraged his participation in athletics. He could have spoken about the fact he was looked after and accommodated as a child, he didn't, he spoke of the need to realise the 'potential' in all of us to achieve our best in our own 'arena'. In our case, in social work and social care in Scotland.

A few weeks earlier I attended an event at Castlemilk High School in Glasgow to highlight and promote the work of Columba 1400, a leadership development programme targeted at people 'who have weathered tough times'. Teaching staff and young people were proud to share their experiences of the programme, the benefit it has individually, within the school, and in the wider community of Castlemilk. (The school shortly thereafter received the best Her Majesty's Inspectors of Education (HMIE) inspection of any in Scotland.) While on holiday, I subsequently met with Norman Drummond, founder of Columba 1400 at Staffin, Isle of Skye, to learn more of the approach and its relevance to my work as the Executive Director of Social Work in South Lanarkshire. His inspirational approach is based on realising the potential of people to grow at a personal level. Through this, participants influence positively, in their school and in the wider community, by building confidence and resilience in young people and adults living and working in communities with challenges.

In recent staff seminars I have spotlighted the idea of realising the potential of people in the work undertaken by practitioners and managers with their teams. I have urged everyone to be aware of their responsibility to empower people who use services, and to continue to advocate for the rights of the people we support.

In theories on leadership, there is a view that good leaders have a number of particular characteristics, qualities and attributes in people based on physical, psychological and demographic variables, such as gender, ethnicity, intelligence or personality. Critics of this approach contest the idea that some people are superior or possess inherent leadership traits. Instead, they argue that emergent leaders are the product of other influences, such as the norms and culture of an organisation (Hafford-Letchfield *et al.* 2008). In this chapter I am suggesting that 'The characteristics of a leader might emerge as a result of an individual's opportunities, experiences and behaviour rather than from an inherent ability or natural flair' (Hafford-Letchfield *et al.* 2008, p.24).

Reflections on my experience of leadership

In reflecting on the development of this chapter I have thought about my own experience of leaders and leadership. I began by thinking about work, particularly social work, but realised this is only a part of my experience. As the eldest of seven children brought up in a loving, caring family, taking responsibility starts at an early stage. A lot of the contribution I made to family life would now be identified as caring duties. The baby of the family was born when I was 16; looking after the needs of my brothers and sisters, shopping and making up the coal fire were just the way it was and had to be. Understanding the family weekly budget was also a part of that. It never felt like a hardship or responsibility, it was what we all did as we grew up. It was something that was within me to do and to accept responsibility early in life was not a burden.

In moving on from school to the shipyards on the Lower Clyde as an apprentice electrician I met many talented, intelligent and, at times, frustrated colleagues: not managers, but journeymen who were seen as being good at the job, experts in their field technically, theoretically or because of their skill level. They were the mentors of apprentices, they 'showed you the ropes' and looked after you. I have many good memories of fellow apprentices and journeymen.

Experience of managers was different. The model of management was command and control. Seddon, in *Freedom from Command and Control* (2005), identifies these features. The model concentrates on a top down hierarchy; the focus is on outputs, targets and standards, on the measures; the ethos is control rather than learning, motivation is extrinsic rather than intrinsic to the organisation. The alternative to this is a model which involves people in decision making, is integrated with work rather than demanded; the view of outcomes is what matters; managing change is adaptive (Heifetz 1994).

I accept that in my role as a very young apprentice there were many things I did not understand. I remember a workplace in which the relationship between staff and managers was not build on respect, participation or a culture which promoted ownership and involvement. I did not appreciate the importance of my role in the huge logistical task of building a ship, partly because this was never explained. In spite of this, there was pride amongst the workforce about building ships, and if harnessed in the right way what an impact could have been made for the individual and for the ship building industry.

Industrial relations were also based on a model of command and control which made adapting to a new competitive environment challenging and which subsequently contributed to the decline of the industry. The approach by trade unions and managers to overcome issues such as demarcation disputes was confrontation, rather than trying to nurture more flexible and efficient approaches. In reality we believed the shipyards would be there forever and we therefore did not need to adopt the changes which would make the process more cost effective in the light of competition from the Far East and then the former Eastern bloc countries.

Within this environment I met a shop steward who encouraged me to take up a career in social care; I went into voluntary work and studied at night-school to attain the qualifications I required to become a social worker. Years later I worked with the son of the man and have wondered if this was his motivation, certainly he offered support which was unexpected and unusual.

As a second-year apprentice we argued because I was the only apprentice in the yard not to have joined a trade union. Older and wiser heads gave me my political and social education and helped me see the errors of my ways!

Working my way into social work as a trainee, qualifying as a social worker and then developing my career as a manager, I met a number of influential figures. Some were peers and others senior managers, each of the latter saw some potential in me and, by committing myself to the work and role, I was fortunate to be given opportunities to develop my skills, educational qualifications and to gain promotions as a manager.

In that time (33 years) the profession has changed and the reasons people enter it are more diverse. We have seen the establishment of a qualified workforce; the registration of staff; the introduction of a degree level qualification; an increase in public expectations; the expanded use of IT; the development of continuous professional development requirements and the further development of research and evidence informed practice. The legislative and policy changes are considerable and we have seen a greater emphasis and recognition on the importance of joint work with other agencies whilst at the same time seeking greater specialisation.

Practitioner leadership

Social work is fundamentally about change in people's lives. Consequently practitioners are required to demonstrate leadership behaviour, styles and approaches which enable, facilitate and support change; this is achieved within a strong value base centred on rights, responsibilities, inclusion, empowerment and equal opportunities.

This raises a question in my mind as I believe all practitioners have the potential to be leaders and yet we do not always see this. How then do we realise their leadership potential for the benefit of people who use social work services?

'Social workers' skills are highly valued and increasingly relevant to the changing needs of society. Yet we are far from making the best use of these skills' (Scottish Executive 2006, p.67). This is one of the conclusions of the Review of Social Work in Scotland, which also recognised a culture of blame had developed in response to systemic failures due to: heavy and inequitable caseloads; demand for services exceeding resources and the constant need to deal with crises affecting the ability to provide early intervention.

This report confirmed the Users and Carers Panel perspective that 'Leaders aren't all at the top. People throughout the organisation should be given the opportunity to lead. Leadership is about doing the right thing. A good leader sticks to their values and isn't knocked off course' (p.67).

The review identified the need for a framework for leadership and management to improve leadership and management across social work, consistent with the needs of all public sector staff. It also recognised the need to promote and develop professional leadership at all levels. It noted 'every frontline practitioner is a leader challenging and developing practice, and looking for opportunities to innovate' (p.66). The report also takes a broader view in relation to academic leadership, political leadership and strategic leadership but, in my view, it fails to make the point that leadership already exists and the following qualities of leadership stressed by the Users and Carers Panel do exist:

- Dedication – this is not just a job but an important job that can make a real difference to people's lives.

- Values – of fairness, equity and inclusion, providing person centred services and never forgetting why they are there.

- Integrity – the ability to keep to their values, even under challenge.

- Charisma – the ability to motivate others, to treat people as they would like to be treated themselves.

- Bravery – being prepared to challenge bad practice whatever it may be.

- Motivation – the ability to encourage others to do the right thing and not just accept the inadequate.

- Credibility – with the firm base of knowledge and experience.

(SSSC 2002)

Throughout my career and certainly in my current role, I hear of and see examples of this approach to leadership in the services we deliver and those delivered on our behalf by other service providers through contracts.

Case study 1

Cath is a social worker in an older people's team in a local office carrying out the task of assessment and care management. In 2006 she completed her Masters degree and her dissertation researched the attitudes of social work practitioners in her team towards local service provision for older people with alcohol problems, on the basis that there appears to be a need for age appropriate services.

I became aware of Cath's work when I attended a lunchtime research seminar where she presented her research findings to colleagues. The meeting was well attended, the presentation was clear and her enthusiasm and knowledge of the subject was striking.

Completing the research and gaining the qualification was not the end of her interest. Using her personal qualities, enthusiasm and networking skills she worked with others to implement the findings of the research into practice and set about improving services to the public.

By motivating others, she successfully applied for funding to address the issues she found in the action research by:

- arranging age-specific training for 150 staff across agencies – this has resulted in a demand for further training

- pursuing joint training for staff on early intervention

- developing staff by raising awareness of growing older and staying healthy. Funding is being sought to work with five groups of older people

- making presentations to strategic joint service management groups and the Community Health Partnership

- establishing a link with the Alcohol and Drug Action Team with a view to developing a Lanarkshire-wide approach to this issue.

Cath has also co-written an article for the *Social Work Practice Journal* on her research which will be published soon.

This case study demonstrates the leadership of an individual social worker prepared to use her skills in communication and networking to go beyond her role.

The Social Work Act 1968 (Scotland) prescribed that local authorities appoint a Director of Social Work to manage and lead departments within local authorities to delivery social work services. Even with the development of integrated service delivery arrangements, Partner Organisations and councils require to recognise the role of the Chief Social Work Officer.

The Scottish Social Services Council (SSSC) produced and monitors the codes of practice for social service workers. As the registration of staff has been introduced, they have been increasingly important for employers, employees and the public. They set out the standards of professional conduct and practice required. These codes confirm workers must:

- protect the rights and promote the interests of service users and carers

- strive to establish and maintain the trust and confidence of service users and carers
- respect the rights of service users whilst seeking to ensure that their behaviour does not harm themselves or other people
- uphold public trust and confidence in social services
- be accountable for the quality of their work and take responsibility for maintaining and improving their knowledge and skills.

(SSSC 2002)

Within the five areas covered by the codes, the level of professional standards is supported by specific guidance. There is a clear match between these and the expectation of the Users and Carers Panel previously described. Interestingly the codes do not refer to leadership specifically or reflect the growing importance of leadership and practitioner leadership in social care. When they are reviewed it will be important to reflect this more explicitly.

Practitioner leadership is not new. In fact, it underpins the core values of social work as much now as it always has.

Leadership potential

Taking responsibility and contributing to family life may have influenced my approach to leadership. I have also had opportunities throughout my adult working life to develop my qualities as a person, social worker and manager, because people believed in me. Which of these experiences has shaped my leadership style?

I would argue it is all of them, as we all have the potential but it needs to be nurtured. One of the definitions of the word 'potential' in the Collins English Dictionary is 'latent' and 'latent' is described as 'potential but not obvious or explicit'.

I believe leadership potential is within all of us and what we need to do is encourage more practitioner leadership, not because it doesn't already exist, but to recognise its existence and its importance for now and the future.

Case study 2

Salena is a social worker in a Child and Family Team working with families who have children with additional support needs. She undertook a postgraduate diploma in Autism at Strathclyde University to improve her understanding of an area of work in which she is very involved.

On completion of the dissertation Salena sent me a copy through the encouragement of our training manager. It is a well-written piece of research that considers the impact of ASD services; informs the reader on the role and remit of the service and informs future practice and service development to benefit children, their families and colleagues from other services. This is another good example of a social work practitioner taking their personal learning further to improve their knowledge and that of the wider organisation.

On receiving and reading the dissertation, I arranged to meet with Salena and was impressed by her professional approach and wider understanding of the needs of families and the implications for service providers. Any further study requires commitment and an acceptance that the learning process and its demands can have an impact on the lives of staff and their families.

In our discussion I asked how she thought the research might be taken forward. Immediately she responded that it would be helpful to translate the research into operational guidance for services. She recognised this would add value to the work she had already carried out and could make a difference to the knowledge and confidence of colleagues in supporting families.

I confirmed I would be delighted if she was prepared to take this forward with a plan for implementation. This work is at an early stage and the process will require collaboration with a range of Salena's colleagues.

This is a good example of a practitioner taking a professional interest, not for academic attainment, but for personal development. Importantly, there was recognition that research has a wider and more important role in improving services to the public and improving current practice within a whole social work service.

How do we realise potential?

In this chapter I have asserted the view and provided evidence that we all have potential as leaders, but the major challenge is how we realise that potential.

I believe there is a responsibility to realise this potential at a practitioner, management and organisational level in social and social care. A framework is under development in Scotland through the *Changing Lives* work stream group which offers all organisations the opportunity to develop the capacity to build their leadership potential. Government has already formally backed a number of leadership development programmes to 'pump prime' the awareness and importance of leadership in the social care sector. None of this will be enough unless we take the issue seriously and build the confidence, resilience and leadership capacity of the workforce. This will in turn build greater confidence with the public and politicians.

If we are to develop a more comprehensive approach to practitioner leadership, social work and social care needs a strategy to address a number of key areas including:

- developing the role of followers and good followership

- agreeing a framework set within the context of public services for leadership development

- considering the organisational approach to leadership and in this context transformational leadership has a lot of merit

- considering leadership as dispersed and not solely the domain of senior managers

- evolving from training to learning organisations

- creating cultures that support staff, take risks and celebrate success

- recognition of partnership work and collaboration in the delivery of services.

A framework to realise potential

I would suggest we begin to consider the leadership model for social care in Scotland and beyond as dispersed or distributed. This model would fit well in 'social care organisations where tasks and goals are shared and based on a common framework of values and where the members of the organisation work together to pool their experience' (Hafford-Letchfield *et al.* 2008, p.24). In the context of professional supervision, this model is described as 'leadership which concentrates on engaging expertise wherever it exists within organisations rather than seeking this only through formal position or role' (p.24).

Distributed leadership is therefore largely equated with teamwork and collaboration, it can, as Hafford-Letchfield *et al.* (2008) argue, contribute towards an ideal culture for learning which can shape the practitioner identity and therefore the organisational culture.

Over the past two years in my current role I have tried to create opportunities at an individual level and through listening seminars to engage staff in understanding the challenges we face and then engaging with them to find solutions. Feedback suggests staff feel more involved and can identify responses to the issues they raise.

The role of reflective practice in professional supervision lends itself in my view to greater emotional intelligence in social care organisations. The characteristics of good followers are the same as those of good leaders. We need to tap this commitment and realise the potential through a dispersed model of leadership in social care organisations. I would argue social care cannot be delivered without this. This approach is focused on people and as stated earlier in this chapter, is compatible with the values of social work. It 'has at its heart a focus on the individual, while being set in an organisational context' (Alimo-Metcalfe and Alban-Metcalfe 2005, pp. 15–16). This transformational leadership model proposed by Beverly Alimo-Metcalfe provides a clear structure for this approach. It is based on the following:

Leadership and developing others

- showing genuine concern
- enabling
- being accessible
- encouraging change

Personal qualities

- being honest and consistent
- acting with integrity
- being decisive, risk taking
- inspiring others
- resolving complex problems

Leading the organisation

- networking and achieving
- focusing on team effort
- building a shared vision
- supporting a developmental culture
- facilitating change sensitively.

In South Lanarkshire Council our leadership competencies cover the communication of our vision; strategic thinking; developing effective partnerships; strategic action and ethical maturity. Like other large organisations we have set out our expectations and these expectations encourage leaders at all levels in the organisation. I feel they have a particular resonance with the leadership approach I favour and are compatible with core social work values.

In implementing this approach there is a need to create a learning culture and the two examples of practitioner leadership highlighted in this chapter illustrate this. Evidence informed practice and identifying outcomes as measure of success push us in this direction – how then do we encourage a learning culture? My experience is that encouraging an enquiry approach in management and leadership is a model staff enjoy and engage with and it leads to a more participative and performance focused organisation.

Looking at the impact of our actions on individuals, families and staff I agree with Garvin *et al.* (2008, p.110) who state 'a learning organisation is a place where employees excel at creating, acquiring and transferring knowledge. There are team building blocks to such institutions (1) a supportive learning environment; (2) concrete learning processes and practices and (3) leadership behaviour that reinforces learning.'

One of the main advantages of a learning organisation is its agility to respond to change and social work needs to operate in an ever changing environment. The demands of the public, politicians and our own expectations set the agenda of improvement, greater effectiveness and value for money.

Within the social work service in South Lanarkshire, the development of this culture operates in a number of ways including professional training; continuing professional development; academic and evidence based learning; a research strategy; research seminars and practitioner research. In addition to this there is a corporate leadership programme as well as a programme for social work staff and more importantly, encouraging innovation, success and a customer focus embodies an approach to improving services to the public that is actively reinforced.

Conclusion

As stated previously, social work is fundamentally about change in people's lives and the values of social work are entirely compatible with the core competencies of practitioner leadership. In this context social work practitioners and managers are well placed to develop a strong leadership culture. However, it needs to be nurtured by managers and embraced by practitioners.

In this chapter I have attempted to reflect on my experience in life and work, from leaving school at the age of 16 as a young adult to my current position as Executive Director of Social Work in South Lanarkshire Council. Since I entered the social work profession we have increased the workforce of qualified staff. With this change the profession has to address the rising public expectations of services and a political environment which is shifting in Scotland. The regulation of the workforce has introduced standards and employers have clear responsibilities to encourage a learning environment which ensures continued professional development.

Practitioners have a responsibility to develop their own professional competence through learning. The approaches to learning are wide ranging, and have gone beyond traditional training approaches, for example action learning, mentoring and coaching. In addition there is greater emphasis on personal and professional development and the use of self in practice.

Working within an agreed framework I believe we can create a consistent approach across Scotland which develops a culture of learning to support positive leadership. Confident practitioners demonstrate this and we all have a responsibility to play our part.

But let us have the decency of a society

That helps those who cannot help themselves

It can be done; it must be done; so do it.

'Brothers and Keepers'
Edwin Morgan
(Reprinted with the kind permission of ADSW)

References

Alimo-Metcalfe, B. and Alban-Metcalfe, J. (2005) 'Leadership: Time for a new direction.' *Leadership 1*, 1, 51–71.

Garvin, D.A., Edmondson, A.C. and Gino, F. (2008) 'Is yours a learning organization?' *Harvard Business Review 86*, 3, 109–116.

Hafford-Letchfield, T., Leonard, K., Bagum, M.M. and Chick, M.F. (2008) *Leadership and Management in Social Care*. London: Sage.

Heifetz, R. (1994) *Leadership with No Easy Answers*. Cambridge, MA: Harvard University Press.

Scottish Executive (2006) *Changing Lives: Report of the 21st Century Social Work Review*. Edinburgh: Scottish Executive. Available at www.scotland.gov.uk/Publications/2006/02/02094408/0, accessed 5 May 2009.

Scottish Social Services Council (2002) *Codes of Practice for Social Service Workers and Employers*. Dundee: SSSC.

Seddon, J. (2005) *Freedom from Command and Control*. New York: Productivity Press.

CHAPTER 3

Supervision, Management and Leadership: Think Piece

Kate Skinner

What are we talking about?

The battle to bottom out the distinctions between these three aspects of public sector life – supervision, management and leadership – has neither been won nor lost, nor has it finally been abandoned. Rather it goes quiet for a while and then re-emerges. New terminology that refers to transactional leadership (exchanging rewards, criticism and sanctions for performance) and transformational or values-based leadership (Alimo-Metcalfe and Alban-Metcalfe 2006, p.293) more recently applied in the public sector does distinguish between management and leadership. Management is held to relate to productivity, efficiency and regulation, whereas leadership focuses on change and motivation. Lawler and Hearn (1995) propose that, in the public sector, the term management has largely been replaced by leadership. Other writers argue that management, while linked to organisational position, requires leadership as one of its component skills. So, management involves leadership but the opposite may not be true. It is certain that managers must be concerned with change and motivation and surely leaders must have an interest in productivity, efficiency and regulation, although not necessarily on a daily basis and to the same degree?

The role of staff supervision

Staff supervision is often described as the 'difference that makes the difference' between social services and other public services. Its roots lie in clinical supervision where staff and supervisor meet to discuss therapeutic work with individuals or families. It was seen as 'a means of developing and controlling the quality of service, taking account of the needs and rights of users and the quality of staff performance' (Hughes and Pengelly 1997, p.6).

Kadushin (1976) proposed three components of staff supervision: management, education and support. Management focuses on staff's account-ability to the organisation and is where the organisation exercises its account-ability to staff. The educational component refers to the organisation's respon-sibility to ensure that staff are developed in order to fulfil their role. The support function acknowledges that the work of social services staff is often unpredictable and difficult. It requires coaching skills, expertise, understand-ing of the environment and concern from a supervisor who models an ethical approach and high standards to encourage and motivate staff. Leadership enters the supervision framework through all three areas of Kadushin's approach. The model is old and has been updated (Kadushin 1992) and reframed by Hawkins and Shoet (1989) – as formative, restorative and normative – but its simplicity is useful in helping to analyse the process.

Research in other industries (see Burke 2001) highlights the role of staff supervision in quality control. In the large public accounting firm studied, su-pervision was used to reinforce the beliefs and values of managers, foster a climate of learning on the job and create a service culture. Findings from the study showed that staff with favourable views of their supervisors' competence reported more supports, fewer barriers, greater job satisfaction and more positive views of their service and product quality. Burke argued in support of earlier writers such as Kotter and Heskett (1992) and Schneider and Bowen (1995) that greater attention to the selection of supervisors to ensure that they bring into the organisation a service culture, a commitment to high quality service and strong supervision skills leads to more satisfied and committed staff.

Staff supervision is seen by some as either (or both) an outdated model or a 'sacred cow'. Its relevance to contemporary practice is questioned in an environment where less therapeutic work is undertaken by staff as care management has superceded direct work with individuals and families. However, there are many points in service delivery where a therapeutic approach by skilled and well-supported staff is needed and we should not forget this. Supervision needs to take account of this by being planned, regular and based on an agreement between staff member and supervisee where reflection, critical thinking and learning link the internal processes of feelings, vision and judgement to external activities such as empathy, intuition, evaluation and objectivity (Heron 1999).

An important factor is that of the supervision needs of supervisors and managers. Promoted staff still require Kadushin's three areas to be attended to, though all three elements do not necessarily need to be provided by one individual. Ollila (2008), in a research study on the role of management supervision, identified evaluation of working methods, crystallising issues, long-range planning, looking after policies, interpreting others' behaviour as aspects usefully covered in supervision between managers and their supervisors. Managers saw supervision as a tool to support their work, prevent burn-out, improve leadership and strengthen their welfare. There are managers in social services who see supervision as something needed only by front-line staff, yet it would be hard to argue that the functions listed by Ollila are unnecessary for managers.

Nearby and distant leaders

Shamir (1995 in Alimo-Metcalfe and Alban-Metcalfe 2006) talks of nearby and distant leaders. Shamir sees nearby leaders as needing to be dynamic, active, sociable; open and considerate; expert and intelligent; physically impressive; original and unconventional and to set high standards. These are positively influential people who impact on motivation, job satisfaction, self-confidence and sense of self-efficacy and development.

Distant leaders are believed to have rhetorical skills, an ideological orientation and a sense of mission; they are consistent in pursuing their vision and courageous in expressing opinions without fearing criticism. They lead from the front but may have less impact on staff and on day to day running of the service than nearby leaders. Much of the North American literature on leadership is based on these distant leaders, often described as charismatic, but there is evidence accumulating that suggests that people with these characteristics are often not good at the detail of organisational life and are easily bored, thus not giving any of Kadushin's three areas their attention and leaving staff unaccountable, unsupported and under-developed. They can also be downright destructive: Buchanan (2005) refers to these 'celebrity bosses' as 'dangerous destabilisers' as, through their interference and grandiose ideas, they frequently foster organisational chaos, low morale and staff burn-out.

What is leadership?

Bass (1990, p.19) defined leadership as 'an interaction between two or more members of a group that often involves a structuring or restructuring of the situation and the perceptions and expectations of members'. This definition gives room for an understanding of management, leadership and supervision which allows for leadership to be encompassed within both management and supervision, so that continuing to focus on leadership as an activity, as opposed to a role, seems entirely appropriate.

Inherent in this definition is that for leaders to lead, there have to be followers, and leaders can only be effective if their followers are prepared to be led. Andrews (1998), in an article on regrounding the concept of leadership, argues that transactional leadership is more appropriate in stable times and transformational leadership more useful in times of change. Andrews' research looked at the role of mental models in leadership behaviour and perceptions. He came to the conclusion that the models held by his research subjects were simpler than those described in much of the literature, and were more likely to be based on transactional leadership. This suggests that staff have a greater appreciation for the nearby leader, the person who supports them in getting work done, rather than more distant leader who may understand less what is required on a day to day basis.

Hamel and Breen (2007) propose that leadership is about multiplying human accomplishment in a world of growing uncertainty, rapid change and growing complexity. As these increase, leadership is created by the interaction of leaders and followers. Binney, Wilke and Williams (2005) argue for leaders leaving models behind and discovering what leadership is possible and needed at this time, with these people, in this organisation and in this environment.

What do leaders and managers do?

Managers and leaders aim to reduce anxieties – their own and others' – in a world of disorder and uncertainty. Everyone wants there to be someone, somewhere, in control. However if leadership is seen as a process that emerges between people, it fits with developments in neuro-science which show that, in our working lives, we exist entirely within a set of relationships and that these regulate our social and emotional behaviour. These relationships are governed by dynamic (emotions, trust, motivation, identity issues), social (group forming and norming), cognitive (perception, learning, knowledge gathering) and coordination/power-related psychological processes (Karp and Helgo 2008). Gardner (2004) uses cognitive research to develop frameworks for helping people to change their perspectives and their behaviour. These may be much more useful in helping to build relationships across the workplace to achieve commonly held goals about what the organisation is for and what its services are trying to do.

Management and its history

Previous managerial 'movements' have included Taylorism, or scientific management, with its authoritarian, rule-laden style. Taylor's ambition was to improve mass production after World War I, trying to find a way to maximise results on factory assembly lines. Parallels have been drawn with the move towards narrowly prescribed roles such as those in call centres and the shift towards a highly proceduralised approach which tends to reduce commitment and lower morale. Taylor emphasised the division between managers and staff by seeing them separately as thinkers and doers. This division could hardly be less suitable for a sector like social services where thinkers are needed in every corner of the organisation and thinking needs to be part of every organisational role.

According to Haynes (2003, p.60), Taylor assumed that public policy can be subjected to routine principles, where causes are linked to effects and can be managed by constant reorganisation, and if the perfect organisational structure were found, contradictions and tensions in working practices would be eradicated. We still seem to be searching for it through repeated reorganisation and, meanwhile, costly mistakes are made with disrupted and diluted services delivered.

The Human Relations movement brought a more participative approach based on a 1920s/1930s ethnographical and anthropological examination – the Hawthorn study – conducted by Mayo in a North American electrical production plant. The study looked at the behaviour of workers and, while challenges to its methods have been made since, its significance and influence have been enormous. Freedom for workers to make decisions about their work environment and work pace was shown by Mayo to trigger, via the informal social pattern of the work group, a huge increase in job satisfaction. Norms of high productivity and co-operation were established in the group, leading Mayo to conclude that the two critical sets of relationships were between group members and between workers and their supervisors.

The 1960s and 1970s brought the growth of technological innovation and global consumerism which created high demand for management science where traditional mechanistic approaches were combined with an understanding of human processes and workforce development. Many business schools were founded at this time, with their leaning towards systems theory which bridged between the complications of people, resources, organisations and the external world and saw organisations as complex entities needing leaders who can engage positively with change (Haynes 2003).

New public management (NPM), which emerged in the late 1970s, has become embedded in the public sector in general and in social services in particular. It emphasises intensification of work, measurement of performance and cost-effectiveness and is associated with performance management, greater surveillance and oversight through regulation and inspection (Pollitt and Bouckaert 2000). There is evidence that one of the unfortunate consequences of the application of these strategies in social services has been that staff are leaving their jobs because the work has become more about 'what can be measured rather than what matters' (Harlow 2004, p.172). Bureaucracy is cited as the reason so many people leave public services, as this conflicts with their desire to make a difference, their main reason for joining in the first place. Haynes (2003, p.83) argues that the public sector should never have allowed itself to move away from an emphasis on the high value of its people, and comments on the tensions introduced by government which claims to appreciate innovation and enterprise at the same time as increasing regulation and narrow performance definition.

The interactions of people make public services complex, and the sector has struggled to find a single model of leadership, while the penetration of the business schools into the sector through graduate and postgraduate leadership programmes has given a much higher profile to interpersonal skills, over and above specialist knowledge and skills. As Haynes points out, an autocratic style may be necessary in limited circumstances, but used in the wrong situation can close down creativity, causing resistance to change and unproductive behaviour, destroying learning and knowledge creation processes.

Lee and Lawrence suggest that:

> it is not sufficient to design jobs, work situations, hierarchies of authority and payment systems. People will interact in much more unpredictable and complex ways than in the formal system which may be designed in line with the classical concepts... This dichotomizing between what should happen – the formal system – and the additional complications due to informal behaviour, emphasizes the perspective of human relations as building on classical ideas rather than working against them. (Lee and Lawrence 1985, p.27)

Knowledge management has become central to the public sector and the task for leaders is how best to value and keep brain power and the creative abilities of staff inside the organisation. Intellectual capital is the life blood of modern post-industrial organisations, replacing the historical emphasis on plant, machinery or industrial production. The task for managers and leaders lies in how to bring this intellectual capital in, maximise its use and impact by valuing it and doing everything they can to develop and hold on to it.

Without people in organisations, despite buildings, technology and money, nothing would get done, so attention to providing social and psychological satisfaction for staff is critical to successful organisational outcomes. In social services this means better outcomes for service users.

The psychological contract and culture

This takes us to the psychological contract. This is the unwritten set of expectations that staff have of the organisation and the organisation has of its staff. It includes issues such as the staff member's commitment to the organisation, perhaps in terms of length of stay or preparedness to work late, and the organisation's commitment to personal development through learning opportunities or increased responsibilities. Mismatch between these expectations may lead to disappointment and frustration, possibly even conflict. Greater job satisfaction, and thus productivity and quality, are closely aligned to the psychological contract and its impact on commitment to staff as exercised through the processes of staff supervision, management and leadership. Neglect of these areas is likely to have a negative and potentially critical impact on both outputs and outcomes.

Berg and Barry (2008), in a study of social work middle managers in Sweden and England, suggest that in mediating between the two paradigms of social work and management, managers accept and support the professional opinions of their staff as they usually work out of sight of managers, within the usual parameters of policy and procedure. Fear of being overruled or of reprisals – negative defensive strategies – may lead to a blame culture and an avoidance of positive approaches to risk, which may in turn be harmful to service users.

Culture is critical to organisational success and the role of supervisors, managers and leaders in setting and maintaining the culture is crucial. Defining culture is not easy, but it is generally accepted to be:

> patterns of behaving, beliefs, ideas, values and knowledge embedded in practices, systems, artefacts and symbols. To belong to culture is to share, often unconsciously, the beliefs and values of that culture – a shared understanding and shared meanings... It refers to the atmosphere or climate within the organisation and to the values that influence the way people work and are managed. (Tyler 2004, p.199)

In addition to the formal way in which it is represented through its mission statement etc. culture will show itself in organisational rituals, the physical layout of the building and its contents. It is experienced or felt as much as seen but reflects what is held to be important in the organisation.

Supervisors, managers and leaders have a vital role to play in setting sustaining or changing organisational culture, one that that is often underestimated or overlooked when prioritising where they direct their effort. Schein (1997, p.5) proposes that: 'the only thing of real importance that leaders do is to create and manage culture and the unique talent of leaders is their ability to understand and work with culture'.

An unfortunate development in organisational culture in social services has revealed itself in recent years. In the last major re-organisation of Scottish local authority services in 1996 after the shift to a greater number of smaller local authorities in Scotland, jobs were re-combined to give flatter structures, with managers having a wider range of responsibilities. There is, in many places, a sense of managers being overwhelmed by their duties. Lateness is often the order of the day, whether it is that there is no expectation that meetings start on time with the full complement of people who should be there; preparation work is often late or not done at all and group members seeming to be at the beck and call of their mobile phones. Decisions disappear into the mire as a consequence of meetings being delayed or cancelled. Conferences expect to run with a high number of non-attenders, especially if they happen to be free of charge. The underlying assumption here is that everyone is extraordinarily busy with insufficient time to do all that they have undertaken and will not even have the time to call ahead and explain their absence or inability to complete their undertakings. Service users and carers now often articulate this on behalf of social services staff: 'well, they're very busy, you know'.

While there is no question that public services are stretched and resources insufficient we should question whether this is how we wish our services to be seen. If managers are exhibiting this kind of behaviour, it is almost inevitable that their staff will accept this as the norm and behave likewise. It is a well-known fact that we model our own behaviour on what we see others do, rather than what they tell us we should do (Skinner and Whyte 2005). 'Informal messages are the more powerful teaching and coaching mechanism' (Schein 1997, p.241).

Ways of being and seeing

Trotter (1999 and 2004) undertook research into improved outcomes for involuntary users of social services. Taking some very tough indicators (fewer offences, less serious offences, fewer injuries to children and less serious injuries to children) he examined factors linked to outcomes. He showed that it was a pro-social approach to service delivery that made the difference to service users: staff turning up on time, returning phone calls, doing what they said they would do, listening to users, working with problems that service users believed were important etc. Using a pro-social approach conveyed to service users that they were valued and respected and this had a significant impact on outcomes. It is not too difficult to see the potential for culture change in social services if supervisors, managers and leaders modelled the kind of behaviour that generates an atmosphere of recognising and valuing the staff who deliver services.

A useful approach to thinking about the role of supervisors, managers and leaders might be to think about an inverted triangle with the apex of the triangle at the bottom, with practitioners ranged along the top, while supervisors, managers and leaders are spread through the rest of the triangle. This nicely, in my view, conveys the notion that everyone else in the organisation is there to support the people who routinely deliver the service.

Practitioners

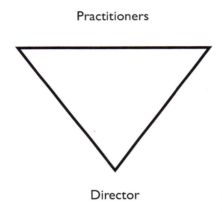

Director

FIGURE 3.1: HIERARCHY AS AN UPSIDE-DOWN PYRAMID

Learning organisations

Senge's (1990) work on learning organisations stimulated much interest in learning as a central aspect of culture. He saw learning organisations as continually expanding their capacity to create their future through adaptive learning – ensuring that organisations change in order to survive – and 'generative learning that enhances the capacity to create' (p.14). The need for public sector organisations to respond to increasing change and complexity requires a learning culture where different perspectives are seen as: 'energising debate and innovation. Making mistakes is seen as an opportunity for review and modification rather than looking for someone or something to blame' (Mullins 1996, p.128).

Mullins quotes Garrett (1994, p.128) as seeing the learning organisation as 'having positive and liberating consequences which include not only enabling organisational efficiency and effectiveness but significantly the generation of a "healthier and more cheerful organisation"'.

Now there's something worth striving for!

Distributed leadership

A chapter on supervision, management and leadership must have, somewhere, something about distributed or dispersed leadership. Decision-making, a significant aspect of leadership, is not an orderly, logical process. It is, according to Hughes and Wearing, messy, unpredictable and chaotic. They go on to remind us that:

> decisions are made on the back steps where the smokers gather...in cars driving to appointments...when people are stressed and when they are feeling anxious...and feeling so overwhelmed that they can't think through all the possible ramifications...when there is a lack of information about the nature of the problem. Sometimes the most important decisions are the ones that are not made, because it's just too difficult to face up to the real problems in the organisation. Thus it is possible to see decision making as a human, active and contingent process. (Hughes and Wearing 2007, p.78)

Dunoon (in Hughes and Wearing 2007, p.80) addresses these points by talking about recognising that leadership behaviours and practices are not solely the preserve of the formally designated leader and that effective leadership involves developing the capacity of others to take on leadership responsibilities. The opportunities for staff in human services who do not have formal responsibility for leading to demonstrate leadership abilities are considerable. Attempts by organisations to create all-encompassing procedures and protocols will never be wholly effective as it is not possible to create a template for action or decision-making in all circumstances, given that human situations are so varied. As a result social service staff often have to use their discretion and act autonomously. Over time, these experiences can be used to question policies and procedures and to argue for change – all aspects of leadership.

Gronn (2008) argues, from his work in education services, that distributed leadership is a notion 'whose time has come' (p.142) and is 'well entrenched into the linguistic furniture' (p.143). The phenomenon is not new, with writers from the 1950s (see Gibb 1954) discussing it. In the main it is part of small group processes, with individuals using certain personal qualities to influence their colleagues, dependent largely on group dynamics and processes. Gronn points out that distributed or dispersed leadership may be more accurately described as hybrid leadership, as usually it exists alongside more traditional hierarchical leadership.

Heifetz (1994) talks of 'leaders without authority' and sees them as 'providing the capacity within the system to see through the blind spots of the dominant viewpoint' (p.183) and cites Martin Luther King Jr. and Gandhi as people who, without formal authority, 'push us to clarify our values, face hard realities and seize new opportunities, however frightening the change may be'. He goes on to talk about leadership emerging 'from the foot of the table, but that is not where we spend our time looking' (p.184).

This kind of leadership may be about an individual expressing a point of view missing from the accepted argument or someone supporting others in a crisis. As progress requires new ideas and innovation to get to new ways of thinking and doing, attitude and behavioural change are necessary. While the formal leader needs to manage the holding environment, direct attention, gather and influence the flow of information, frame the terms of the debate, distribute responsibility, regulate conflict and distress and structure decision processes, the absence of authority permits latitude for creative deviance by 'gaining the fine grain of people's hopes, pains, values, habits and history' (Heifetz 1994, p.188).

The danger for people in this situation is that in raising difficult issues they may receive the opprobrium of group members as they attempt to 'kill the messenger'. Stimulating and maintaining the support of the group will be essential for informal leadership in adverse circumstances. In a more benign environment distributed leadership can be seen and experienced as increasing capacity and therefore as positive.

Leadership and partnership

A significant change in social services has been the series of strong imperatives for partnership and inter-disciplinary working. Inquiries into the operation of social services triggered by deaths of service users have often mentioned in their reports failures in working with others as contributory factors, and exhortations to do better at this aspect of work have followed. The complexity of working in this way has, though, often been overlooked. Haynes (2003) talks of permeable boundaries, mutual dependence and entanglement, where processes are iterative, evolving and dynamic, often unlikely to result in a single conclusion. Senior managers need a vision of direction and then to allow leadership and judgement to take over from the 'desire to monitor and control every detail' (p.42) as relationships and communication between staff become mission critical and 'disorder and tension create new opportunities for dealing with challenging social issues' (p.43). Huxham and Vangen (2005, p.202) draw attention to the potential for lack of clarity about who the partners are and real difficulty in specifying collaborative aims. Working alongside others is difficult and staff often need help in understanding why it is important and how best to do it. Huxham and Vangen refer to distributed leadership as useful in working across discipline and organisational boundaries and the need to take an inclusive approach.

The most likely path to success in collaborative working lies in the use of strong interpersonal skills. Goleman (1999) has spent much of his working life dispelling the myth that what really matters for successful work is intelligence, generally known as IQ. He argues that IQ is necessary but not sufficient and the missing ingredient is emotional intelligence (EQ). Goleman quotes a great number of research studies, two of which are Hunter *et al.* (1990) and McClelland (1994) and goes on to explain that simply being high in EQ does not guarantee a person will have learned the emotional competencies that matter for work.

The five elements of emotional intelligence are: self-awareness, motivation, self-regulation, empathy and adeptness in relationships and from these are derived 25 emotional competencies. Goleman explains that none of us have all 25, as the ingredients for outstanding performance are strengths in about six or so, spread across all five areas of emotional intelligence. The same competencies can contribute to excellence in different roles, but almost certainly senior positions may require the development of different competencies as people move through their careers. The Continuous Learning Framework developed jointly by the Scottish Social Services Council (SSSC) and Institute for Research and Innovation in Social Services (IRISS) (2009) calls on work on emotional and social intelligence by Goleman and others to show what the workforce need to be able to do to do their job well and describes what employers need to do to support them.

Skills for leadership

What seems inescapable is that EQ is closely linked to individual effectiveness and makes a substantial contribution to the workforce. The presence of these capabilities in supervisors, managers and leaders will enable them to become more effective in what they do to support, guide, motivate and lead their staff and staff's emotional intelligence will enable them to perform at their best, especially in areas such as collaborative working and distributed leadership.

Gardner in his book on 'how people learn, how they create, how they lead, how they change the minds of other persons or their own minds' (2006, p.1) describes five kinds of minds we should develop for the future. The first is the *disciplined* mind where expertise in a particular discipline is developed and sustained. Gardner's *creating* mind builds on the first two to pose questions, develop new ideas and so on. The *respectful* mind appreciates differences and works effectively with them. The *synthesising* mind makes sense of information and the *ethical* mind conceptualises connections between the work of individuals and the needs of society as a whole. He argues that these minds span both the cognitive spectrum and the human enterprise, and in referring to his earlier work on theories of multiple intelligences (1983), suggests that the five minds draw on the multiple intelligences. They can be cultivated 'at school, in the professions or in the workplace...[and this] constitutes a major challenge to all individuals who work with other persons' (pp.4–5).

Gardner's approach might have been written for those who work in the social services, talking as he does about maximising human potential, which neatly captures the essence of what social services, in all their various aspects, duties and responsibilities, were set up to do. *Changing Lives* (Scottish Executive 2006), having taken evidence from across the sector and beyond, argues for the reduction of administrative duties for front-line staff in favour of greater emphasis on the interpersonal aspects of the work. Gardner's five minds speak to this aspect of the work, and to all those in supervision, management and leadership roles who support service delivery.

Conclusion

This chapter explores the relationship between supervision, management and leadership within a social services environment. Perhaps distinctions between them are both artificial and immaterial in the final analysis. Much more important is that all in the workforce are equipped with the emotional competencies and the minds to work in the complex and turbulent social services environment to create a positive and dynamic culture with highly motivated and competent people to deliver services and to support service users.

References

Alimo-Metcalfe, B. and Alban-Metcalfe, J. (2006) 'More (good) leaders for the public sector.' *International Journal of Public Sector Management 19*, 4, 293–315.

Andrews, J.P. (1998) 'Regrounding the concept of leadership.' *Leadership and Organization Development Journal 19*, 3, 128–136.

Bass, B.M. (1990) *Bass and Stogdill's Handbook of Leadership.* 3rd edn. New York: Free Press.

Berg, E.B. and Barry, J.J.J. (2008) 'New public management and social work in Sweden and England.' *International Journal of Sociology and Social Policy 28*, 3/4, 114–128.

Binney, G., Wilke, G. and Williams, C. (2005) *Living Leadership: A Practical Guide for Ordinary Heroes.* Harlow: Pearson Education.

Buchanan, D.A. (2005) *Effective Organizations and Leadership Development.* London: NHS Leadership Centre.

Burke, R.J. (2001) 'Supervision and Service Quality.' *Measuring Business Excellence 5*, 4, 28–31.

Gardner, H. (1983) *Frames of Mind: The Theory of Multiple Intelligences.* New York: Basic Books.

Gardner, H. (2006) *Changing Minds: The Art and Science of Changing Our Own and Other People's Minds.* Boston, MA: Harvard Business School.

Garrett, B. (1994) *The Learning Organisation.* London: Harper Collins.

Gibb, C.A. (1954) 'Leadership.' in Lindzey, G. (ed.) *Handbook of Social Psychology.* Reading, MA: Addison Wesley.

Goleman, D. (1999) *Working with Emotional Intelligence.* London: Bloomsbury.

Gronn, P. (2008) 'The future of distributed leadership.' *Journal of Educational Administration 46*, 2, 141–158.

Hamel, G. and Breen, B. (2007) *The Future Management.* Boston, MA: Harvard Business School Press.

Harlow, E. (2004) 'Why don't women want to be social workers any more? New managerialism, postfeminism and the shortage of social workers in social service departments in England and Wales.' *European Journal of Social Work 7*, 2, 167–179.

Hawkins, P. and Shoet, R. (1989) *Supervision in the Helping Professions.* Milton Keynes: Open University Press.

Haynes, P. (2003) *Managing Complexity in the Public Services.* Maidenhead: OUP and McGraw-Hill.

Heifetz, R.A. (1994) *Leadership without Easy Answers.* Cambridge, MA: Belknap Press of Harvard University Press.

Heron, J. (1999) *The Complete Facilitator's Handbook.* London: Kogan Page.

Hughes, L. and Pengelly, P. (1997) *Staff Supervision in a Turbulent Environment.* London: Jessica Kingsley Publishers.

Hughes, M. and Wearing, M. (2007) *Organisation and Management in Social Work.* London: Sage.

Hunter, J.E., Schmidt, F.L. and Judiesch, M.K. (1990) 'Individual differences in output variability as a function of job complexity' *Journal of Applied Psychology 75*, 1, 1128–1137.

Huxham, C. and Vangen, S. (2005) *Managing to Collaborate.* Abingdon: Routledge.

Kadushin, A. (1976, 1992) *Supervision in Social Work.* New York: Columbia University Press.

Karp, T. and Helgo, T. (2008) 'The future of leadership: The art of leading people in a "post-managerial" environment.' *Foresight 10*, 2, 30–37.

Kotter, J.P. and Heskett, J.L. (1992) *Corporate Culture and Performance.* New York: Free Press.

Lawler, J. and Hearn, J. (1995) 'UK public sector organizations: The rise of managerialism and the impact of change on social services departments.' *International Journal of Public Sector Management 8*, 7–16.

Lee, R. and Lawrence, P. (1985) *Organizational Behaviour: Politics at Work.* London: Hutchinson.

McClelland, D.C. (1994) 'The knowledge-testing-educational complex strikes back.' *American Psychologist 49*, 66–69.

Mullins, L.J. (1996) *Management and Organisational Behaviour,* 4th edn. London: Pitman Publishing.

Ollila, S. (2008) 'Strategic support for managers by management supervision.' *Leadership in Health Services 21,* 1, 16–27.

Pollitt, C. and Bouckaert, G. (2000) *Public Management Reform: A Comparative Analysis.* Oxford: Oxford University Press.

Schein, E.H. (1997) *Organizational Culture and Leadership,* 2nd edn. San Francisco: Jossey-Bass.

Schneider, B. and Bowen, D.E. (1995) *Winning the Service Game.* San Franciso: Jossey-Bass.

Scottish Executive (2006) *Changing Lives: Report of the 21st Century Social Work Review.* Edinburgh: Scottish Executive.

Scottish Social Services Council and Institute for Research and Innovation (2009) *Continuous Learning Framework.* Dundee: SSSC and IRISS.

Senge, P. (1990) *The Fifth Discipline.* London: Century Business.

Skinner, K. and Whyte, B. (2005) 'Going beyond training: theory and practice in managing learning.' *Journal of Social Work Education 25,* 1, 367–383.

Trotter, C. (1999) *Working with Involuntary Clients.* London: Sage.

Trotter, C. (2004) *Helping Abused Children and Their Families.* Crows Nest, NSW: Allen and Unwin.

Tyler, S. (2004) *The Manager's Good Study Guide.* Milton Keynes: Open University.

CHAPTER 4

Leadership and Management: Not Losing Sight of Both

Anne Cullen

Summary

The context of this chapter is the challenge that is being issued to those responsible for the planning and delivery of services for children and families and adult social care to achieve transformational change. It begins by discussing some key reports, policy documents and legislation in order to try to elucidate this context and its implications in terms of leadership need. It goes on to consider some recent discussions and developments in relation to the social work role, and some leadership literature that identifies an apparent convergence between a particular direction in leadership theory and current discussions of social work. This leads to the rather paradoxical suggestion that social work might be regarded as a profession whose status is equivocal, and whose role is in question, but whose practitioners and managers may nevertheless operate from a perspective and use skills that are well attuned to the needs of the current agenda. Some suggestions are made as to the role of managers in providing a framework to support the realisation of the suggested potential of social work practice.

Introduction

Section 1 of this chapter reviews material that identifies key features of policy for children's services and adult social care and leadership needs associated with these. It discusses two highly influential British public reports: first, the report into the events leading up to the death of Victoria Climbié (Laming 2003), which identified systemic failures within and across agencies, including inadequate leadership at all levels of services for vulnerable children, and second, the report commissioned by the King's Fund into the funding of social care for older people (Wanless 2006), which focused on demographic and economic imperatives. It goes on to discuss how these different influences appear to have converged to shape policy, legislation and structural changes that focus on the achievement of closer integration of services, personalised provision and the development of individual, family and community capacity. It concludes by noting some explicit calls for leadership associated with this.

Section 2 looks at material relating to the position of social work as a profession. It begins by discussing a recent publication that proposes an account of the core role and tasks of social workers (General Social Care Council 2008), which suggests that social workers have characteristic skills and values that are highly relevant to the delivery of the current agenda for public services. This is followed by a consideration of material relating to the recent history and current context of social work practice, which highlights some particular issues relating to the identity and status of social work.

Section 3 discusses some suggested parallels between aspects of social work practice and the 'New New Paradigm' of transformational leadership, which reflects a direction in leadership theory towards an interest to direct, close by, rather than more distant charismatic leadership relationships.

Finally, Section 4 draws on material relating to distributed leadership and supervision in social work to suggest some elements of a framework for managers in supporting the delivery of leadership within social work practice.

Section 1: The current agenda for public services
Introduction

This section reviews some key reports, policy and legislation which set out the current agenda for aspects of public services that involve, or have implications for, social work, and which articulate an acute concern to secure leadership that is relevant to this agenda. The report of the Victoria Climbié Inquiry (Laming 2003) and the report *Securing Good Care for Older People* commissioned from Derek Wanless (Wanless 2006) by the King's Fund, are examined as seminal documents that identify the major drivers for services for children and families, and for adult social care services, respectively. Resulting policy and legislation is reviewed to identify the directions that are being set and their implications, especially expectations in relation to both social work and leadership.

The Reports

THE VICTORIA CLIMBIÉ REPORT

The inquiry that was conducted by Lord Herbert Laming (Laming 2003) was triggered by the death of one child, Victoria Climbié, but comprised a much wider review of the state of services for children and families throughout England. The ensuing report identifies a series of significant failings of practice and management within and between all the organisations that were, or in the view of the inquiry team should have been, involved in her care and protection. The report highlights multiple individual and system failures, in terms of both professional practice and operational management, including those of social workers and their immediate supervisors (see Laming 2003, pp.208–214, points 6.5–6.6). By far the most powerful and far reaching concerns, however, relate to what are regarded as severe and systematic failures of leadership and management at all levels, leading to what is considered to have been a collective failure of staff and elected members to take responsibility for ensuring the delivery of good quality support to children and families (e.g. Laming 2003, p.4, point 1.23).

The report concludes by providing far reaching recommendations designed to improve standards of practice and achieve greater integration of provision between universal and specialist services, across agencies and occupational groups, and to secure clearer lines of accountability. A key role is envisaged for local authorities in community development and combating social exclusion (Laming 2003, p.6, point 30; p.8, point 1.37; p.11, point 1.54).

THE WANLESS REPORT INTO FUNDING OF SOCIAL CARE FOR OLDER PEOPLE

Starting from a basis of very different concerns, the review commissioned by the King's Fund into the funding of care for older people (Wanless 2006) reaches a number of conclusions that are broadly congruent with those of the report of the Victoria Climbié Inquiry. The review examined social and health care policy, services and spending and analysed demographic, social and technological trends, in order to project need and costs over the ensuing 20-year period.

The resulting report highlights the economic and practical implications of a projected increase in the number of people in England aged 85 and over of more than two thirds, especially an anticipated rise in the number of people with impairment and disability, associated with heart disease, sensory loss, arthritis, dementia and depression. It draws attention to evidence that social care provided in the community can delay the need for more intensive and expensive services, such as nursing homes, and that improved joint working between health and social care services can reduce the rate of both hospital admissions and delayed discharges. This leads to a conclusion that there are likely to be both economic and social benefits in moving more resources into community-based social care services, but only if this is done on the basis of more effective integration of services and coordination of arrangements (Wanless 2006, p.xxiii–xxiv).

Policy and legislation

The majority of the recommendations of the report of the Victoria Climbié Inquiry have been taken up through a series of policy documents, guidance and legislation, beginning with the green paper *Every Child Matters* (Department for Education and Skills 2003), moving through the Children Act 2004 (HM Government 2004), to the recently published *The Children's Plan* (Department for Children, Schools and Families 2007).

Similarly, the considerations set out in the Wanless report clearly inform the green paper on social care, *Independence, Well-being and Choice* (Department of Health 2005) and the white paper *Our Health, Our Care, Our Say* (Department of Health 2006). This agenda has been further developed in subsequent guidance, including, for example, *Transforming Social Care* (Department of Health 2008a) and in the 'concordat' between central and local government *Putting People First: A Shared Vision and Commitment to the Transformation of Adult Social Care* (Department of Health 2008b)

Several key threads can be detected across these documents and are summarised below.

ENABLING AUTONOMY AND INDEPENDENCE

All the documents express an aspiration to move away from a culture where provision is driven by historical service structures to more flexible arrangements that focus on the needs, aspirations and capacities of the individual, family and community.

From the perspective of services for adults this is presented as involving 'a radical and sustained shift in the way in which services are delivered – ensuring that they are more personalised' (Department of Health 2006, pp.14–15), and from that of services for children and families the commitment is expressed: 'to put children at the heart of…policies, and…organise services around their needs' (Department for Education and Skills 2003, p.9, point 15).

INTEGRATION OF SERVICE DELIVERY SERVICES ACROSS LEVELS AND DISCIPLINES

In relation to both children's and adults' services there is a strong emphasis on local, integrated services, across an extensive continuum of need. Thus, for example, for children and families: 'early years settings, schools and colleges must sit at the heart of an effective system of prevention and early intervention working in partnership with parents and families...integrated with more specialist provision' (Department for Children, Schools and Families 2007, p.144, point 7.8).

In relation to adult care services local authorities are required to undertake: 'key strategic and leadership roles...with a range of partners including Primary Care Trusts and the independent and voluntary sectors, to provide services which are well planned and integrated, make the most effective use of available resources, and meet the needs of a diverse community' (Department of Health 2005, p.10).

This includes integrated delivery across health and social care, for example joint teams to support people with the most complex needs (Department of Health 2006, p.17, points 21–24).

The call for leadership

The need for value-driven, creative, dynamic and integrative leadership, to redress the perceived deficits in existing public services and to drive service transformation, is a strong theme throughout the documents.

The report of the Victoria Climbié Inquiry asserts that: 'What is needed are managers with a clear set of values about the role of public services, particularly in addressing the needs of vulnerable people, combined with the ability to "lead from the front"' (Laming 2003, p.5, point 1.28). *The Children's Plan* (DCSF 2007) calls for: 'strong, effective and supportive leadership and management at all levels in the system...[of]...inter-agency and multi-disciplinary teams' (Department for Children, Schools and Families 2007, p.52, point 7.37).

Finally, a report on the status of social care provided to the Department of Health by the Chair of the Commission for Social Care Inspection is prefaced with the statement that: 'the service lacks confidence...it is timid in its vision and ambition for...adult social care services...The services call for imagination, excitement and enthusiasm. This requires leadership across the sector and at all levels within it' (Platt 2007, covering letter).

Section 2: Social work

This section reviews some discussions about social work as a profession. It looks first at material relating to both the potential relevance of the skills, orientation and values of its protagonists to current aspirations for public services. It then moves on to a consideration of material relating to the context in which social work is practised, including organisational structure, management and the particular status of the profession.

The role and potential of social work

Following an extensive period of collaborative development, which engaged a range of representative organisations and service users, the General Social Care Council, as the registration and regulatory body for social work in England, recently published a document entitled *Social Work at Its Best: A Statement of Social Work Roles and Tasks for the 21st Century* (General Social Care Council 2008). This aim was to provide a current and authoritative account of the purpose and functions of social work in England.

One of the sources for this statement was an academic paper, *The Changing Roles and Tasks of Social Work* (Blewett, Lewis and Tunstill 2007), which reviewed professional and policy literature relating to social work over a period of approximately 25 years.

A striking feature of this paper is the authors' declaration of 'the impossibility of reaching one comprehensive, uncontested definition of social work' (Blewett *et al.* 2007, p.6). It is equally notable, however, that this finding is construed in positive terms, as evidence of 'social work's capacity for adaptability and responsiveness' (p.6) and indeed as testimony to the particular vitality and relevance of the profession: 'In contrast to other professional groups social work has always sought to adapt to the social and individual needs of a rapidly changing demographic, economic and social structure' (p.6).

A similar position is taken by Payne in his book, *What is Professional Social Work?* (2006). Arguing from an explicitly social constructionist perspective, Payne expresses the view that social work can most helpfully be understood as an evolving tradition that is characteristically both situated and personalised 'social work emerges from a particular place's history and social environment… As [individual social workers] embody their enactment or performance of the culture of their locality…they change social work by interpenetrating social work and the local' (p.189).

From this perspective *Social Work at Its Best* should perhaps be understood as an attempt to extract from the variety of accounts of theory and practice

available, a summary account of the credentials of social work, in its contemporary incarnation, in relation to the current agenda for public services.

The statement suggests that these credentials are substantial – that social
work provides an orientation, distinctive values and specialised skills that are
closely attuned to the requirements of this agenda. In terms of orientation, the
statement suggests that social work 'looks at people's lives and circumstances in
the round, and works with them to personalise social care responses to fit their
own individual circumstances' (General Social Care Council 2008, p.1, point
2). From a value perspective, it is suggested that social work, 'embodies a set of
core values and principles...is committed to the rights of the child; respects
equality, worth and human rights of people' (p.1, point 4, emphasis original).

In relation to the agenda of partnership working and local service delivery
it is suggested that 'social work is increasingly making its distinctive contribution in inter-disciplinary teams and multi-agency settings. It is good at building
bridges with other disciplines and agencies, and helping overcome some of the
barriers and gaps between different professions' (p.5, point 10).

Finally, social workers are identified as an important source of expertise in
the delivery of personalised services, and the proactive management of situations requiring sensitive balancing of the respective capacities, rights and vul-
nerabilities of individuals, families and communities: 'Social work applies
expert knowledge and skills to analyse complex individual, family and social
situations where there is a need to assess high levels of risk and uncertainty...to make judgements...and to take action' (p.11, point 26).

Alongside these optimistic assertions of the potential for social workers to
make an important contribution to the delivery of the current agenda that has
been identified for public services, however, it seems important to consider
some potential challenges and inhibitions associated with the organisational
setting and occupational identity of social work.

The fragmentation of social work

Payne (2006) draws attention to the significance of recent legislation, the
Health Act (HM Government 1999), Health and Social Care Act (HM Government 2001) and the Children Act 2004 (HM Government 2004) in conferring
powers and responsibilities on the National Health Service (NHS) and local
government that encourage new forms of partnership and collaboration but at
the same time contribute to an increasingly fragmented delivery of social
work. He notes, for example, trends towards the co-location of social work
services for children and families with education services, and for social
workers specialising in areas of medical social work to be employed by and

based within health-led facilities. An additional source of fragmentation is detected in the increasingly significant role that is played by both voluntary and private sector organisations within an increasingly mixed economy of social care provision.

Such changes are clearly in keeping with the directions of policy outlined earlier in this article. However, as Payne observes, they can be seen as reinforcing the movement away from the model of integrated social work delivery that was recommended by the Seebohm committee (Seebohm 1968), and which informed the development of local authority social services departments in 1971. As a result, such developments can be seen as contributing to the effective demise of the institution that was uniquely identified with social work as a profession and in which it had been, at least originally, 'the dominant occupational voice' (Lymbery 2001, p.371, summarising Hill 1993).

The status of social work

A further potential source of insecurity relating to the identity and status of social work is suggested by Lymbery's article *Social Work at the Crossroads* (2001). Drawing on the work of Parry and Parry (1979), Lymbery observes that, unlike more powerful and established professions such as law and medicine, social work operates within the parameters of a '"bureau-professional" compact' (p.377) in which authority is conferred and the remit of activity defined primarily by the state; without the potential balancing influence of a formally empowered professional representative body.

Lymbery illustrates the practical significance of this status in his discussion of the impact of 'managerialism'. Clarke and Newman (1997) have characterised managerialism as being driven by a concern, originating in the politics of the 'New Right', to adopt principles developed primarily from, and for the benefit of, private sector organisations, by authors such as Peters and Waterman (1982), and to apply them within public sector organisations, as a means of remedying the perceived inefficiencies of this sector. They suggest that one of the characteristic features of the managerialist agenda was to reshape public institutions: 'around a command structure which privileges the calculative framework of...how to improve efficiency and organisational performance' (Clarke and Newman 1997, p.76).

Pollitt identifies the priority placed within this framework on the manager's 'right to manage' (Pollitt 1993, p.3), and Lymbery suggests that this resulted in 'the management task' becoming identified as being: 'essentially different from and superior to the professional one' (2001, p.375). In the case of social work he suggests that this resulted in a significant 'shift of power from social work practitioners to a managerial elite' (pp.377–378). He goes on to detail the impact of this, including a progressive diminution in the status and level of involvement of senior professionals in line management, a devaluing of professional supervision, and a progressive reduction in the scope of the social work practice, associated with an increasing focus on gatekeeping of resources. Lymbery suggests that these factors contributed significantly to an impoverishment of practice and to a widespread demoralisation within the social work profession, amounting to a 'condition of crisis' (p.369).

It may be reasonably suggested that other material reviewed here could be interpreted as evidence of the declining influence of managerialism and the emergence of a potentially more supportive environment for social work. However, the issues raised by Payne and Lymbery appear to be potentially important in highlighting, first, the relatively unsettled position of social work currently and, second, the potentially limited capacity of its protagonists, individually and collectively, to influence the scope and nature of its remit.

The force of these comments would appear to be emphasised by the fact that at government level responsibility for social work in England is now split between two different departments – the Department for Children, Schools and Families and the Department of Health. The significance of this is illustrated by the statement issued by the two departments to coincide with the publication of the General Social Care document on the roles and tasks of social workers. The statement welcomes the document as a valuable source of information but suggests that it has been substantially superseded by separate developments within the agendas of each department:

> Since this work started…the Government has published *Putting People First*, on the transformation of adult social care and the Children's Plan, which sets direction for children's services…further work which will be needed to align the content of the statement with the emerging workforce strategies for adult and children's services. (Department for Children, Schools and Families and Department of Health 2008)

Section 3: Social work and leadership

This section explores material that proposes a potential convergence between characteristic features of social work practice and a recent line of development of discussions of 'transformational' leadership. The discussion is influenced in particular by Lawler's article *Leadership in Social Work: A Case of Caveat Emptor?* (2007). In this article the author identifies an awakening interest in social work leadership but comments on both the sparseness of UK-based studies on the subject and the limited relevance of the remaining, predominantly US-based, studies to the UK experience.

A revised account of transformational leadership

Lawler draws attention, however, to a recent UK-based study by Alimo-Metcalf and Alban-Metcalf (2005), which focuses on public sector leadership. This study appears to be of interest and potential relevance to the agendas identified in previous sections of this paper, due to this public service focus, as well as the authors' concern to explore 'close' or 'nearby' rather than 'distant' leadership.

In adopting this focus Alimo-Metcalf and Alban-Metcalf acknowledge, in particular, the influence of Shamir's (1995) study of charismatic leadership, which marked a shift of interest within such studies towards a focus on the nature of the influence exerted by leadership figures of whom the subjects had direct personal experience. The study demonstrated that these figures were differently and more significantly influential of the attitudes and behaviour of respondents than were their more distant hero figures.

Following this lead, Alimo-Metcalf and Alban-Metcalf's study focuses on descriptions by public sector professionals and managers of people within their direct line of reporting. Robustness and reliability were pursued by means of a rigorous methodology including the specification of the size and structure of the study sample, to include 3,500 public sector professionals and managers, employed at different levels within the UK NHS and local government services, and the use of a sampling approach that secured proportionate representation of the perspectives of women and members of black and minority ethnic groups. Further reliability was pursued through a follow up study of respondents working in the private sector.

Alimo-Metcalf and Alban-Metcalf report findings that show the single most important factor associated with their account of 'transformational' leadership was 'valuing others'. This factor is defined as encompassing a 'genuine concern for others' well-being and development' and a commitment to developing the capacity of both the individual and the wider team (Alimo-Metcalf and Alban-Metcalf 2005, p.57).

The remaining significant factors identified by the study are: inspirational communication and networking; enabling others through delegation and development of potential; acting with integrity; being accessible; and being prepared to take risks and make decisions (p.56).

Suggested parallels with social work

It appears notable that there is a considerable similarity between the features of leadership as presented by Alimo-Metcalf and Alban-Metcalf and both the leadership needs identified within Section 1 of this chapter and the orientations, values and behaviours ascribed to social workers in the material reviewed in Section 2.

Lawler draws explicit attention to similarities between accounts of leadership such as that of Alimo-Metcalf and Alban-Metcalf and characteristic features of social work practice. He argues, for example, that 'social work practitioners operate within a framework of values and ethics; focus their practice on empowerment; and encourage a vision for their users through effective communication' and, further, that a concern to develop the potential of others and the proactive management of risk are 'as important to social work practice as they are to leadership' (Lawler 2007, p.130). As a consequence he suggests that: 'some of the components of leadership as identified…might already be present but overlooked in the [social work] profession' (p.123).

These considerations appear to be further reinforced by Alimo-Metcalf and Alban-Metcalf's concluding comments on the implications of their research, which highlight a distinction proposed by Stone, Russell and Patterson (2003) between, on one hand, the earlier, US-based 'New Paradigm' of leadership associated with accounts of 'transformational' leadership, for example Bass (1985), or 'charismatic' leadership, for example Conger (1989) and House (1971) and, on the other, descriptions of 'servant' leadership (see Greenleaf 1970, 1996). The critical distinction proposed lies in the primary focus of the leader. Stone *et al.* suggest that while the 'New Paradigm' of transformational leadership locates the leader's main focus as being on building follower commitment to organisational objectives, the focus of servant leaders is characteristically towards the interests and concerns of followers.

Alimo-Metcalf and Alban-Metcalf adopt this criterion of leader focus as the basis for proposing that their own account constitutes a 'New New Paradigm' of transformational leadership; but propose a further modification to the account of the 'servant' leadership relationship as follows: 'We would stress the importance of the intention and the impact of servant leaders to affirm the leadership potential of those they serve, and would prefer to use the term "servant and partner"' (2005, p.64). This appears to have strong resonances with descriptions of effective social work practice, for example Beresford, Adshead and Croft's summary of appreciative feedback from users of palliative care services, who identified the distinctive contribution of social workers as: 'helping individuals to develop their own expertise and genuinely working in ways that service users want' (2007, p.197).

Section 4: Social work leadership – the role of management

This section looks at the role of managers in providing a framework that is supportive of the realisation of the leadership potential that has been suggested for social work. Two elements are considered: organisational context and the role of supervision.

Creating an organisational context

Section 2 of this chapter highlighted the current climate of change and uncertainty in relation to social work practice. The role of management appears to be important here in influencing whether this becomes a source of insecurity and inhibition, or an opportunity to exercise professional judgement and creativity. Some relevant insights would appear to be provided by findings from a systematic review of studies of distributed leadership, in the related setting of education, undertaken by Woods *et al.* (2004). This identifies the importance of the role of senior managers in 'enabling resources (of legitimacy as well as material) to be made available' (p.451) to enable staff at all levels to develop innovative and participative approaches to service delivery. Specifically this involves creating first, an overall framework of expectations, second, specific systems of permissions and delegations and, third, securing the necessary practical resources.

Supervision and performance management

The discussion of the Victoria Climbié Report (Laming 2003) in Section 1 drew attention to the vital importance placed on the responsibility of managers to exercise effective accountability for the quality of front line practice. Lymbery's (2001) article, considered in Section 2, however, suggested the demoralising and ultimately self-defeating effect of an overly restrictive approach to the management of resources and performance.

In considering what might form the basis of a more constructive approach, Lymbery's reference to the diminished role of professional social work supervision, under the domination of a managerialist culture, appears to sharpen the significance of Oko's description of supervision as 'the mediator between the worker and the tasks of the organisation' (Oko 2008, p.87). This theme is taken up by McDonnell and Zutshi, who argue that supervision provides a mechanism through which it is possible to 'integrate performance management…with a dynamic, empowering…relationship to improve the quality of practice, support the development of integrated working and…impact on personal development' (2006, p.1).

Oko describes how the supervision process provides the social worker with a context in which to critically review and develop their practice and to access personal support, and, at the same time, delivers accountability by means of the supervisor's delivery of their responsibility to ensure that: 'practice is judged, in line with the organisation's task of providing client centred services' (2008, p.87).

McDonnell and Zutshi draw out the more explicitly managerial aspects of supervision: its role in enabling resource and workload management, as well as staff development, including the identification of specific learning needs. They acknowledge that practitioners may need to access other sources of specialist clinical, therapeutic or personal consultation, but argue that this should be seen as an adjunct and not a substitute for the main supervision process.

Eby underlines the significance of this argument. She acknowledges the potential tension within a process that combines the three different elements of personal support, review of professional practice and specifically managerial functions, and additionally arising from the differential status and power of the respective parties involved. She suggests, however, that such tensions are inherent features of the work and context, that are reflected, rather than created, by the supervision process, which in fact provides 'a very effective mechanism for holding and mediating some of these tensions' (Eby 2000, p.67). Relatedly, Oko identifies the supervision process as an important source of feedback, challenge and ideas that contribute to the development of the organisation and its services.

Section summary

This section has highlighted the role of managers in providing a framework that supports the realisation of the potential of social work practice as a source of innovation and leadership. It has been suggested, first, that senior managers have a significant role in setting overall parameters and effective systems of delegation and accessing resources. Second, it has been suggested that a robust system of supervision appears to provide an apposite means of equipping and enabling social workers, not only to deliver the quality of practice that is needed to fulfil essential responsibilities, in terms of protecting vulnerable children and adults, but also to contribute significantly to the development of personalised and integrated services.

Conclusion

In this chapter I have considered material relating to the current policy context in England in relation to services for children and families and adult social care, the factors driving this and the associated leadership needs. Material has been explored suggesting that social work provides a potential exemplar of the orientation and skills required, but that members of the profession may have limited autonomy to negotiate the scope and nature of their remit. I have also considered some suggested parallels between social work practice and the 'New New Paradigm' of transformational leadership, which presents leadership as a relationship of service and partnership. Finally I have considered the role of management in providing a framework that supports the realisation of the potential suggested for social work practice.

At this stage I would suggest that the question remains open as to whether social work is imperilled in various ways by the absence of an appropriate source of leadership, or provides within its own practice a potential source of leadership that is well attuned to the current zeitgeist. I suggest that this provides a worthwhile direction for further research, and hope to contribute to this.

References

Alimo-Metcalf, B. and Alban-Metcalf, J. (2005) 'Leadership: Time for a new direction.' *Leadership 1*, 1, 51–71.

Bass, B.M. (1985) *Leadership and Performance Beyond Expectations.* New York: The Free Press.

Beresford, P., Adshead, L. and Croft, S. (2007) *Palliative Care, Social Work and Service Users.* London: Jessica Kingsley Publishers.

Blewett, J., Lewis, J. and Tunstill, J. (2007) *The Changing Roles and Tasks of Social Work: A Literature Informed Discussion Paper.* General Social Care Council. Available at www.gscc.org.uk/News+and+events/Consultations, accessed 7 May 2009.

Clarke, J. and Newman, J. (1997) *The Managerial State: Power, Politics and Ideology in the Remaking of Social Welfare.* London: Sage Publications.

Conger, J.A. (1989) *The Charismatic Leader: Beyond the Mystique of Exceptional Leadership.* San Francisco, CA: Jossey-Bass.

Department for Children, Schools and Families (2007) *The Children's Plan.* London: Stationery Office.

Department for Children, Schools and Families and Department of Health (2008) Statement on General Social Care Council website to accompany publication of General Social Care Council 2008. Available at www.gscc.org.uk/News+and+events/Consultations, accessed 7 May 2009.

Department for Education and Skills (2003) *Every Child Matters.* Available at www.everychildmatters.gov.uk, accessed 7 May 2009.

Department of Health (2005) *Independence, Well-being and Choice.* London: Stationery Office.

Department of Health (2006) *Our Health, Our Care, Our Say.* London: Stationery Office.

Department of Health (2008a) *Transforming Social Care,* Available at www.dh.gov.uk/en/Publicationsandstatistics/Lettersandcirculars/LocalAuthorityCirculars/DH_081934, accessed 7 May 2009.

Department of Health (2008b) *Putting People First.* Available at www.dh.gov.uk/en/Publicationsandstatistics/Publications/PublicationsPolicyAndGuidance/DH_081118, accessed 7 May 2009.

Eby, M. (2000) 'Understanding Professional Development.' In A. Brechin, H. Brown, and M. Eby *Critical Practice in Health and Social Care.* London, Los Angeles and New Delhi: Sage Publications.

General Social Care Council (2008) *Social Work at Its Best: A Statement of Social Work Roles and Tasks for the 21st Century.* General Social Care Council. Available at www.gscc.org.uk/ NR/rdonlyres/4EDB6D7E-C18C-4A38-8BEA-D271E9DFFC06/0/RolesandTaskssta tementFINAL.pdf, accessed 7 May 2009.

Greenleaf, R.K. (1970) *The Servant as Leader.* San Francisco, CA: Jossey-Bass.

Greenleaf, R.K. (1996) *On Becoming a Servant Leader.* San Francisco, CA: Jossey-Bass.

Hill, M. (1993) *The Welfare State in Britain.* Aldershot: Edward Elgar.

HM Government (1999) *Health Act.* London: Stationery Office.

HM Government (2001) *Health and Social Care Act.* London: Stationery Office.

HM Government (2004) *The Children Act 2004.* Available at www.opsi.gov.uk/acts/ acts2004/ukpga_20040031, accessed 7 May 2009.

House, R.J. (1971) 'A path–goal theory of leadership effectiveness.' *Administrative Science Quarterly 16,* 3, 321–328.

Laming, H. (2003) *The Victoria Climbié Inquiry.* London: Stationary Office. Available at www.victoria-climbie-inquiry.org.uk, accessed 7 May 2009.

Lawler, J. (2007) 'Leadership in social work: A case of caveat emptor?' *British Journal of Social Work 37,* 123–141.

Lymbery, M. (2001) 'Social work at the crossroads.' *British Journal of Social Work 31,* 369–384.

McDonnell, F. and Zutshi, H. (2006) 'Manage Effective Supervision.' In Skills for care (2006) *Leadership and Management – A Strategy for Social Care.* Leeds: Skills for Care.

Oko, J. (2008) *Understanding and Using Social Work.* Exeter: Learning Matters.

Parry, N. and Parry, J. (1979) 'Social Work, Professionalism and the State.' In N. Parry, M. Rustin and C. Satyamurti (eds) *Social Work, Welfare and the State.* London: Edward Arnold.

Payne, M. (2006) *What is Professional Social Work?,* 2nd edn. Bristol: Policy Press.

Peters, T. and Waterman, R. (1982) *In Search of Excellence: Lessons from America's Best Run Companies.* New York: Harper and Row.

Platt, D. (2007) *Raising the Status of Social Care.* London: Department of Health. Available at www.dh.gov.uk/en/Publicationsandstatistics/Publications/PublicationsPolicyAndGuida nce/DH_074217, accessed 7 May 2009.

Pollitt, C. (1993) *Managerialism and the Public Services,* 2nd edn. Oxford: Basil Blackwell.

Seebohm, F. (1968) *Report of the Committee on Local Authority and Allied Personal Social Service.* Cmnd 3703. London: HMSO.

Shamir, B. (1995) 'Social distance and charisma: Theoretical notes and an exploratory study.' *Leadership Quarterly 6,* 1, 19–47.

Stone, A.G., Russell, R.F. and Patterson, K. (2003) 'Transformational versus servant leadership – A difference in leader focus.' Paper from the Servant Leadership Round Table, October. Available at www.regent.edu/acad/cls/2003Servant Leadership Roundtable/Stone.pdf, accessed 7 May 2009.

Wanless, D. (2006) *Securing Good Care for Older People.* London: King's Fund.

Woods, P.A., Bennett, N., Harvey, J. and Wise, C. (2004) 'Variabilities and dualities in Distri- buted Leadership: Findings from a systematic literature review.' *Educational Management Administration and Leadership 32,* 4, 439–457. Available at http://emasagepub.com/cg/ content/refs/32/4/439, accessed 7 May 2009.

PART II
Leadership for Collaborative Advantage

CHAPTER 5*

Doing Things Collaboratively: Realising the Advantage or Succumbing to Inertia?

Chris Huxham and Siv Vangen

The project has worked out, but oh boy, it has caused pain. (Senior health promotion officer, health promotion partnership)

Decisions are made by the Alliance Executive, but they keep procrastinating over big decisions…you can't afford to procrastinate over spending a million pounds. (Information manager, retail property development alliance)

Multi-agency work is very slow…trying to get people moving collectively rather than alone is difficult. (Project officer, young offender community organisation)

I am under partnership attack from my colleagues. (Operations manager, engineering supply chain)

The long catalogue of failed JVs – lcatel/Sharp, Sony/Qualcomm, Lucent/Philips – demonstrates the enormous difficulties in pulling companies like these together. (A Gartner analyst quoted in the *Financial Times*, 10 December 2002, p.8)

Not everyone who works daily in collaborative alliances, partnerships or networks reports such negative experiences as those quoted above. Indeed the *Financial Times* (24 June 2003, p.14) reports a Nokia executive as saying that

---

*   Originally published in *Organizational Dynamics 33*, 2, 190–201. Reprinted here by permission of Elsevier.

their linkages are paying off. Others talk similarly enthusiastically about their partnership experiences: 'When it works well you feel inspired…you can feel the collaborative energy.' However, very many do express frustration. There has been much rhetoric about the value of strategic alliances, industry networks, public service delivery partnerships and many other collaborative forms, but reports of unmitigated success are not common. In this article we explore the nature of *the practice of collaboration*, focusing in particular on some of the reasons why collaborative initiatives tend to challenge those involved. Two concepts are central to this exploration. The first is *collaborative advantage*. This captures the synergy argument: to gain real *advantage* from collaboration, something has to be achieved that could not have been achieved by any one of the organisations acting alone. This concept provides a useful 'guiding light' for the purpose of collaboration. The second concept, *collaborative inertia*, captures what happens very frequently in practice: the output from a collaborative arrangement is negligible, the rate of output is extremely slow, or stories of pain and hard grind are integral to successes achieved.

Clearly there is a dilemma between advantage and inertia. The key question seems to be: If achievement of collaborative advantage is the goal for those who initiate collaborative arrangements, why is collaborative inertia so often the outcome? To address this question, and the question of what managers can do about it, we will present a set of seven overlapping perspectives on collaborative management. This is extracted from the theory of collaborative advantage, which has derived from extensive action research over 15 years. We have worked with practitioners of collaboration, in the capacity of facilitators, consultants and trainers, in a wide variety of collaborative situations. We have kept detailed records about the challenges and dilemmas faced by managers, and of comments they make in the course of enacting their collaborative endeavours. Many such statements are reproduced as illustrative examples in this article.

Perspective 1: We must have common aims but we cannot agree on them

Agreement on aims is an appropriate starting point because it is raised consistently as an issue. *Common wisdom* suggests that it is necessary to be clear about the aims of joint working if partners are to work together to operationalise policies.

Typically individuals argue for common (or at least compatible), agreed or clear sets of aims as a starting point in collaboration. *Common practice*, however, appears to be that the variety of organisational and individual agendas that are present in collaborative situations makes reaching agreement difficult. For example, a board member of an alliance of 120 charities commented on the difficulty of reconciling members' interests. Invariably someone would call to say, 'We don't want you to do that.'

The reasons behind the struggles for agreement may not be obvious. Organisations come together bringing different resources and expertise to the table, which in turn creates the potential for collaborative advantage. Yet organisations also have different reasons for being involved, and their representatives seek to achieve different outputs from their involvement. Sometimes these different organisational aims lead to conflicts of interest. Furthermore, for some organisations the joint purpose for the collaboration is perceived as central to achieving organisational purposes, whereas others are less interested and perhaps only involved (reluctantly) as a result of external pressure. Tensions often arise, therefore, because some organisations are very interested in influencing and controlling the joint agenda, and some are reluctant to commit resources to it, and so on. Similarly, individuals too will join the collaboration with different expectations, aspirations and understandings of what is to be achieved jointly. It follows that whilst at first glance it may appear that partners only need be concerned with the joint aims for the collaboration, in reality organisational and individual aims can prevent agreement because they cause confusion, misunderstanding and conflicts of interest. In addition, while some of these various aims may be explicit, many will be taken for granted (assumed) by one partner but not necessarily recognised by another, and many will be deliberately hidden: 'My company is really most interested in having access to, and experience of, the Chinese business environment and cares little for the formally declared purpose of the alliance.' On reflection then it is not so surprising that reaching agreement can be very difficult.

Managing aims in practice

Figure 5.1 is a simplified version of a framework of aims in collaborative situations. Its purpose is to facilitate a better understanding of the motivations of those involved, and the ways in which multiple and (sometimes even) conflicting aims can prevent agreement and block progress. In turn, this sort of understanding can help in finding ways of addressing the concerns of all involved. The framework distinguishes between the various types of aims mentioned above and emphasises that some aims will be assumed rather than explicitly acknowledged, and many will be deliberately hidden.

(One participant's perspective)	Explicit	Assumed	Hidden
Collaboration aims	The purpose of the collaboration		By definition these are perceptions of joint aims and so cannot be hidden
Organisation aims	What each organisation hopes to gain for itself via the collaboration		
Individual aims	What each individual hopes to gain for him/herself via the collaboration		

FIGURE 5.1: A FRAMEWORK FOR UNDERSTANDING AIMS IN COLLABORATION

This framework can be used as an effective tool for gaining insight about the motivations of members of a collaboration – even of one's own! Obviously it is not possible to know others' hidden agendas, but it is possible to speculate on the possibility that they might have some – and even have a guess at what they might be. Trying to 'fill in' each of the cells of the framework for each other partner can be enlightening, whether it is done quickly, 'back of an envelope' style, or as a major investigative exercise. Gaining this kind of insight into partners' expectations and aspirations can be very helpful in understanding and judging how best to work with them.

At the general level, the obvious conclusion to be drawn from the framework is that it is rarely going to be easy in practice to satisfy fully the common wisdom. Therein lies the dilemma – clarity of purpose provides much needed direction, yet open discussion can unearth irreconcilable differences! Difficulties that arise out of the need to communicate across different professional and natural languages and different organisational and professional cultures are unlikely to assist the negotiation process. Likewise, concerns about accountability of participants to their own organisations or to other constituents are unlikely to make it easy for individuals to make compromises. Often, the only practical way forward is to get started on some action without fully agreeing the aims. In the words of the manager of an urban regeneration partnership engaged in writing a bid for funding, the task for managers can be to: 'find a way of stating the aims so that none of the parties can disagree.'

Perspective 2: Sharing power is important, but people behave as if it's all in the purse strings

As with the previous perspective, the 'pain' associated with issues of power is often raised by practitioners of collaboration. *Common wisdom* is that 'the power is in the purse strings', which suggests that those who do not have control of the financial resource are automatically deprived of power. Viewed dispassionately, these perceptions quite often seem at odds with 'reality' since most parties do, minimally, have at least the 'power of exit'. A manager in an automotive industry joint venture commented: 'The balance of power was seemingly with the UK company, who had a majority shareholding, but in reality it was with US company, who knew how closely the investment analysts were watching the joint venture. The threat of pulling out was always in the background.' However, the *common practice*, unsurprisingly, is that people act as though their perceptions are real and often display defensiveness and aggression.

Looking more closely at where power is actually used to influence the way in which collaborative activities are negotiated and carried out, it is possible to identify different *points of power*. Many of these occur at a micro level in the collaboration, and would often not be particularly obvious to those involved. One example of a point of power is the naming of the collaboration, since this is likely to influence what it does. Those who are involved in the naming process are therefore in a powerful position at that time. Other examples concern invitations to join a collaboration; those who choose who to involve are obviously powerful, but those who choose the process of whom to involve are even more so.

Many points of power relate to communication media and processes. One set of examples concerns the arrangements for meetings. Clearly, any person taking the role of chair or facilitator in a meeting is in a position of power whilst the meeting is in place, but those who get to choose which facilitator to appoint are more subtly and perhaps more significantly powerful. Those who choose the location of a meeting may be in a powerful position, particularly in terms of determining whether it will be on the premises of one of the participants. Those who choose the timing of the meeting are also powerful. It is possible to identify many more points of power that typically are present during collaborative activities.

An important characteristic of points of power is that they are not static. In collaborative situations, power continually shifts. At the macro level, for example, in a pre-start-up phase those who get to draw up contracts, write bids for funding or who have direct access to a customer may be powerful. In a start-up phase however, once money is available, those who are given the task of administering the collaboration may be highly powerful in determining many parameters concerned with direction and ways of working. It may only be at later stages that the actual members become active and have the chance to exert power.

Less obvious, but very significant, are the continuous shifts of power at a micro level during all phases. For example, network managers are often in powerful positions between meetings because they are the only people formally employed by the network – and hence the only people who have its agenda as their main concern. They may also have access to the network funds. During meetings, however, members can shift many of the points of power in significant ways, often determining new members, times and locations of meetings as well as influencing agreements about action. Those less centrally involved, such as facilitators or consultants, can be in powerful positions for short periods of time. External influences, such as those from government, can sometimes be extremely powerful in a short-term way as they make demands for reports or responses to initiatives.

Managing power in practice

Issues concerned with control of purse strings are significant, but there are many other points at which power is, in practice, enacted in collaborative settings. All participants have power at one time or another and may frequently have the option to empower themselves. Understanding and exploring the points of power can enable assessment of where and when others are unwittingly or consciously exerting power, and where and when others may view them as exerting power. It also allows for consideration of how and when deliberately to exert power. Responding to these insights, however, requires a willingness to accept that manipulative behaviour is appropriate, which some would argue is against the spirit of collaborative working. We will return to this point later.

Perspective 3: Trust is necessary for successful collaboration, but we are suspicious of each other

Issues relating to trust are also commonly raised by participants. The *common wisdom* seems to be that trust is a precondition for successful collaboration. However, while the existence of trusting relationships between partners probably would be an ideal situation, the *common practice* appears to be that suspicion, rather than trust, is the starting point. Often participants do not have the luxury to choose their partners. Either imposed (for example government) policy dictates who the partners must be or, as expressed by the business development manager of the Far East operation of a major oil producer below, the pragmatics of the situation dictate that partners are needed where trust is weak: 'You may have to jump into bed with someone you don't like in order to prevent a competitor coming into the market.' This suggests that it is appropriate to pay attention to trust *building* between partners.

One way of thinking about trust building is through the loop depicted in Figure 5.2. This argues that two factors are important in getting started in a trusting relationship. The first is concerned with the formation of expectations about the future of the collaboration; these will be based either on reputation or past behaviour, or on more formal contracts and agreements. Given the earlier remarks about the difficulty of agreeing on aims in collaborative settings, this in itself is a non-trivial starting point. The second starting point involves risk taking. The argument is that partners need to trust each other *enough* to allow them to take a risk to initiate the collaboration. If both of these initiators are possible, then the loop argues that trust can gradually be built through starting with some modest but realistic aims that are likely to be successfully realised. This reinforces trusting attitudes between partners and provides a basis for more ambitious collaboration.

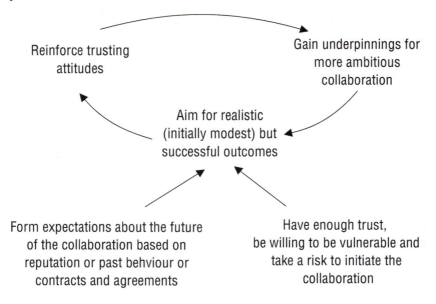

FIGURE 5.2: THE TRUST-BUILDING LOOP

Managing trust in practice

The practical conclusion from the trust building loop is very similar to that concerning the management of aims: sometimes it is better to get started on some small but tangible action and then to allow trust to develop slowly. This incremental approach to trust building would obviously not be relevant if an immediate need to attain a major objective is paramount. In those situations, expectation forming and risk taking would have to be managed simultaneously and alongside other trust-building activities. However, in other situations building trust incrementally is, in principle, appealing. We shall return to it later.

Perspective 4: We are partnership-fatigued and tired of being pulled in all directions

In this perspective it is not so much the common wisdom but the *taken for granted assumptions* that are to be challenged. One of the most surprising observations about collaborative situations is the frequency with which clarity about who the collaborators are is lacking. Different members often list different partners from each other, and staff who are very centrally involved in managing collaborations often cannot name partners without referring to formal documentation. Reasons for this include the different statuses or commitment that people or organisations have with regard to the network: 'They were only involved to provide the financial support… (rather than as a proper member)', and ambiguity about whether people are involved as individuals or on behalf of their organisations: 'Members were invited to join because of their ethnic background, but the organisations they worked in (which were not specifically concerned with ethnicity issues) then became partners.'

The lack of clarity about who partners are is often compounded by the complexity of collaborative arrangements in practice. The sheer scale of networking activities is one aspect of this. Many organisations are involved in multiple alliances. One major electronics manufacturer, for example, is said to be involved in around 400 strategic alliances. Clearly, even with the most coherent alliance management practices, no individual manager is likely to know which partner organisations are involved. Clearly also, multiple alliances must pull the organisation in a variety of different directions. As one senior manager in a division of a multinational computer hardware manufacturer put it: 'We have separate alliances with two companies (worldwide operating system providers) that are in direct competition with each other…there is a lot of conflict within the company over these alliances...the people involved try to raise the importance of theirs.'

The same issue arises in the public sector context, with ever increasing numbers of partnerships and inter-agency initiatives appearing in localities. In this case, however, the problem that is most commonly voiced is 'partnership fatigue', with individuals often regularly attending meetings of five or six collaborative schemes. More extreme cases occur in this sector too. For example, a manager from a community-based careers guidance organisation commented: 'When I heard of the person attending meetings of five partnerships, I thought "Is that all?!"... My organisation is involved in 56 partnerships.'

There are many other consequences of these multiple initiatives apart from fatigue. One is that some participants try to link agendas across the initiatives, but the links they see relate to the particular combinations of initiatives that they are involved in, which generally do not overlap precisely, if at all, with involvements of other members. Another is that it is hard for any individual to judge when another is inputting the views of their employing organisation or bringing an agenda from another partnership.

In addition to the volume of relationships, there is frequently complexity in the networks of relationships between organisations. For example, the complexity of interacting supply chain networks – in which every supplier has multiple customers, every customer has multiple suppliers, and suppliers have suppliers and customers have customers – is potentially infinite. Many networks of collaborations are, in addition, hierarchical in the sense that collaborations are members of other collaborations. For example, a local government organisation may be a member of a regeneration partnership but also a member of several community collaborations which are in turn members of a community 'umbrella group', which is in turn a member of the regeneration partnership. Similarly, joint ventures may be members of strategic alliances, trade associations may represent their members in policy networks, and so on.

Managing ambiguity and complexity in practice

Clearly, it is hard for managers to agree on aims, build mutual understanding and manage trust and power relationships with partners if they do not unambiguously know who their partners are. Equally, it is difficult to manage collaborative working in complex systems in which different elements must be affecting each other but there is little clarity on the nature of the inter-relationships.

Hierarchies of collaboration

Key
Circles represent collaborations
Arrows indicate members of collaborations

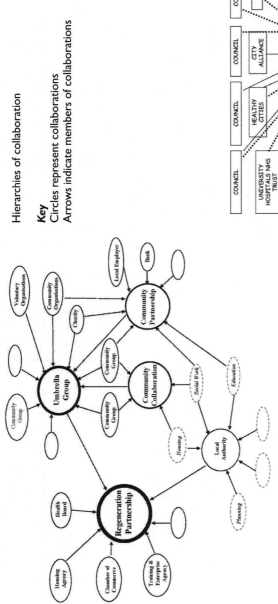

Mapping an organisation's partnerships

Key
Centre box represents the organisation
All other boxes represent parties with which
it has collaborative relationships

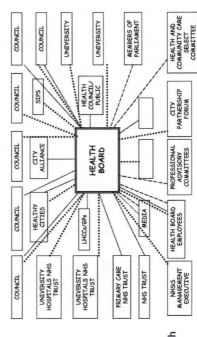

FIGURE 5.3: EXAMPLE DIAGRAMMING METHODS FOR MAPPING THE COMPLEXITY OF COLLABORATIVE STRUCTURES

Diagramming techniques can help in mapping the structure of partnerships. Figure 5.3 provides two possible ways of doing this. Obviously this cannot remove the ambiguity and uncertainty completely, but it is generally enlightening at the point of construction and useful as a long-term reminder. As with the aims framework, this exercise can be done in more or less detail.

At a general level, learning how to identify, live with and progress despite ambiguity and complexity is probably the key challenge of this perspective. A careful approach to nurturing relationships must be an essential aspect of this.

Perspective 5: Everything keeps changing

Collaborative structures are commonly talked about as though stability of membership can be *taken for granted*, at least for a tangible period. The ambiguity and complexity indicated in the previous section would be difficult enough for participants to cope with if that were the case. In practice, however, policy influences, which may be internal but are frequently imposed externally, often generate restructuring of member organisations. Merger and de-merger, new start-ups and closures, acquisitions and sell-offs, and restructurings are all commonplace. In turn, these imply a necessary restructuring of any collaboration in which they participated.

Equally, policy changes in the individual organisations or the collaboration affect the purpose of the collaboration. These may be generated internally – for example, as the result of a revision of strategic direction. Or they may be generated externally – for example, as a result of government policy or major market disturbances. Either way, this in turn implies a shift in the relevance of the collaboration to its members. New members may join and others may leave, and sometimes such changes are imposed: 'The problem isn't that their collaboration is not working, but that because of the new policy we are asking them to work differently, which means breaking up established successful and effective working relationships and building new ones.'

Another source of dynamic change comes with individual movements. The manager of a company that was delivering a major service for an alliance partner, for example, commented that the relationship with the partner organisation had been both helped and hindered because: '...the chief executive in the partner organisation was, until recently, my boss in my own organisation.'

The relationships between individual participants in collaborations are often fundamental to getting things done. This makes collaborations highly sensitive to changes in individuals' employment, even if these are simply role changes within one of the participating organisations. Finally, even if all of the above stood still there is often an inherent dynamic. If an initial collaborative purpose is achieved, there will usually be a need to move to new collaborative agendas, and these are likely to imply different membership requirements.

All organisations are dynamic to the extent that they will gradually transform. However, collaborations are sensitive to transformations in *each* of the partner organisations and therefore may change very quickly. In one example, a collaborative group with an ambiguous structure involving many partners went through three identifiable reincarnations over a three-year period and ended up as a very controlled partnership between two organisations. Its final stated purpose was related to, but definitely not the same as, the original one. It would be reasonable to argue that the final partnership was a different one from the original collaborative group, but it is possible to trace a clear lineage from one to the other.

Managing collaborative dynamics in practice

One obvious conclusion that derives from recognition of the dynamic nature of collaborations is that the appealing trust-building loop (Figure 5.2) is inherently extremely fragile. Effort put into building mutual understanding and developing trust can be shattered, for example, by a change in the structure of a key organisation or the job change of a key individual. A practical conclusion, therefore, for those who want to make collaboration work is that *the nurturing process must be continuous and permanent.* No sooner will gains be made than a disturbance, in the form of a change to one of the partners, will shatter many of them.

Perspective 6: Leadership is not always in the hands of members

Given the inherent difficulties with collaborative forms that have been discussed so far, the issue of leadership seems highly relevant. Because traditional hierarchies do not exist in collaborative settings, it is appropriate to consider leadership in a general sense, rather than as specifically the realm of senior executives or prominent public figures. Here, we consider leadership as being concerned with *the mechanisms that lead to the actual outcomes of a collaboration.* Put simply, we are concerned with what *makes things happen* in a collaboration. More formally, this concern is with the formation and implementation of the collaboration's policy and activity agenda.

Looked at from this perspective, leadership, interestingly, becomes something that is not only enacted by people. Structures and processes are as important in leading agendas as are the participants involved in the collaboration. Thus, for example, a structure in which two organisations only are involved in partnership should allow both organisations good access to the agenda, but clearly excludes others. To take an extreme contrast, a collaboration in which any organisation that wants to be a member may send a representative allows wide access to the agenda in principle, but it can be difficult for any individual to have much influence in practice. Similarly, in the context of collaborative processes, a collaboration for which a major form of communication is through open meetings is going to allow a very different form of access to the agenda from one whose principal mode of communication is through e-mail and/or telephone. Thus, agendas may be led by the type of structure that is in place and the type of processes used. Once again, this challenges a *taken for granted* presumption about the nature of leadership. Agendas can, of course, also be led by participants, though generally these are emergent, informal leaders rather than those who lead from a position of authority.

Structures, processes and participants can be thought of as different *media* through which collaborative leadership is, in practice, enacted. An important point about these media is that all three are largely not controlled by *members* of the collaboration. Structures and processes are sometimes imposed externally, for example, by government, a corporate headquarters or a funding body. Even if this is not the case, they often emerge out of previous action rather than being explicitly designed by members. Even in the context of 'participants' as the leadership medium, leadership is not solely the role of *members* of the collaboration. External stakeholders such as customers or local public figures often strongly direct the territory of a partnership or alliance. A strong lead is often also given by support staff who are not strictly members. For example, the information manager of a retail property development alliance commented about his role in moving the alliance members towards agreement about action: 'I find that attrition helps... I am a stubborn old devil.'

Managing leadership media

This perspective demonstrates the ease with which collaborations can move out of the control of their membership. Recognising the at least partial inevitability of this and working around it is part of the practical response required. Diagramming techniques such as those in Figure 5.3 may be helpful in exploring the nature of the structure as a first step towards gaining an understanding of its leadership consequences.

For managers who wish to lead more actively, the implication appears to be that part of their activity must be concerned with the design of structures and processes that are effective for the particular purpose, and with monitoring their performance and evolution. We look further at active leadership in the final perspective.

Perspective 7: Leadership activities continually meet with dilemmas and difficulties

Despite the strong contextual leadership derived from structures and processes, participants (whether or not they actually are members) do carry out *leadership activities* in order to move a collaboration forward in ways that they regard as beneficial. In carrying out these activities, they do affect the outcomes of collaborative initiatives. However they are frequently thwarted by difficulties, so that the outcomes are not as they intend. For example, despite his war of attrition, the information manager quoted above was continuously thwarted in his attempts to create events in which key members of the partnering organisations would jointly consider their modes of thinking and working. Several dates set aside for group workshops were ultimately used for other kinds of meetings, as issues needing immediate attention emerged.

In practice, much of what is done by those who aim to take a lead in moving a collaboration forward may be said to be fundamentally *within the spirit of collaboration*. Activities of this sort are highly facilitative and are concerned with embracing, empowering, involving and mobilising members. However, the same people are also engaged in activities that, on the face of it, are much less collaborative. Many of them are adept at manipulating agendas and playing the politics. We have characterised these kinds of activities as being *towards collaborative thuggery* after the member of a city partnership who told us that a partnership that he was involved with had been successful: '...because the convenor is a thug...if people are not pulling their weight he pushes them out.' He appeared to be arguing that this was a positive and effective mode of leadership.

Managing leadership activities

Does this, then, suggest a dilemma between the ideology of collaborative working and the pragmatism needed to get things done? Not necessarily. One way of thinking about this is to consider the nature of nurturing. Nurturing is often talked about in the context of the gentle care required for fragile plants. However, rather more decisive tactics have to be taken if the object is to nurture an overgrown garden back to health. Chopping down of excess growth and pulling up of weeds are likely to be key activities, in addition to the nurturing back to health of individual plants that have become overpowered by others. Whilst it is not possible to produce hard evidence of this, those who lead more successfully seem to operate from both perspectives – the *spirit of collaboration* and *towards collaborative thuggery* – and to continually switch between them, often carrying out both types of leadership in the same act.

Realising collaborative advantage

Our aim here has been to convey some of the complexity that underlies collaborative situations in a way that should seem real to those involved. Obviously the set of seven perspectives does not, in itself, provide any precise recipes for managerial action. It does, however, provide a dual basis for thoughtful action.

The first basis is through legitimising the pain and addressing the isolation that people often feel when trapped in collaborative inertia: 'I have been working in a health–education partnership…for about a year, and it is a relief and a reassurance to see that the 'pain and grind' of partnership work exists in other partnerships, not just my situation.' Like this person, many managers are empowered simply by understanding that the problems they are experiencing are inevitable. This is partly because this awareness increases self-confidence, and partly because it immediately highlights the need to tackle the problem at a different level. Legitimising a degree of manipulative and political activity through the notion of *collaborative thuggery* can also be helpful in this respect.

The second, and perhaps more significant, basis for action is through the conceptual handles that the perspectives provide. As presented here in summary, the combined picture gives a sense of the kinds of issues that have to be managed (a more detailed version of each perspective is available). Like the summary, the detailed perspectives do not provide a recipe for good practice, because to do so would be to over-simplify. Rather, they are intended to alert managers to challenges of collaborative situations that will need active attention and nurturing if problems of collaborative inertia are to be minimised. Each perspective provides a particular view on this, and can be used in isolation to stimulate thinking about that in particular. However, the issues raised by each perspective overlap with those raised by others, so the combination of perspectives always needs to be in the background, even if the focus at a particular time is a specific one. Many of the challenges are inherent, and there are often tensions between directly opposed possible ways of tackling them. This approach to practical support regards the action to be taken as a matter for managerial judgement. This includes making informed judgements about the resource that needs to be available to support the nurturing activities.

Don't work collaboratively unless you have to

One definite conclusion can, however, be drawn. That is, that making collaboration work effectively is highly resource-consuming and often painful. The strongest piece of advice to managers (and policy makers) that derives from the above perspectives, therefore, is 'don't do it unless you have to'. Put rather more formally, the argument is that unless potential for real collaborative advantage is clear, it is generally best, *if there is a choice*, to avoid collaboration. It is worth noting, however, that collaborative advantage sometimes comes in non-obvious forms and may be concerned with the process of collaborating – for example from the development of a relationship with a partner – rather than the actual output.

Selected bibliography

This article draws on the *theory of collaborative advantage*, which we have developed gradually from extensive research with practitioners of collaboration over the last 15 years. The notions of Collaborative Advantage and Collaborative Inertia are central to this theory. *Collaborative Advantage* was first used in this way in the early 1990s. See for example, C. Huxham and D. Macdonald, 'Introducing Collaborative Advantage,' *Management Decision*, 1992, 30(3), 50–56. Rosabeth Moss Kanter used the term differently in her 1994 article 'Collaborative Advantage: The Art of Alliances,' *Harvard Business Review*, 72(4), 96–108. *Collaborative inertia* was introduced in C. Huxham, 'Advantage or Inertia: Making Collaboration Work,' in R. Paton, G. Clark, G. Jones, and P. Quintas (eds), *The New Management Reader* (London: Routledge, 1996, 238–254).

Theory relating to the aims framework of perspective one can be found in C. Eden and C. Huxham, 'The Negotiation of Purpose in Multi-Organizational Collaborative Groups,' *Journal of Management Studies*, 2001, 38(3), 351–369. A detailed discussion on the points of power in perspective two can be found in C. Huxham and N. Beech, 'Points of Power in Interorganizational Forms: Learning from a Learning Network,' *Best 10%, Proceedings of the Academy of Management Conference*, 2002. The development of the trust-building loop and its implication for the management of trust in perspective three is explored in S. Vangen and C. Huxham, 'Nurturing Collaborative Relations: Building Trust in Inter-organizational Collaboration,' *Journal of Applied Behavioral Science*, 2003, 39(1), 5–31. A detailed exposition of perspectives four and five can be found in C. Huxham and S. Vangen, 'Ambiguity, Complexity and Dynamics in the Membership of Collaboration,' *Human Relations*, 2000, 53(6), 771–806. For a detailed discussion on the conceptualisation and enactment of leadership in perspectives six and seven see C. Huxham and S. Vangen, 'Leadership in the Shaping and Implementation of Collaboration Agendas: How Things Happen in a (Not Quite) Joined Up World,' *Academy of Management Journal (Special Forum on Managing in the New Millennium)*, 2000, 43(6), 1159–1175; and S. Vangen and C. Huxham, 'Enacting Leadership for Collaborative Advantage: Dilemmas of Ideology and Pragmatism in the Activities of Partnership Managers,' *British Journal of Management*, 2003, 14, 61–74.

Acknowledgements

Colin Eden and Nic Beech have been involved in developing specific elements of this theory. Their perspectives and styles of researching have provided invaluable insights. We would also like to thank Murray Stewart and Robin Hambleton for the research collaboration that led to our work on collaborative leadership. Many, many practitioners have been wittingly and unwittingly involved in the development of this theory; they are too numerous to name, but our thanks are due to them all. We would like to acknowledge the support for this research of the U.K. Economic and Social Research Council (ESRC) and Engineering and Physical Sciences Research Council (EPSRC) under ESRC grant numbers 000234450 and L130251031 and the ESRC/EPSRC Advanced Institute of Management Research grant number RES-331-25-0016.

CHAPTER 6

Leading Partnerships: Learning from Study and Practice

Patrick Leonard

Introduction

Social work professionals, and others working in public services, have found themselves facing an increasing requirement to work together 'in partnership'. Partnership working has been viewed as the preferred means of tackling intractable problems arising from poverty, such as crime, ill health and family dysfunction. For the public sector managers involved this creates a context in which they are challenged to lead collaboratively, and often without authority. This chapter reports on the author's recent reseach, which explores how leadership operates in partnerships by drawing on the experiences of a group of managers who work across the Scottish public service. The record of their discussions as they studied for a postgraduate diploma devised by Lancaster University Management School in conjunction with the Scottish Leadership Foundation reveals something of the paradoxes and limitations associated with collaborative leadership. The managers pointed to romantic, idealised notions of leadership and to the realities of power and resistance in partnership working. The research concludes that collaborative leadership does not appear to provide a solution to all leadership problems.

Collaborative leadership in theory

Mainstream leadership theories have been predicated on the widely held view that 'leadership' equates to the traits, behaviours, characteristics and actions of the person 'in charge'. Such a perspective has a long lineage that can be traced back to Plato's assertion that we would best be led by 'philosopher-kings'. Machiavelli revived the classical tradition, reinforcing a view of leadership as a property of an individual. In the nineteenth century Thomas Carlyle asserted 'the history of what man [*sic*] has accomplished in this world, is at bottom the history of the Great Men who have worked here' (1993, p.3). This heroic view of leadership has a powerful grasp on the public imagination, at least in Western, and especially Anglo-Saxon societies. Throughout the twentieth century this leader-centric approach became more nuanced, suggesting that leadership style might emphasise more people-oriented or task-oriented approaches. It was recognised that leadership outcomes might be contingent on context. By the 1980s these theories crystallised into a distinction between 'transactional' and 'transformational' leaders, with a suggestion that nurturing behaviours typically associated with female roles were becoming more highly valued by followers. This presumed cause–effect relationship between the leader and their followers is the source of conventional knowledge of leadership and has remained the dominant paradigm within leadership studies – a view of leadership as 'human capital'.

More recently, however, alternative voices have been heard that challenge this dominant concept of leadership. They start by recognising that *all* leaders rely on the collaboration of those who follow them. If not, the relationship is clearly coercive. This view has been reinforced by growing dissatisfaction with an inability of conventional studies to pin down what exactly it is individual leaders need to do to be effective. For example, one study listed 499 traits and dimensions of leadership behaviour. The implication appears to be that more or less *anything* the person 'in charge' thinks or does will end up being labelled 'leadership'! An alternative perspective considers leadership as 'social capital' – the product of the interactions between many individuals within organisations. It has been suggested that this may reflect the particular times in which we live. 'The micro transition we are in, multifaceted global transformation [driven by the Information Revolution]...has changed the dynamics – who leads whom, and how – within the big organizations so characteristic of modern society: they look top-heavy but have to diffuse authority and initiative broadly to work at all' (Cleveland 2002, p.xv). In other words, nobody is, or can be 'in charge'! The core issue is a paradox of participation: how do you get everybody who needs to be in on the act working together and still get some action? On the other hand it may simply be that there are some organisations, for example in education or health care that, by nature of their multi-hierarchical, 'collegial' structures, lend themselves more readily to adopting the forms of distributed leadership that emphasise collaboration.

When groups of people are interacting there are necessarily conflicting values because they have different individual histories. The process that aligns these individual ethics towards a shared idea of the common good is the phenomenon often experienced as leadership. The process of leadership is stimulated by some perceived differential between what people collectively want and what they currently have. When the differential is large enough it motivates people to act. 'Leadership, then, can be defined as a process of transformative change where the ethics of individuals are integrated into the mores of a community as a means of evolutionary social development' (Barker 2002, p.106). Leadership as a social process can be viewed as a dynamic collaboration, where individuals and organisations authorise themselves and others to interact in ways that experiment with new forms of meaning, making discussible what is usually undiscussible. In this way collaborative leadership has an important potential role in promoting the potential for people to work together more effectively.

Chrislip and Larson (1994) argued that the purpose of collaborative leadership is to create shared vision and joint strategies to address concerns that go beyond the purview of any particular party. They described this as a profound shift in our conception about how change is created and requires an equally profound shift in our conception of leadership. Rather than heroes who tell us what to do they argue for leadership that helps us to do the work ourselves. They suggest that blaming individual leaders may be a convenient, but ultimately fruitless alternative to engaging *ourselves* in the difficult work of public problem solving, avoiding quick fixes to complex issues. Indeed they considered contemporary challenges are so complex one person cannot supply the necessary leadership to get results. We need to discover new ways of interacting that helps us collectively address issues of shared concern. What makes collaborative leadership difficult is that many people have the power to say 'No!' yet no one person or group has the power to act alone. The primary task of collaborative leadership is to create a constituency for change that can reach implementable agreements on problems and issues of shared concern, not impose specific solutions that an individual leader has defined. This argument appears prescient in the light of contemporary responses to the challenges of global warming.

The Scottish Programme

The delivery of a Post-Graduate Diploma in Public Service Leadership (course title: *Collaborative Leadership for Scotland*), provided by Lancaster University Management School in conjunction with the Scottish Leadership Foundation, provided an opportunity to observe a group of public service managers. The Scottish Programme included five four-day residential sessions comprising a mix of lectures and smaller discussion groups. The Programme content ensured that the focus was on leadership, collaboration or partnership, and learning. The author sat in on these sessions and manually recorded over 160 hours of talk relevant to the topic. Sixteen students, including police and fire officers, social and health care professionals, representatives from local government and the voluntary sector participated in an 18-month exploration of leadership, collaboration and enquiry. Participants drew on their extensive experience of partnership working to describe their prior experiences of collaborative leadership. In addition, on a number of occasions participants attempted to collaborate in the production of shared work. This created the opportunity not only to draw from what they said about collaborative leadership, but also to observe the exercise of collaborative leadership in 'real time'.

Since the 1980s 'partnership working' has been viewed as an essential attribute of public services. A recent report, Governing Partnerships (Audit Commission 2005, p.4) confirmed that partnerships are big business. The report defined partnerships as 'an agreement between two or more independent bodies to work collectively to achieve an objective'. Partnerships are a significant feature of public service delivery. Around 5500 partnerships exist in the UK, accounting for some £4 billion of public expenditure. Given this, it is remarkable that there is so little hard information about their impact. Partnerships can bring significant benefits. They are a response to the complex and multi-faceted problems that face society and that cannot be tackled effectively by any individual body working alone. They can provide flexibility, innovation and additional financial and human capital resources to help solve problems. These are powerful incentives for organisations to work together and now all public bodies work in partnership to different degrees. But partnerships also bring risks. Working across organisational boundaries brings complexity and ambiguity that can generate confusion and weaken accountability. This report recommended that public bodies should be much more constructively critical about partnership working and recognise it may not be the best solution in every case. They need to be clearer about what they will achieve and how they will achieve it. Problems arise when governance and accountability are weak: leadership, decision-making, scrutiny and systems and processes such as risk management are all under-developed in partnerships. Integration without clear agreements can lead to confusion. Partnership working among Scottish public services has created an original perspective from which to explore collaborative leadership.

What method could be used that would reveal the processes of collaborative leadership at work in public sector partnerships? For the purposes of this research, social reality has been viewed as an accomplishment, created by people through their day-to-day interactions. Human life is essentially a life of meaning, of language and reflective thought and communications. 'Leadership' is not an objectively defined concept, but one lifted from the cultural, linguistic vernacular of commonly employed concepts that social actors use to make sense of the world around them. This makes it permissible, perhaps even desirable, to return leadership study to a focus on what actors and observers construct as a normal part of their social experiences. This is to suggest that both the managers being researched and in turn the researcher are trying to construct the very social features (in this case of collaborative leadership) we are trying to make sense of.

'Some say talk *is* the work of managers' (Woodilla 1998, p.31). The point about paying attention to the language of leadership is not about identifying 'good' or 'bad' communications. Rather it is about trying to understand the functions of communication patterns, their causal effects upon, and change in, people (their beliefs, attitudes, etc.), actions, social relations and the material world. Given the view of leadership set out above as a dynamic social and political relationship, and public sector partnerships as dynamic collaborations, it is clear that the study of language used in relation to collaborative leadership could have good explanatory power. A formidable barrier to the legitimacy of language analysis is the deeply rooted cultural preference for action over 'mere talk'. Indeed, a characteristic criticism of public sector partnerships has been to describe them as 'mere talking shops'. Yet talk is action, especially in the ways it enables and constrains meaning. Human interactants continually display to each other, in the course of their conversation, their own understanding of what they are doing. By trying to explore the context of human action we can gain a nuanced understanding of the historical and place-specific operation of collaborative leadership practice.

The aim of this study, then, has been to elaborate and make intelligible the meanings constructed by the people studied. It seeks to do so in a way that strives to be 'critical', not in the sense of being negative but, rather, trying to reveal the taken-for-granted understandings that, without reflection, can serve simply to reproduce the status quo. Studying critically involves challenging and disrupting this accepted knowledge in ways that opens up the possibility of unrealised alternatives (Choulariaki and Fairclough 1999). The aim is to reveal something of the underlying operation of power and influence which privileges certain views of leadership at the expense of others (Western 2008). As a result it becomes possible to imagine other meanings including those which promote the collective creation of conditions more conducive to the fulfilment of human potential. Theory becomes an aid to think about new possibilities – in this case, to transcend the limitations derived from mainstream leadership theory and begin to imagine *'how do you lead when not "in charge"?'*

Collaborative leadership in practice
The romance of collaborative leadership

Participants in the Scottish Programme highlighted a number of public documents emerging from arms of the devolved government (Audit Scotland, the Scottish Parliament Audit Committee and the Scottish Executive, as it titled itself at the time) that explicitly addressed leadership and leadership development. This included calls for the exercise of: 'strong, visible and dynamic leadership' to promote collaboration across different organisations within the Scottish public services (Scottish Executive 2006). In the view of participants these documents would significantly influence their practice in future. However, their own constructions of leadership, as experienced in collaborative partnerships, showed marked contrast. They talked instead about 'using a broken concept of leadership' and 'faceless leadership', and, with reference to the Joint Future programme (intended to promote collaborative working between health and social care agencies to deliver better outcomes for vulnerable, elderly people and for community care as a whole) 'absent leadership'.

Participants were constructing a very different notion of collaborative leadership from those who held authority over them. The evidence from the two contrasting discourses of leadership highlights the romanticised notion of 'strong, visible and dynamic leadership' advocated in official publications.

How did this view of collaborative leadership affect peoples' ability to work together? Participants first came together in the Highland Resort of Aviemore. A classroom exercise involved working together to carry out a study of the regeneration of the area examining in particular the role of collaborative leadership in the town's current revitalisation. Few of the participants had met before and inter-personal relations were relatively undeveloped. The record of their spoken interactions demonstrates that participants rapidly formed effective working groups. They clarified the task, developed a plan, allocated tasks to different group members and collaborated, for example by sharing mobile phone numbers so that they could communicate with one another.

'What is the problem/issue we are looking at?'

'Decide what we are doing, we are going to be splitting tasks.'

'Negotiating time to come together and share data.'

During these interactions there was no sense of one individual dominating the discussion. Participants appeared to be exercising collaborative leadership as defined by Chrislip and Larson (1994), leading one another to reach an implementable agreement on an issue of shared concern.

Some months later, around half the participants expressed a desire to work together to produce a piece of collaborative work with the aim of influencing the devolved government. This time the language oscillates between proposing reasons why they may collaborate, followed by a counter proposal why they may not.

'Recent experience of students doing work on my organisation – we'll act on some of the things they said.'

'It might just sit on someone's desk.'

'I don't think it will just be ignored – could be exciting...'

'I don't expect it will be ignored.'

'I think it will need a lot of planning and setting deadlines we must meet...I wouldn't like to do the project management.'

'Might be ignored – maybe it would.'

'Could be a series of bits of individual work that form parts of a planned collaboration...'

'It's like a real partnership!'

This later evidence suggests that, if a context is created in which there is nobody in charge, what you may get is not 'strong, visible and dynamic leadership' as the romance promoted in *Transforming Public Services* suggests but rather, as the participants expressed it, 'absent leadership'.

There may be a number of reasons for this. Participants demonstrated they could exercise distributed leadership when faced with the task of carrying out a case study on the regeneration of Aviemore. The discourse recorded seems to reflect the concept of 'swift trust' (Meyerson, Weick and Kramer 1996). Traditional concepts of trust suggest that it builds incrementally and accumulates – in other words, requires time and a history of mutually beneficial exchanges. Temporary groups, typical of contemporary organisations, lack the requisite history on which such incremental confidence-building measures are predicated. The authors suggest that swift trust is most likely to develop when the level of interdependency of group members is kept to a minimum with a focus on roles rather than relationships.

In short, swift trust works when the focus is on *doing*. The context of undeveloped relationships, a restricted timescale and a clearly defined task all appear to have contributed positively to enabling what was, in effect, a group of strangers to work together to produce something meaningful. Indeed, it may be significant that, in the post-Programme evaluation, participants looked back favourably on the Aviemore residential as the time when the group collaborated most effectively together.

On the other hand, the classroom environment is not the same as the (partnership) working environment where these managers would find themselves representing their organisations, with an externally imposed requirement that they collaborate. The classroom, particularly on a postgraduate course, may include the assumption that the contribution of each participant is as valid as any other. The smaller group in the second sequence of dialogue represented those self-selected as being most committed to collaborating together, yet their discourse suggested a number of doubts about both the validity and the practicality of joint working that, in the end, appeared to create the dominant voice. In contrast, in many partnership contexts there will be a 'taken-for-granted' understanding of different individual's positioning within the social hierarchy of their own organisation and therefore, by comparison, within the Scottish Public Service as a whole. The point is that this might promote conditions more or less conducive to collaborative leadership than the classroom setting that was observed.

Power/resistance in collaborative partnerships

Power theory in social and political science comprises several traditions (Flyvbjerg 2001, p.115). Mainstream management theory avoids reference to 'power'. The right of managers to exercise authority is taken for granted. 'Power' becomes equated with resistance and is viewed as, in some ways, illegitimate (Hardy and Clegg 1999, p.376). This conventional approach can be seen to be reflected in the language of collaborative public sector partnerships (Scottish Executive 2006). For the purposes of this study an alternative perspective was utilised. Lukes (2005) adopted a three-dimensional concept of power. A one-dimensional perspective is similar to Weber's conception and involves 'power over' another – equivalent to a social actor's opportunity to impose their will on another, even against the other's resistance. A two-dimensional view of power involves the above plus the power to decide which issues are key and which issues are suffocated before they are even voiced. In other words, from this perspective one examines who has the power to, literally, set the agenda. In a three-dimensional view of power A may exercise

power by shaping B's wants through control of information, media, socialisa-
tion and so on. As a result of the identification of shared culture and values, B
feels they have been consulted and that their interests have been taken into
account.

Participants in the Scottish Programme spoke of the 'traditional' exercise
of power in collaborative partnerships (i.e. one dimensional, in Lukes' construction):

> 'The Scottish Executive is becoming so prescriptive...'

> 'We are subject to micromanagement – they are playing the 'Big Adult'
> role – its creeping centralism.'

The tools deployed in this exercise of 'power over' local partnerships included
ring-fencing of finance and the passing of legislation (on Community
Planning, the Joint Future programme in health and social care, the requirements for localities to establish Community Justice Partnerships, and so on.)

'We are forced to the table...', this despite the talk of 'parity of esteem
between Scottish and local elected representatives'. While participants
believed that the priorities in local partnerships were 'driven by the Scottish
Executive's themes', one participant believed that this approach had proved
counter-productive:

> I have had experience of a voluntary partnership involving health and
> social services. This subsequently had to be formalised following the im-
> position of more controls by the Executive. I felt it was becoming less ef-
> fective as a result – people hiding behind the rule book – whereas previ-
> ously the informal arrangements, with their focus on meeting the needs of
> service users, had been perfectly adequate.

Another suggested that resistance could be exercised without overtly
opposing central Government requirements:

> 'The default position is we must collaborate – or we must *look* as if we
> are collaborating – give the appearance.'

> '[It was a] pseudo aim – do what we were going to do anyway but
> brand it as "partnership".'

Previous studies have suggested that subordinates have available a variety of
options, knowledges, cultural resources and strategic agencies through which
they can and do initiate oppositional practices (Collinson 2000, p.180).
However, it should be recognised that resistance is not always the result of
rationally organised strategic planning and instrumental calculation and that
even those who resist might not identify, explain or even recognise their

actions as explicitly oppositional. In addition, unforeseen consequences may result, including paradoxical effects whereby apparent resistance reinforces the very domination it is intended to oppose.

There was some scepticism about the ability of Government to exercise formal control. Participants argued that there was a:

'Lack of a joined-up picture from the Executive.'

'It's a shambles – a guddle.'

and expressed some frustration with trying to turn a range of policies into meaningful local service delivery:

'I wish there *were* a Master Plan!'

'Are we part of a big cosmic experiment here?'

'The idea that one size fits all Scottish communities is questionable – they are too diverse in terms of their capacity and capability – bespoke solutions [are needed].'

On the other hand, there was some individual accountability, recognising that, '[If we treat the] Executive as a 'bête noire' – externalising, stop looking at what we can do ourselves… If we work better together we will improve services.'

Another tool in the exercise of 'power over' collaborative partnerships involved monitoring of targets and inspection: 'Reality is – partnership – we are going to be *measured* on this…the alternative is not very desirable.'

Rather than objecting to such an approach there was sympathy:

'In fairness reflects Ministers' accountability – their way of managing risks – [a] mind set of ensuring shit doesn't stick to *them.*'

'[We are] criticising Scottish Executive – know in my head they are between a rock and a hard place.'

It was clear that participants had experienced occasions where power was exercised in setting agendas and deciding what could, or could not, be the subject for discussion (consistent with Lukes' two-dimensional forms of power).

'Because the local authority has a statutory duty as "lead organisation" in Community Planning this can lead to suspicion.'

'Health bigger but narrow/deep… Councils a bit broader. Infrastructure of agendas/minute writing/action plans/[preparing] papers – unless Council did all these things [they] would not happen.

Staff draft papers and other organisations comment...as a result matters of strategic importance to the Council end up being the partnership's priority.'

'[The talk is of] equal partners but some are more equal than others, for example statutory organisations with greater authority and money.'

At the same time, some participants recognised that, beyond these rather transparent exercises of power in collaborative partnerships, much occurred out of view:

'[It's like an] iceberg...majority of stuff is below the surface.'

'A lot of business [is] done outside collaboration – some overt, some covert. You don't know what you don't know.'

'Who's in and who's out needs to be carefully managed...'

'Go back to "awaydays" – who chose who attended ...'

'In [named city] a small executive took the key decisions to move the whole partnership.'

'There is a core group and a wider group – it's very difficult to negotiate decisions when everyone is watching – the core group negotiated out difficulties.'

Such an approach was described as 'The Big Cheeses round the table with the Crackers'[!]

Although it was recognised that 'Some people feel excluded', there was a sense that these types of covert exercises of power were understandable – even, perhaps, inevitable:

'The organisation probably has a clear statement of values and behaviour but then they manipulate meetings.'

'A benign meaning [is used to describe this] – "facilitative".'

'Manipulative – facilitative...how distinguish? Different words for same behaviours.'

'Getting key partners to meetings – evil techniques for greater good.'

'Who decides? But you have to do it.'

'Does everybody know you are doing this anyway?'

'Do collaborations need to be amoral? A very political environment...'

'Becomes deeply manipulative...people using opportunity to further *own* aims rather than partnership.'

There were some appeals for the application of individual, heroic leadership in collaborative partnerships: '[We are like] Israelites in the desert – we need a Moses', and reports of occasions when this had been significant:

'Symbolism of Leader [of Council] or Chief Executive attending/not attending.'

'Personal involvement of Leader/Chief Executive has real significance for other partners...political leader bring[ing] people on board.'

'Realpolitik – what we can't renegotiate.'

'Reason is these people can really bugger it up.'

But risks inherent in this approach were acknowledged:

'[My] boss can be very powerful and forceful.'

'One or two difficult individuals behaving like psychopaths.'

As part of their course of study, participants in the Scottish Programme considered case studies of two contrasting regeneration partnerships: one, in an urban area, had been written up as a 'pioneering' example of a collaborative approach to tackling de-industrialisation; the other, in the rural Highlands, was explored as a more current example of a public/private sector collaboration intended to boost economic prosperity through tourism. In the first it was acknowledged that 'There were clear references in the case study to multiple and shifting leadership roles as the [partnership] evolved.'

The second case study provided an opportunity to contrast:

'Collaborative leadership led by the community led to stagnation and decline...the public bodies didn't know what they wanted.'

'Local people [seemed] incapable of collaborating...how hard to get people together...'

with

'The autocratic approach of the entrepreneur who was prepared to invest in employment and regeneration.'

'It took one person to drive it forward – "my way or no way" approach.'

Nevertheless, participants acknowledged that this entrepreneur was also involved in collaboration: with banks lending him money; with the Council as planning authority; and with the enterprise agency that committed £8 million of public money to the regeneration programme. This same individual had subsequently been instrumental in fostering the development of an 'Attractions Group', aimed at getting a range of service providers associated with the same destination to collaborate in providing an integrated experience for the tourist customer. As one of the participants reflected, 'Local people *can* see the benefits [of the development]…but could the process have avoided putting their noses out of joint?'

This might be viewed as an appeal for the exercise of 'soft power' (equivalent to Lukes' three-dimensional perspective), seeking to persuade people that the intended outcome would benefit them; indeed, that supporting the regeneration programme would be in their own self-interest.

Implications

The report *Governing Partnerships* (Audit Commission 2005) recommended that public bodies should be much more constructively critical about partnership working and recognise it may not be the best solution in every case. This study suggests that social work and other public service managers might exercise leadership by being more prepared to challenge notions of partnership as self-evidently a 'Good Thing'. Not only does it require enormous time and effort to overcome differences in inter-organisational languages, but from the accounts of participants in the Scottish Programme, partnership working appears to be prone to subversion and to the exercise of one and two-dimensional power, as individuals attend to their own and their organisations' priorities at the expense of better outcomes for service users.

The group of managers in this study considered what alternatives might be available. They suggested that, since it can be so difficult to work across boundaries, consideration might be given to redrawing the boundaries. They quoted as an example the integration of four previously independent but supposedly collaborating forensic laboratories into a single hierarchical structure under the Scottish Police Services Authority, with the intention of improving accountability. They explored, as another possibility, the private sector model of the Joint Venture. In this the 'rules' for the collaboration are spelled out in contractual terms, including the divorce arrangements that would apply if and when it proved necessary or desirable to bring the collaboration to an end.

A second implication is that managers might give more consideration to leadership as a social, rather than an individual phenomenon. Do people at all levels in your organisation have an impact on its future direction, for example through adapting to or seeking to resist change initiatives? If we thought differently about leadership might it, as Chrislip and Larson (1994) suggested, encourage us to engage *ourselves* in the difficult work of public problem solving, avoiding quick fixes to complex issues? Might it also reduce the tendency to scapegoat individual leaders as a convenient but ultimately fruitless reaction to the continued social, economic and environmental challenges presented by the impacts of rapid globalisation on local communities?

Conclusion

Collaborative and other forms of distributed leadership provide alternative concepts to the dominant mainstream in leadership theory. Taking the social aspects of leadership seriously can provide refreshing insights into the operation of leadership both within and between organisations. This study has shown how it can reveal romantic ideas that do not necessarily assist the difficult business of finding better ways of working together. These idealisations might, in turn, make collaborative partnerships particularly prone to subversion and vulnerable to the exercise of both one and two-dimensional forms of power. It becomes clear, then, that while collaborative leadership may provide a useful way of thinking differently, especially about the interactions between social actors in cross-organisation partnerships, it does not provide a solution to all leadership challenges (Grint 2005).

References

Audit Commission (2005) *Governing Partnerships: Bridging the Accountability Gap.* Available at www.audit-commission.gov.uk/reports/NATIONAL-REPORT.asp?CategoryID=&Prod ID=1CDA0FEF-E610-463c-B3F3-220F607B1A2C, accessed 8 May 2009.

Barker, R.A. (2002) *On the Nature of Leadership.* Lanham, MD: University of America Press.

Carlyle, T. (1993) *On Heroes, Hero-Worship and the Heroic in History.* Oxford: University of California Press. (Original work published in 1856.)

Choulariaki, L. and Fairclough, N. (1999) *Discourse in Late Modernity: Rethinking Critical Discourse Analysis.* Edinburgh: Edinburgh University Press.

Chrislip, D.D. and Larson, C.E.(1994) *Collaborative Leadership: How Citizens and Civic Leaders Can Make a Difference.* San Francisco: John Wiley.

Cleveland, H. (2002) *Nobody in Charge.* San Francisco: Jossey-Bass.

Collinson, D. (2000) 'Strategies of Resistance: Power, Knowledge and Subjectivity in the Workplace.' In K. Grint (ed.) *Work and Society: A Reader.* Cambridge: Polity Press.

Flyvbjerg, B. (2001) *Making Social Science Matter: Why Social Inquiry Fails and How It Can Succeed Again.* Cambridge: Cambridge University Press.

Grint, K. (2005) *Leadership: Limits and Possibilities.* Basingstoke: Palgrave Macmillan.

Hardy, C. and Clegg, S.R. 'Some Dare Call It Power.' In S.R. Clegg and C. Hardy (eds) *Studying Organization: Theory and Method.* London: Sage.

Lukes, S. (2005) *Power: a Radical View,* 2nd edn. Basingstoke: Palgrave Macmillan.

Meyerson, D., Weick K.E. and Kramer R.M. (1996) 'Swift Trust and Temporary Groups.' In R.M. Kramer and T.R. Tyler *Trust in Organisations: Frontiers of Theory and Research*. London: Sage.

Scottish Executive (2006) *Transforming Public Services, the Next Phase of Reform*. Edinburgh: Scottish Executive. Available at www.scotland.gov.uk/Publications/2006/06/15110925/0, accessed 8 May 2009.

Western, S. (2008) *Leadership: A Critical Text*. London: Sage.

Woodilla, J. (1998) 'Workplace Conversations: the text of organising.' In D. Grant, T. Keenoy and C. Oswick *Discourse and Organisation*. London: Sage.

CHAPTER 7

The Work of Leadership in Formal Coalitions: Embracing Paradox for Collaboration

Sonia Ospina and Angel Saz-Carranza

I'm just thinking of the tension sometimes between Rainbow Network[1] and its partner agencies, as we try to work within a coalition framework, an active coalition, you know? Part of my work right now…is exactly that… And that is difficult…is challenging, there's times [when] we all just clash because we're moving from a director's model, 'here, we want to give you a helping hand' to an organizing model, to 'how can you empower yourself?' So there's bound to be clashes and we're not going around demanding 'Look you've got to change your ways,' but we're trying to work with other groups that have been through a different type of framework, and that requires a lot of cooperation and patience, and being willing to negotiate and figure out what their interests are… (Rainbow Network executive director)

This chapter explores challenges associated with the paradoxical nature of coalition work, as illustrated by the quote above from the executive director of one of the coalitions studied. We draw from a study about how leaders in successful coalitions face collaboration demands to ensure member engagement

---

1   Real names of the coalitions have been changed to protect confidentiality.

so as to make things happen. We used narrative inquiry (Dodge, Ospina and Foldy 2005; Reissman 2002) – a kind of qualitative interpretive research based on stories – to illuminate these challenges in a particular type of successful action network, urban immigrant coalitions, in a particular US policy arena, immigration.[2]

Formal coalitions like those in our study are inter-organizational action networks (Ebers 1997; Ring and Van de Ven 1994). Their coordinating units[3] advance the network's goals by promoting collaborative work among coalition members and supporting their activities to influence external actors. In the context of action networks, these efforts correspond respectively to inward work (engaging inside actors) and outward work (engaging outside actors) (Shortell et al. 2002). In this chapter we explore the inherent tensions leaders in these coordinating units faced when addressing contradictory but necessary requirements of collaboration with internal and external stakeholders. Scholars define these generic tensions as paradoxes (Ford and Backoff 1988; Lewis 2000; Ofori-Dankwa and Julian 2004; Smith and Berg 1987).

We found that coalition leaders faced the unity and diversity paradox when doing inward work, and the confrontation and dialogue paradox when doing outward work. However, rather than trying to reduce, resolve or cope with these paradoxes, leaders seemed to engage in a type of work that allowed them to fully embrace them. They thus developed what we call *leadership practices* (Ospina and Foldy 2008) that honored both sides of the paradox at the same time, in the name of the broader organizational mission – in this case, enhanced quality of life for immigrant communities.

Paradox has been an important area of interest in organization science (Ford and Backoff 1988; Lewis 2000; Poole and Van de Ven 1989). Managing paradox has also been identified as a key dimension of coalition work (Mizrahi and Rosenthal 2001). But there is little empirical work in the context of inter-organizational collaboration (Faulkner and DeRond 2000; Huxham 2003). Attention to *how* inherent challenges and tensions associated with action networks are managed successfully is an exception rather than the rule (Huxham and Beech 2003).

That most people attribute failure in networks to poor management (Park and Ungson 2001) suggests the urgency of learning from effective leaders.

---

2   For information about the broader national, multi-year, multi-method research project about social change leadership in the United States, please go to www.leadershipforchange.org (accessed 8 May 2009).

3   The coordinating unit is 'a separate administrative entity…set up to govern the network [and] plays a key role in coordinating and sustaining' it (Provan and Kenis 2007, p.236). It is also known as the network administrative organization (NAO).

This is particularly true given the relevance of this governance mechanism (Agranoff and McGuire 2001) to address acute social problems in a shared-power world (Crosby and Bryson 2005). Empirical studies of successful cases offer an opportunity to produce actionable knowledge about effective leadership of formal coalitions.

The chapter is structured as follows. We first introduce the concept of paradox and connect our research question to the received literature. Next we briefly describe the methods used in our study, as well as the cases and their policy context. We then present the findings, structuring them around the challenges of inward and outward work. A discussion and a conclusion highlight the implications and promise of linking leadership, paradox and collaboration when considering the challenges of inter-organizational work. We then offer, in a post-script, some personal reflections about the practical implications of accepting the notion that embracing paradox might help to effectively address the challenges of collaboration.[4]

Paradox, inter-organizational collaboration and leadership

Lewis (2000) defines paradox as some 'thing' that denotes contradictory yet interwoven elements (for example, perspectives, feelings, messages, demands, identities, interests, or practices) – elements that seem logical in isolation but absurd and irrational when appearing simultaneously. A paradox, then, is a duality – consisting of two parts – of opposing poles, poles standing in contradiction, which create a tension or a strained condition.[5] The paradoxes explored in this paper are empirical realities, 'demands' that occur when organizations need to collaborate. Leaders experience their impact directly, because, while contradictory, these demands coexist. Organization and management theory offers valuable insights about paradoxes, but few studies have explored empirically how organizational actors respond to them.

Paradox in organizational studies

That paradox has gained considerable momentum is reflected in the special issue of the *Academy of Management Review* dedicated to 'paradox, spirals, and ambivalence' (Eisenhardt 2000). The construct itself is complicated and scholars use it differently, as it is only emerging as a subject of theoretical

---

4   We choose to frame these final reflections as a post-script to signal our awareness of the tentativeness of our findings, and the fact that we cannot make definitive statements based on our research.

5   A dilemma, on the other hand, is the choice between two alternatives (poles), either of which is equally (un)favorable.

and empirical study.[6] Nevertheless, it offers great promise to illuminate the dynamics of organizing in today's complex and interdependent world.

Paradox has been considered in a variety of organizational arenas. For example, Smith and Berg (1987) argue that group life is inherently paradoxical. They document instances where individuals pursue conflicting goals and engage simultaneously in contradictory processes of equal relevance for organizational life. At a more macro-level, the idea of the network society (Castells 2000) is grounded in the contradicting yet simultaneous realities of high fragmentation but also interdependence (Kickert et al. 1997).

Between these two levels of action, scholars in the strategic alliance field highlight the tensions between vigilance and trust and between individualism and collectivism (de Rond and Bouchikhi 2004). Similarly, the strategic management literature documents the tension between competition and cooperation (Brandenburger and Nalebuff 1996). Managers' responses to the challenges posed by these paradoxes are less interesting to these scholars, given their focus on organizational strategy.

Paradox in inter-organizational contexts

Ambiguity and complexity in the network governance form underscores the pervasiveness of paradox in networks and their management. Given the multiple factors associated with network formation, the resulting governance structures are the repository of a diverse and often contradictory set of expectations, aspirations, and goals (Huxham 2003; Huxham and Beech 2003; McGuire 2002; Saz-Carranza 2007; Saz-Carranza and Serra 2006).[7]

Scholars of inter-organizational collaboration acknowledge the presence of conceptual paradoxes, anomalies, and ambiguities (Huxham and Vangen 2000; Rainey and Busson 2001). For example, Vangen and Huxham argue that managing trust in network collaborations demands 'dealing with many paradoxes inherent in collaborative activities' (2004, p.23). They are inherent because the potential for collaborative advantage depends on each partner's ability to bring different resources (Huxham and Beech 2003). This need is,

---

6　　For example, some scholars use 'paradox' to identify contradictory yet valid and coexisting theories regarding organizational phenomena, while others refer to a concrete and identifiable phenomenon in organizational life, and yet others use the term when contradictory findings are empirically documented (Poole and Van de Ven 1989).

7　　Factors associated with goal attainment include ownership over goals (by the network, its members, and individual representatives), openness of the aims (implicit, explicit, and hidden), and means of achieving them (using the network, its members or individuals) (Huxham and Vangen 2000). Goal complexity has practical implications. For example, goal clarity influences which tasks a network manager decides to undertake (McGuire 2002).

however, a function of differences in organizational purpose, which reduces the incentives for collaboration (Eden and Huxham 2001). Moreover, diversity slows progress towards common goals because adjustments, such as trust and familiarity, take time and energy (Mizrahi and Rosenthal 2001). Inter-organizational action networks – such as coalitions – need both unity and diversity.

Social work scholars Bailey and Koney (1996) discuss paradoxical management in coalitions. This is a way, they argue, for managers to address tensions such as the need to be both responsive to and assertive with the membership. Nevertheless, despite some exceptions, exploring how social actors experience and address paradox in a context characterized by dynamic tensions remains a rare occurrence in the received literature.

Responding to paradox

If addressing paradox is not the object of empirical work, organizational scholars do discuss theoretically the forms it may take. An actor can simply favor one pole over the other, or she can try to reach a balance between poles. Moreover, managing each pole could be alternated (Poole and Van den Ven 1989; Van den Ven and Poole 1988) – as when two companies have their development departments cooperate in product design and compete in product sales. Similarly, poles may be applied at alternate times according to context, as suggested by the situational leadership literature (Hersey and Blanchard 1982).

Another way of managing paradox is to make the inherent tensions apparent and to accept them (March and Weil 2005). Some scholars argue that the edge of chaos created in coping with paradox is healthy (Eisenhardt 2000), and that specific mindsets and dispositions, competencies and skills can be developed to reframe and live with paradox (Quinn and Cameron 1988). March and Weil (2005) lament that the potential benefits of ambiguity for organizational performance are undermined because rational frameworks dominate organizational studies. Similarly, Kaplan and Kaiser (2003) call for versatile leadership, that is, the capacity to function well while holding opposites.

But how is this done? What does the work look like when leaders encounter paradox on a daily basis and respond to it? How does this relate to the work that advances the mission? And how does it happen in contexts that are inherently paradoxical? Despite an increasing awareness of the presence of paradox and its potential role in organizational performance, these questions have yet to be answered. One way of exploring them in action networks, particularly in coalitions, is by focusing on the work of leadership (Heifetz 1994).

The work of leadership in managing paradox

A focus on the work of leadership presupposes a particular approach to leadership. Traditional understandings tend to emphasize leaders' attributes or the relationship between leaders and followers, what Uhl-Bien (2006) calls an 'entity' perspective of leadership. More appropriate to the task is a 'relational' (Uhl-Bien 2006) or constructionist (Ospina and Sorenson 2006) approach, which represents novel thinking in the leadership field (Jackson and Parry 2008).

In a constructionist approach, leadership is relational, emergent and contextual (Ospina and Sorenson 2006). It is a collective process of meaning making that produces shared direction, commitment and alignment to achieve agreed upon common purposes (Drath 2001). Leaders and followers *construct* each other as leadership *happens* when the group agrees upon ways to move forward to achieve these (Hosking 2007). When leadership happens it is thus a collective achievement and, as such, it belongs to the group (Dachler and Hosking 1995). It is found in the group's work, not in specific individuals'. This meaning making in communities of practice (Drath and Palus 1994) is embedded in historically grounded structures of power and influenced by the dynamics of exclusion that characterize social relationships (Ospina and Sorenson 2006; Schall *et al.* 2004).

That leadership is socially constructed does not imply always taking a collective form. Always rooted in collective processes, leadership can nevertheless emerge in the form of strong charismatic individuals; or in dyads, as in the case of co-leaders; or in committees with decision-making authority; or in organizations with democratic governance structures where it is made collective by design. Similarly, the work of leadership can be distributed among individuals taking up different roles, it can also be rotated over time or it can occur in many places within a given system. Finally, all social actors have the capacity to exercise leadership, but not all do. Those who do may enact different styles, such as democratic, autocratic, laissez-faire and so on (Ospina and Sorenson 2006).

Illuminating leadership work in coalitions made up of multiple organizations requires focusing on the efforts that emerge in response to situations that call forth what some scholars call 'relational work' (Fletcher 2008). Relational work aims to promote conditions for concerted action by fostering connectedness and emphasizing interdependence (Fletcher 2008). We can illuminate the actions associated with this type of work by inquiring into what we call 'leadership practices.' As a social construct, 'practice' is located within the collective rather than the individual realm. Practices are the outcome of collective meaning making; they rest upon a shared knowledge, largely implicit, historically and culturally specific, which transcends individual cognition (Reckwitz 2002; Swidler 2001). A focus on leadership practices offers a way to make operational the work of leadership, viewed as a social construction.

To sum up, interest in paradox ranks high in organizational studies, and it is considered an important dimension of collaborative work in the received literature. But how leaders address paradox when confronted with it has not received sufficient research attention, and even less in the context of inter-organizational collaboration. We contribute to this agenda by illuminating the leadership practices of staff in the coordinating units of formal coalitions supporting immigrant organizations. A relational approach to leadership allows us to draw from practice theory to explore the work of leadership as it emerges in response to the challenges of collaboration.

Methods

Our study used narrative inquiry as the primary methodology (Clandinin and Connelly 2000; Ospina and Dodge 2005; Reissman 2002) to answer the research question 'how do leaders in successful coalitions manage collaboration challenges to make things happen?' We collected data – stories about inter-organizational collaborative work – from members of two coalitions that supported immigrants in large urban centers of the US. These coalitions had public recognition as successful networks achieving effective change in their domain.

The cases

The studied coalitions supported the immigrant communities of two large cities in the US. Immigrant Policy Network (IPN) and Rainbow Network (RN) were respectively located in two major urban centers, one on the north east coast and the other in the midwest. Both represented large portions of their city's immigrant population, including the traditional Mexican, Dominican, Eastern European and Chinese immigrants as well as Latin American, African, South Asian and the Middle Eastern newcomers. Both networks aimed to improve immigrants' quality of life and to provide a forum for their voice and collective action. Figure 7.1 offers a description of the coalitions' mission and work.

These coalitions represent a specific inter-organizational governance mode – a network, that is, a long-term cooperative relationship among organizations, in which each entity retains control over their own resources, but jointly decide on their use (Brass *et al.* 2004; Ebers 1997).[8] Coalitions are a specific type of action network (Agranoff 2003).

SAMPLING CRITERIA

The decision to focus on only two cases responded to the exploratory nature of a topic with scant empirical research: the work of *leadership* in response to collaboration challenges in a type of action network, *coalitions*. These are not representative cases, but a purposive sample, chosen to explore in depth the richness and complexity of inter-organizational collaboration and to surface themes that merit further research.

The coalitions were comparable along two key dimensions: policy domain (immigration) and location (large urban centers). Their governing bodies were also similar, including a core coordinating unit with an executive director accountable to a board of directors that included membership representation.

There were also key differences. Their local and state policy contexts differed. Despite comparable annual budgets ($1.3 million and $1 million, respectively), their funding sources also differed slightly.[9] Their membership size and structure (20 and 150 members) and the complexity and size of the staff working in the coordinating unit (9 and 17) also differed. Their age (5 and 15 years) evidenced different life cycle stages, one relatively young and maturing (Rainbow Network), and the other well established (Immigrant Policy Network).

Data collection and analysis

Stories were collected via two rounds of individual and group in-depth interviews during site visits to the coalition coordinating units. Individual leaders from this unit were interviewed independently and then joined group interviews with representatives of stakeholder members (such as other staff from the coordinating unit, and representatives of the board, member organizations, clients, funders, allies and public officials). Twelve hours of conversation with 12 individuals associated with the coalitions yielded about 500 pages of transcripts. These were complemented with archival material such as

---

8   Similar cooperative arrangements have been studied under the rubrics of partnerships,
     strategic alliances, inter-organizational relationships, cooperative arrangements, or
     collaborative agreements (Provan, Fish and Sydow 2007, p.480).
9   Immigrant Policy Network depended almost entirely on foundations, while Rainbow
     Network drew also on government and corporations. Only the latter accepted
     governmental money, reflecting ideological differences.

Immigrant Policy Network

Mission: 'to provide a forum for the immigrant community to discuss urgent issues and provide a vehicle for collective action in addressing these issues.'

Programs:

- Policy Analysis and Advocacy – practices, policies and laws affecting the quality of life of immigrant communities
- Civic Participation and Voter Education – large-scale voter registration project, multiple voter education events, recruitment of bilingual poll workers
- Immigrant Concerns Training Institute – workshops and seminars on relevant issues to immigrant communities
- Community Education – develops multi-language educational materials on immigration law, the citizenship process, school registration, health care access and voting rights

Rainbow Network

Mission: 'to improve the quality of life for immigrants and refugees and to ensure dignity and respect by organizing and uniting communities through education, leadership development and direct services and by promoting a voice of community in public policy.'

Programs:

- English Literacy and Civics – integrated English literacy and civics education to immigrant and other limited-English-proficient population with a focus on promoting active community participation
- Community Organizing – develops community groups to work towards social justice for immigrants and refugees
- Independent Monitoring Board – active participation to ensure that the Immigration and Naturalization Service (INS) is accountable to the public
- Computer Technology Project – bridges the Digital Divide for its partner agencies
- Citizenship and Voter Training School – a 'gathering place' where community leaders share their concerns

FIGURE 7.1: DESCRIPTION OF THE IMMIGRANT COALITIONS' MISSION AND WORK

independent analytical memos about the leadership challenges in each coalition and documentation of the organizations' accomplishments.[10]

Data collection and analysis focused on organizational strategies and activities revealed in the stories, including evidence of collaboration challenges. Interview protocols included questions about the organizations' issue focus, the activities conducted to attain the mission, and leadership challenges in their particular arenas of operation. They did not include explicit questions about collaboration, which nevertheless emerged spontaneously in the stories. Neither were there questions about paradox, which also emerged as a pattern in the analysis.

The analysis identified and explored patterns grounded in the data. We canvassed interview transcripts to explore the challenges of collaboration within the context of the organizations' work. The method was interpretive, with systematic and recurrent readings of the narratives to find meaning and identify patterns. We alternated deductive and inductive analysis, first coding categories using concepts from the received literature, and then developing 'grounded' codes reflecting ways to address the challenges of collaboration emerging from identified stories. Embracing paradox as a way to address the challenges of collaboration was an unexpected finding.[11]

Policy context and organizational achievements

Immigrant Policy Network and Rainbow Network represent successful efforts of immigrant communities to participate in the polity and offer a new model of work with immigrants in their respective cities.

Urban political machines, religious institutions, social service nonprofits and settlement houses have offered assistance to immigrant communities over the past 200 years in the US. Immigrant service and advocacy organizations focusing on services for refugees and targeted immigrant groups (for example legal assistance involving citizenship and work permits) have mostly worked independently and in isolation.

The Immigration Reform and Control Act of 1986 (IRCA) altered the demographic landscape of many urban and rural areas of the US, including those of the studied coalitions. IRCA made 3 million undocumented workers and

---

10   These materials were drawn from the data set of the Leadership for a Changing World
      program's Research and Documentation Component. The coalitions participated between
      2001 and 2003.
11   The literature identifies many paradoxes of organizing, including the ones described in
      this paper. Only two emerged from the stories as a concern of leaders in the studied
      coalitions. This does not imply the absence from their work of other paradoxes, but we
      cannot consider them given our inductive approach.

their families eligible for legal status, broadening the demand for services and collaboration among organizations (Federation for American Immigration Reform 2003; Moran and Petsod 2003). Service organizations quickly adapted to include assistance in language skills, workforce integration, training and other social services.

Emerging from this fertile ground that created many new nonprofits, a small group of immigration reform advocates in a large north-east city gave birth to Immigrant Policy Network in 1987. The new locally based immigrant advocacy organization offered support to immigrants and newly made citizens, while also responding to IRCA's goal to deter illegal immigration to the US. In a large Midwest urban center twelve years later, propelled by the anti-immigrant tone of the 1996 federal welfare reform initiative, several immigrant groups coalesced around an unresponsive local Immigration and Naturalization Service (INS)[12] office and became the Rainbow Network.

IPN and RN developed within the dispersed, atomized and isolated immigration environments in two of the largest US cities. Their sustainability, the stability of their staff, boards and budgets and the strong reputation and public credibility they enjoy are evidence of their success. Figure 7.2 illustrates mission specific achievements for each coalition.

Both coalitions have received prestigious awards, one of which characterizes their work as effective, systemic, strategic and able to sustain results beyond individual efforts. Their ability to engage in effective inter-organizational collaboration to attain their goals makes these coalitions excellent cases for study.

Findings: Addressing paradox for inter-organizational collaboration

In answering our original question – how do leaders in successful coalitions manage collaboration challenges to make things happen? – paradox emerged as a key reality of the work.

As staff in the coordinating units of the studied coalitions tried to respond to the challenges of collaboration within a network governance structure, they spent time and energy doing leadership work that was distinct from, but supported, the critical tasks required to address the public problem of concern.

---

12   After the interviews, in 2003, the functions of the former Immigration and Naturalization Service (INS) were incorporated into the US Citizenship and Immigration Services (USCIS) of the US Department of Homeland Security.

This leadership work was meant to ensure that apparently competing demands, which seemed essential to advance the mission, were honored. In particular, coalition leaders faced and addressed the paradoxes of unity and diversity and of confrontation and dialogue. In describing their work, leaders thought of themselves as solving puzzles around what one of them called 'the ironies of the work', what we call here the artful management of paradox.

We have structured this section around Shortell *et al.*'s (2002) distinction between inward and outward work in organizational networks. Inward work refers to explicit efforts to build community, that is, to nurture and maintain the network and the effective coordination of members' work. Outward work is about actions to influence external actors in order to achieve the network's goals.

Immigrant Policy Network

- Immigrant voter education and mobilization campaign for the 2000 elections (enrolled over 60,000 members of immigrant families; registered more than 200,000 new citizens)

- Won millions of city and state dollars in recent years to expand legal services and English classes for its city's immigrants

Rainbow Network

- Organized a petition campaign for INS reform (more than 19,000 signatures collected), contributing to create a watchdog and reform organization (Independent Monitoring Board)

- By 2000 the board had sent approximately 800 documented cases to INS and to members of Congress, detailing the experiences of immigrants and refugees with INS backlog

---

FIGURE 7.2: SELECTED ACHIEVEMENTS

Inward work: Honoring the competing demands for unity and diversity

Rainbow Network worked with 13 different communities, and programs for its 20 organizational members were executed in 11 different languages. This coalition included organizations whose clients ranged from a couple of thousand up to 20 thousand a year. Members in Immigrant Policy Network also covered most ethnic communities in the city, and included, at one end of the spectrum, a federation of 81 Latino health and human services agencies, serving more than 800,000 vulnerable Latinos annually, and a small Korean neighborhood organization serving a narrow catchment area, at the other end.

Membership and size differences were exacerbated by the coalitions' focus on immigration. Organizations served people of multiple ethnicities, with diverse religions, cultural and linguistic characteristics. Some member organizations provided services and others did organizing or advocacy work. Problems tackled ranged from comprehensive services to very specialized issues, like health, ageing, problems for specific immigrant communities, or very narrow issues like HIV. Given this diversity, it is no wonder that an education specialist at Rainbow Network argued: 'There's a lot of politics among the [coalition members] and to get everybody to agree [is] not easy.'

While making agreement potentially hard, this diversity accounted for the coalitions' strength. At Immigrant Policy Network, a cofounder argued that internal diversity was a key factor for effectiveness: 'whatever the process has been, we've been able, for the most part, to bring so many different groups to the table that don't normally advocate together'. The executive director reinforced this: 'we had all of these different groups coming...with the shared message on these issues, and then they [actors of the target agency] all scratched their heads saying: "So, Central American Refugee Center is...in on this with UJA and with...?" ...and that's when they realize that they have to pay closer attention.' Diversity thus played a strategic role in the coalition's attaining sufficient leverage as an interlocutor at the policy table.

However, if not managed, this diversity could hinder the unity required for the coalitions to act with a single voice. The diverse characteristics, strengths, goals and hence interests of the membership made reaching common ground and collaboration harder. The basic experience afforded by the common 'immigrant' identity provided a starting point to build community, but it was not enough. The advocacy director at Immigrant Policy Network said about the differences between big and small organizations: 'all of them don't really get along [but] they're all together because there is a strong consensus, you know, on the agenda, as it really brings people together.'

Creating common ground required managing differences in a creative way, such as finding agreement in respecting disagreements by taking no position in regard to controversial issues. This is the case when the Immigrant Policy Network carefully assessed the consequences of addressing school vouchers as part of its education reform work. After analyzing the pro-voucher position, the anti-voucher position and the no-position, the coalition agreed to take no position, thus upholding the ideological diversity while finding unity in the way the decision was made. The executive director commented: 'It would have really been a "make or break" issue for [some organizations], and we just decided that "vouchers" wasn't an important enough issue on our agenda for us to lose major players of the Coalition over it.'

The functional need to maintain and honor the needed diversity without threatening the needed unity to ensure collaboration required deliberate and strategic work. Three leadership practices emerged from the analysis: nurturing and facilitating member interaction, fostering openness and participatory processes and paying attention to personal relationships.

FACILITATING INTERACTION

The coordinating unit played a facilitating role that encouraged member interaction. Activities like setting up a press conference, identifying and proposing immigration-related issues as the source for common work, or setting the structure and processes for organizational exchanges reminded coalition members of a shared platform geared toward united action.

Coalition members appreciated the coordinating unit staff's constant follow up, setting of the stage, and looking at the small details, while giving each organization enough space to showcase its separate identity. A Rainbow Network member indicated that the message was not just of being welcome, but of understanding that 'if you're not here, there is going to be something missing. And it started a trend of feeling like you all needed to contribute in order to make something as successful as it turned out to be.' The practices to facilitate interaction also reinforced the importance of member participation. A staff member at Immigrant Policy Network said: 'it is less about [the executive director] being a leader than nurturing other leaders and setting up the processes to nurture them.' The value of participation highlighted in this comment represents the second leadership practice.

PROMOTING OPENNESS AND PARTICIPATION

The Immigrant Policy Network's board discussion about school vouchers described above illustrates the importance of devoting efforts to ensure that all perspectives were heard before a decision was made. The process used reflects openness and participation. Decision making in both coalitions took the form of participatory processes, in particular when the stakes were high. A member of Rainbow Network claimed: 'The way we work together is [we] build consensus among us. And sometimes that takes longer.' Yet these lengthy deliberation processes ensured that the outcome was not arrived at at the expense of either unity or diversity.

Participation reflected the value of diversity and at the same time created ownership and commitment among coalition members, thus promoting unity. A staff member of the Immigrant Policy Network said: 'It's been really essential for us to show that we care just as much about the Russian, Korean, Chinese, Haitian and South Asian votes as we do about the Latino vote,' and as a consequence, 'we've been able to maintain the sense of...multi-ethnic participation, and our agenda has always been inclusive.'

'There doesn't feel like a dominance of power in Rainbow Network [so] that one group has more say than the other group,' claimed a member. Promoting a relatively balanced power distribution was at the core of the work of leadership in these coalitions. The Immigrant Policy Network's executive director described her efforts to ensure that small grass roots organizations were not overpowered by the large powerful multi-service organizations represented on the board, while giving the latter their due. She explained: 'Instead of trying to take away power or suppress those that are powerful, you just elevate the emerging groups so that they're more on equal grounds. So you don't alienate, you know, some of the more established groups.' Inclusiveness, participation and open processes allowed leaders to turn differences that could produce conflict into sources of strength for the coalition, thus honoring both sides of the unity and diversity paradox.

CULTIVATING PERSONAL RELATIONSHIPS

'And when you get a group that's diverse as we are, staying...fairly friendly and really not having a tremendous difference of opinion about who did this and who didn't do that, that's pretty good testimony to your ability to keep us all on track,' said a representative of a member organization to the executive director of Rainbow Network during an interview. This comment illustrates the consequences of the recurrent work he did to pay personal attention to each member, and investing time 'into building relationships with local leaders,' as a coalition staff of the Immigrant Policy Network said.

This emotional work helped to build trust and respect in the face of differences. The advocacy director of Immigrant Policy Network described the executive director as very attentive to each new coalition member. She was always trying to help them find their way and their voice, sometimes, in the words of the staff, creating 'a little personalized plan' that helped them best use their potential within the coalition. The advocacy director experienced directly the impact of this type of work when her small neighborhood organization first started working with the coalition, and the executive director sent them a personal note congratulating them for their contribution to their first campaign. She recalls, 'I just didn't expect the executive director of this large, broad-based group to be doing that, so I felt like she was really welcoming and seeking out our involvement.' She was impressed: 'we didn't know anybody and here she is writing us a letter...' and 'putting in that time to cultivate relationships and to take the time to have the conversations...'

The three leadership practices associated with embracing the unity and diversity paradox interact to produce the synergy required to create a sense of community, while maintaining diversity as a resource. A participatory process needs facilitation and nurturing. Similarly, personal relationships are an outcome of, as well as an input to, participatory processes. Together, these leadership practices helped to foster unity, despite the tremendous differences among coalition members, thus creating the fertile soil for collaboration. As a community, coalition members were then ready to influence key external organizations.

Outward work: Managing dialogue and confrontation to facilitate external collaboration

Members in coalitions spent considerable energy engaging actors from the institutional targets that the coalition intended to influence. The goal of improving immigrants' quality of life demanded that coalitions influence the regional and federal offices of a public agency over which they had no direct power, the Immigration and Naturalization Service. This agency's power was far superior to that of either coalition, given its legal mandate and role in implementing immigration policy, the favorable political climate towards increased control and the irregular legal status of some of the coalition's constituents.

To successfully influence the behavior of this powerful target, coalition leaders could not just engage in frontal attack or direct resistance. They also had to engage representatives of the target agency in dialogue and collaboration. This meant combining two contradictory engagement forms in the same relationship. Immigrant Policy Network's executive director justified the simultaneous use of dialogue and confrontation when she said: 'You're no good to anybody if you're someone's friend all the time. But you're also no good if you're the enemy all the time…' In her view, the trick was to 'intelligently and ethically strike the balance between…maintaining relationships being important to people, and at the same time being able to be critical of them,' so as to get them 'to do what you want them to do.'

In practice, confrontation implied questioning the target agency publicly regarding unacceptable behavior, inhumane policies or defective outputs of immigration processing tasks. But confrontation would not exclude collaboration efforts with either the INS or other administrative and political bodies. Leadership work was required to manage these competing demands. We identified three leadership practices that helped leaders embrace this paradox of engagement with influential targets: maintaining credibility, working at multiple levels and cultivation of multiple relationships.

MAINTAINING CREDIBILITY

Credibility played an important role in using dialogue and confrontation successfully, in two different ways. General credibility made the coalitions more reliable in the eyes of the target organization. The coalitions' threats were more powerful during confrontation, and their offers for collaboration more convincing during dialogue. A Rainbow Network founder, currently the director of one of its member organizations, described the potential for dialogue as follows: 'We've demonstrated that we have the credibility… In fact, the INS regional office local director…has continuously sought out this body to communicate with…because he realizes that we're representing the voices of his customers.' Credibility represented a form of political capital that allowed coalitions to engage legitimately in confrontation as needed, without then being discounted as a potential collaborator by the same agency.

MULTI-LEVEL WORKING

Working at local, state and national levels via campaigns, lobbying and partnering with other nonprofits allowed the coalitions to keep up with the INS's own multi-level presence and operating arenas. The strategic importance of information was multiplied when the sources were broadened, as illustrated in the comment of the director of training and legal service at Immigrant Policy Network: 'We were the only group that knew what was going on because of our relationship with people in DC.'

Acting on and linking different levels of action allowed these coalitions to combine simultaneously, although at different levels, the engagement strategies of dialogue and confrontation within the same agency, as when

Immigration Policy Network staff confronted federal officials while maintaining dialogue with the district office.

CULTIVATING MULTIPLE RELATIONSHIPS

Having relationships at different layers of an agency and with multiple actors in the environment prevented 'burning bridges' (using the words of Immigrant Policy Network's executive director) and safeguarded opportunities to introduce dialogue before or after confrontation. Moreover, relationships helped the coalitions stay in a political environment characterized by internal mobility associated with political changes. Forecasting a change of commissioner in the INS, the executive director of Immigrant Policy Network said: 'There we would draw on our relationships with other groups around the country, the other immigration coalitions, and our partners nationally. Veronica goes to regular meetings down in DC that a lot of the groups have with the INS.'

In sum, maintaining credibility in the policy field, working with multiple actors from the same agency and from different jurisdictions, as well as maintaining an extended network of external relationships facilitated the simultaneous engagement in confrontation and dialogue. This way, leaders embraced rather than resolved paradox.

Discussion and conclusions

The competing demands posed by the unity and diversity paradox, when doing inward work, and the confrontation and dialogue paradox, when doing outward work, represented significant collaboration challenges as coalition leaders tried to make things happen.

The functional need to honor both sides of each paradox demanded explicit and deliberate efforts – what we have called here leadership practices – for leaders to be able to leverage the coalitions' collaborative advantage (Huxham 2003; Huxham and Macdonald 1992).

This leadership work was distinct from the instrumental tasks and activities associated with effective management, like strategic planning or budgeting, and from the expressive strategies associated with social change work, like organizing, advocating or developing community. As *practices,* they were organic and purposive social interventions (Polkinghorne 2004) – embodied and routinized ways of *understanding, knowing how and desiring* (Reckwitz 2002, p.250) – that the group, bound together by collaborative challenges, enacted when making meaning out of their experience. As *leadership* practices, they mixed elements of both instrumental and expressive logics of action (Polkinghorne 2004). Moreover, these practices informed the managerial and strategic social change work.

Leaders embraced paradox through six leadership practices. Purposively facilitating membership interaction, promoting openness and participation and cultivating personal relationships ensured both unity and diversity inside the coalition. Purposively managing the coalition's credibility, working at various levels of action (multi-level), and cultivating multiple external relationships enabled them to engage successfully in confrontation and dialogue with the target.

Independently, each of these activities has been traditionally identified in the received literature as a way to effectively manage networks of organizations. For example, in the case of practices associated with unity and diversity, facilitating interaction has been viewed as a nurturing process to ensure inter-organizational collaboration (Agranoff and McGuire 2001; Huxham 2003; Kickert, Klijn and Koopenjan 1997). Similarly, openness is considered key to effective management in networks (Agranoff 2003), and cultivating personal relationships is a prerequisite to building trust (Agranoff and McGuire 2001; Mattessich, Murray-Close and Monsey 2001; Ospina and Yaroni 2003; Ring and Van de Ven 1994). However, scholars have not linked these activities to the paradoxical demands of inter-organizational collaboration. Our contribution lies in viewing them as practices embedded within a broader logic: together, they represent the work of leadership in the context of a complex governance structure characterized by paradox.

In the case of confrontation and dialogue, our findings also resonate with activities previously identified in the received literature. But they gain explanatory power when seen in the context of the need to address paradox. For example, scholars have indicated that collaboration represents only one of several possible strategies to engage a coalition's external environment (Mizrahi and Rosenthal 2001). Other strategies include compliance, contention and contestation (Hardy and Phillips 1998). Selection of a given strategy is contingent on factors like the nature of previous relationships with the target, its power and the coalition's capacity to influence it. Our findings suggest that these engagement strategies functioned in an interdependent way: they belong to a coherent set of strategic practices reflecting a choice to embrace and live with paradox.

Together, the identified practices document the work of leadership as it emerges over time to face the challenges of collaboration. These practices are not just isolated tasks or activities, but visible, publicly enacted patterns of action (Swidler 2001) that have become habitual yet are quite purposive (Polkinghorne 2004). They reflect internalized collective understandings of how to perform the work (Drath 2001; Hosking 2007; Reckwitz 2002) to attain, in this case, collaborative work for social change.

The two sets described – for embracing unity/diversity and confrontation/dialogue respectively – seem to represent the purposive yet taken for granted responses to the contradictory pulls for the leaders' attention and energy in different directions. If such is the case they evidence the artful management of paradox, a type of leadership work that may be required for successful coalition building.

These findings are fairly tentative, given the data and design limitations of our exploratory study. For example, we did not include explicit questions about collaboration, so we might have missed other paradoxes and practices not captured by the data. Similarly, we do not know if the identified phenomena are specific only to immigration coalitions. Finally, our findings about the relationship between collaboration, paradox and leadership were unexpected. Hence the next step is to explore deductively that effective collaboration in formal coalitions involves explicit leadership work that allows embracing, rather than resolving, paradox. Research designs with more cases and different policy areas are needed to further develop and test this proposition.

If our findings hold, however, the implications for practice are exciting: awareness of the pervasiveness of paradox and its implications for the work of leadership can better prepare coalition participants to address the inherent challenges of collaborative work. Instead of viewing paradox as a problem to be resolved, practitioners can view it as a natural feature of coalition work that, embraced and honored, can contribute to develop collaborative advantage (Huxham 2003; Huxham and Macdonald 1992) and enhance collaborative capacity in the coalition and its organizational members (Bardach 1998).

At the risk of oversimplifying, we offer below some practical considerations for embracing paradox in the context of networked governance structures typical in today's world:

- Recognize that paradox is a normal state of organizational life, not something problematic or to be avoided.

- Identify those areas of the work where demands direct your attention in opposing directions: these are areas of paradox, and they are context specific.

- Understand the nature of the demands that pull you in different directions: Why do they exist? How does each help to move the work forward? What are the tradeoffs of *not* addressing each demand? Of addressing them simultaneously? How can these be minimized?

- Recognize that addressing both demands simultaneously will take time, energy and effort; be aware of the tradeoffs and of their consequences, and be prepared to manage them.

- Devise, or learn from others, leadership practices that you can adapt to honor both sides of the identified paradoxes.

And, finally, reframe, for yourself and for those to whom you are accountable, what it means to be effective and efficient. After all, embracing paradox means living with complexity and uncertainty in ways that may take the work through longer paths or may demand alternative logic. This contrasts with the quicker and more expedient ways to respond to paradox, such as favoring one pole over the other, or alternating their management, or focusing on each according to context. These ways of resolving the paradox might lead to simpler work, but not necessarily better, considering the potential benefits of honoring both poles of the paradox as part of your leadership work.

Post-script: A metaphor to explore the implications of embracing paradox

A mathematician confided

That a Möbius band is one-sided

And you'll get quite a laugh

If you cut one in half

For it stays in one piece when divided[13]

This poem refers to the curious and counterintuitive Möbius band (Emmer 1980; Peterson 2000a and b), discovered by the mathematician August Möbius[14] and popularized by M.C. Escher's etching of ants crawling indefinitely on an eight-figure surface. Escher's ants walk indefinitely on a flat area with no edge in the direction of their movement, in what is clearly a Möbius band, with one side, one surface and one edge. The Möbius band offers a perfect metaphor to imagine what it means to face and embrace the paradoxical challenges of inter-organizational collaboration.

---

13   Anonymous poet (cited in Emmer 1980, p.110).
14   Simultaneously discovered by the mathematician J.B. Listing in 1858 and then by the visual artist Max Bill in 1936 (Emmer 1980).

To create a Möbius band (or strip) half twist a strip of paper (a 180 degree twist) and secure together its ends to form a loop. The enigmatic result is a shape that has only one continuous side: if you place your finger in one side (point A) and follow the shape along without lifting it, you will return to a point marked in what appeared to be the other side of the band (point B). Both sides of the paper are actually the same side, or one continuous side. Moreover, if you try to cut a straight line in the middle of the strip (parallel to its two edges) instead of two parallel strips as expected, the result will be one single longer strip, also with a twist. As stated in the poem above, 'it stays in one piece when divided.'

In a sense, embracing the identified paradoxes of collaboration means treating them not as a reality with two separate poles, but instead viewing the poles as two dimensions of the same 'one-sided' reality. For example, honoring the poles of unity and diversity is like moving the finger from point A to B along the Möbius band without 'lifting the finger,' to experience a one-sided, continuous loop, as unity turns into diversity, turns into unity, and so on, thus creating the desired result of *unity in diversity* (Saz-Carranza 2007). In contrast, in a normal strip with two sides, one for unity and one for diversity, the poles would coexist but never interconnect.

The Möbius band metaphor clarifies the practical implications of our findings about how to address the challenges of inter-organizational collaboration. The point is not to figure out how to resolve these inherent paradoxes, but to live them fully. This is particularly true when we refer to leadership at the network level of analysis, that is, leadership of organizing forms such as formal coalitions. Using the metaphor of the Möbius band to think of embracing paradox means inviting leaders to think of paradox counter-intuitively – as in the case of a band that has a three-dimensional shape but only one side that simultaneously captures all dimensions. Once this happens, it is only natural to consider both demands as part of the same reality. Moving carefully and deliberately through the enigmatic experience of thorough and concurrent consideration of what appear to be contradictory demands may contribute to support the coalitions' ability to carry out collective action.

References

Agranoff, R. (ed.) (2003) *Leveraging Networks: A Guide for Public Managers Working across Organizations.* Arlington, VA: IBM Endowment for the Business of Government.

Agranoff, R. and McGuire, M. (2001) 'Big questions in public network management.' *Journal of Public Administration Research and Theory 11*, 3, 295–327.

Bailey, D. and Koney, K.M. (1996) 'Interorganizational community-based collaboratives: A strategic response to shape the social work agenda.' *Social Work 41*, 6, 602–611.

Bardach, E. (ed.) (1998) *Getting Agencies to Work Together. The Practice and Theory of Managerial Craftsmanship*. Washington: Brookings Institution Press.

Brandenburger, A. and Nalebuff, B. (1996) *Co-opetition*. New York: Doubleday.

Brass, D.J., Galaskiewicz, J., Greve, H.R. and Wenpin Tsai (2004) 'Taking stock of networks and organizations: A multilevel perspective.' *Academy of Management Journal 47*, 6, 795–817.

Castells, M. (ed.) (2000) *The Network Society*. Oxford: Blackwell.

Clandinin, D.J. and Connelly, F.M. (eds) (2000) *Narrative Inquiry: Experience and Story in Qualitative Research*. San Francisco: Jossey-Bass.

Crosby, B. and Bryson, J. (2005) *New Leadership for the Common Good*. San Francisco: Jossey-Bass.

de Rond, M. and Bouchikhi, H. (2004) 'On the dialectics of strategic alliances.' *Organization Science 15*, 1, 56–69.

Dachler, H.P. and Hosking, D.M. (1995) 'The Primacy of Relations in Socially Constructing Organizational Realities.' In D.M. Hosking, H.P. Dachler and K.J. Gergen *Management and Organization Relational Alternatives to Individualism*. Brookfield: Avebury.

Dodge, J., Ospina, S.M. and Foldy, E.G. (2005) 'Integrating rigor and relevance in public administration scholarship: The contribution of narrative inquiry.' *Public Administration Review 65*, 3, 286–302.

Drath, W.H. (ed.) (2001) *The Deep Blue Sea: Rethinking the Source of Leadership*. San Francisco: Jossey-Bass.

Drath, W.H. and Palus, C.J. (1994) *Making Common Sense: Leadership as Meaning-Making in a Community of Practice*. Washington: CCL Press.

Ebers, M. (1997) 'Explaining inter-organisational network formation.' In M. Ebers (ed.) *The Formation of Inter-organisational Networks*. Oxford: Oxford University Press.

Eden, C. and Huxham, C. (2001) 'The negotiation of purpose in multi-organizational collaborative groups.' *Journal of Management Studies 38*, 3, 373–393.

Eisenhardt, K.M. (2000) 'Paradox, spirals, ambivalence: The new language of change and pluralism.' *Academy of Management Review 25*, 4, 703–722.

Emmer, M. (1980) 'Visual art and mathematics: The Moebius Band.' *Leonardo 13*, 2, 108–111 (limerick on page 110).

Faulkner, D. and de Rond, M. (ed.) (2000) *Cooperative Strategy: Economic, Business and Organizational Issues*. Oxford and New York: Oxford University Press.

Federation for American Immigration Reform (2003) New York: Census Bureau Data.

Fletcher, J. (2008) 'Reflection on leadership, race and power.' Essay commissioned for the Symposium on Race and Leadership at the Intersections, 29–30 May 2008, Research Center for Leadership in Action, Wagner Graduate School of Public Service, New York University: New York.

Ford, J.D. and Backoff, R.W. (1988) 'Organizational Change in and out of Dualities and Paradox.' In K.S. Cameron and R.E. Quinn (eds) *Paradox and Transformation: Toward a Theory of Change in Organization and Management*. Cambridge, MA: Ballinger.

Hardy, C. and Phillips, N. (1998) 'Strategies of engagement: Lessons from the critical examination of collaboration and conflict in an interorganizational domain.' *Organization Science 9*, 2, 217–230.

Heifetz, R.A. (1994) *Leadership without Easy Answers*. Cambridge, MA: Harvard University Press.

Hersey, P. and Blanchard, K. (1982) *Management of Organizational Behavior Utilizing Human Resources*. Englewood Cliffs, NJ: Prentice-Hall.

Hosking, D. (2007) 'Not Leaders, Not Followers: A Post-modern Discourse of Leadership Processes.' In B. Shamir, R. Pillai, M. Bligh and M. Uhl Bien (eds) *Follower-Centered Perspectives of Leadership: A Tribute to the Memory of James R. Meindl.* Greenwich, CT: Information Age Publishing.

Huxham, C. (2003) 'Theorising collaboration practice.' *Public Management Review 5*, 3, 401–424.

Huxham, C. and Beech, N. (2003) 'Contrary prescriptions: Recognizing good practice tensions in management.' *Organization Studies 24*, 1, 69–93.

Huxham, C. and Macdonald, D. (1992) 'Introducing collaborative advantage: Achieving inter-organisational effectiveness through meta-strategy.' *Management Decision 30*, 2, 50–56.

Huxham, C. and Vangen, S. (2000) 'Leadership in the shaping and implementation of collaboration agendas: How things happen in a (not quite) joined-up world.' *Academy of Management Journal 43*, 4, 1159–1176.

Jackson, B. and Parry, K. (2008) *A Very Short, Fairly Interesting and Reasonably Cheap Book About Studying Leadership.* London: Sage.

Kaplan, R.E. and Kaiser, R.B. (2003) 'Developing versatile leadership.' *MIT Sloan Management Review 44*, 4, 19–26.

Kickert, W.J.M, Klijn, E.H. and Koopenjan, J.M.F. (1997) 'Introduction: A Management Perspective on Policy Networks.' In W.J.M. Kickert, E.H. Klijn and J.M.F. Koppenjan (eds) *Managing Complex Networks; Strategies for the Public Sector.* London: Sage.

Lewis, M.W. (2000) 'Exploring paradox: Toward a more comprehensive guide.' *Academy of Management Review 25*, 4, 760–775.

March, J.G. and Weil, T. (2005) *On Leadership.* Malden, MA: Blackwell.

Mattessich, P.W., Murray-Close, M. and Monsey, B.R. (eds) (2001) *Collaboration: What Makes It Work.* Saint Paul, MN: Amherts H. Wilder Foundation.

McGuire, M. (2002) 'Managing networks: Propositions on what managers do and why they do it.' *Public Administration Review 62*, 5, 599–610.

Mizrahi, T. and Rosenthal, B.B. (2001) 'Complexities of coalition building: Leaders' successes, strategies, struggles, and solutions.' *Social Work 46*, 1, 63–78.

Moran, T.T. and Petsod, D. (eds) (2003) *Newcomers in the American Workplace: Improving Employment Outcomes for Low-Wage Immigrants and Refugees.* Sebastopol, CA: Grantmakers Concerned with Immigrants and Refugees and Neighborhood Funders Group.

Ofori-Dankwa, J. and Julian, S.D. (2004) 'Conceptualizing social science paradoxes using the diversity and similarity curves model: Illustrations from the work/play and theory novelty/continuity paradoxes.' *Human Relations 57*, 11, 1449–1477.

Ospina, S. and Foldy, E. (2008) 'Building bridges from the margins: The work of leadership in social change organizations.' Paper presented at the Academy of Management Research Conference, Anaheim, August 2008.

Ospina, S. and Sorenson, G. (2006) 'A Constructionist Lens on Leadership: Charting New Territory.' In G. Goethals and G. Sorenson (eds) *In Quest for a General Theory of Leadership.* Cheltenham: Edward Elgar Publishers.

Ospina, S. and Yaroni, A. (2003) 'Understanding Cooperative Behavior in Labor Management Cooperation: A Theory-Building Exercise.' *Public Administration Review 63*, 4, 455–472.

Ospina, S.M. and Dodge, J. (2005) 'Narrative inquiry and the search for connectedness: Practitioners and academics developing public administration scholarship.' *Public Administration Review 65*, 4, 409–424.

Park, S.H. and Ungson, G. (2001) 'Interfirm rivalry and managerial complexity: A conceptual framework of alliance failure.' *Organization Science 12*, 1, 37–54.

Peterson, I. (2000a) 'Möbius and his Band.' *Science News Online 158*, 2. Available at www.sciencenews.org/articles/20000708/mathtrek.asp, accessed 9 May 2009.

Peterson, I. (2000b) 'Möbius at Fermilab.' *Science News Online 158*, 10. Available at www.sciencenews.org/articles/20000902/mathtrek.asp, accessed 9 May 2009.

Polkinghorne, D. (2004) *Practice and the Human Sciences: The Case for a Judgment-based Practice of Care.* Albany: State University of New York Press.

Poole, M.S. and Van de Ven, A.H. (1989) 'Using a paradox to build management and organization theories.' *Academy of Management Review 14*, 4, 562–578.

Provan, K.G. and Kenis, P. (2007) 'Modes of network governance: Structure, management, and effectiveness.' *Journal of Public Administration Research and Theory 18*, 229–252.

Provan, K.G., Fish, A. and Sydow, J. (2007) 'Interorganizational networks at the network level: A review of the empirical literature on whole networks.' *Journal of Management 33*, 3, 479.

Quinn, R.E. and Cameron, K.S. (1988) *Paradox and Transformation: Toward a Theory of Change in Organization and Management.* Cambridge, MA: Ballinger.

Rainey, G.W. and Busson, T. (2001) 'Assessing and Modelling Determinants of Capacity For Action In Networked Public Programs.' In Myrna Mandell (ed.) *Getting Results Through Collaboration: Networks and Network Structures For Public Policy and Management.* Greenwood: Quorum.

Reckwitz, A. (2002) 'Toward a theory of social practices.' *European Journal of Social Theory 5*, 2, 243–263.

Reissman, C.K. (2002) 'Narrative analysis.' In A.M. Huberman and M.B. Miles (eds) *The Qualitative Researcher's Companion.* Thousand Oaks, CA: Sage.

Ring, P. and Van de Ven, A. (1994) 'Developmental processes of cooperative inter-organisational relationships.' *Academy Management Review 19*, 1, 90–119.

Saz-Carranza, A. (2007) 'Managing inter-organizational networks: Leadership, paradox, and power.' Doctoral dissertation, ESADE.

Saz-Carranza, A. and Serra, A. (2006) 'La gestión de redes inter-organizativos desde el sector público: El caso de los servicios sociales de barcelona.' *Territorios Revista de Estudios Regionales y Urbanos 15*.

Schall, E., Ospina, S., Godsoe, B. and Dodge, J. (2004) 'Appreciative Narratives as Leadership Research: Matching Method to Lens.' In D.L. Cooperrider and M. Avital (eds) *Advances in Appreciative Inquiry.* Oxford: Elsevier Science.

Shortell, S.M., Zukoski, A.P., Alexander, J.A., Bazzoli, G.J., Conrad, D.A., Hasnain-Wynia, R., Sofaer, S., Chan, B.Y., Casey, E. and Margolin, F.S. (2002) 'Evaluating partnerships for community health improvement: Tracking the footprints.' *Journal of Health Politics, Policy and Law 27*, 1, 49–92.

Smith, K.K. and Berg, D.N. (eds) (1987) *Paradoxes of Group Life: Understanding Conflict, Paralysis, and Movement in Group Dynamics.* San Francisco: Jossey-Bass.

Swidler, A. (2001) 'What Anchors Cultural Practices.' In T.R. Schatzki, K.K Cetina and E. Von Savigny (eds) *The Practice Turn in Contemporary Theory.* London: Routledge.

Uhl-Bien, M. (2006) 'Relational leadership theory: Exploring the social processes of leadership and organizing.' *Leadership Quarterly 17*, 654–676.

Van de Ven, A.H. and Poole, M.S. (1988) 'Paradoxical Requirements for a Theory of Organizational Change.' In R.E. Quinn and K.S. Cameron (eds) *Paradox and Transformation: Toward a Theory of Change in Organization and Management.* Cambridge, MA: Ballinger.

Vangen, S. and Huxham, C. (2004) 'Enacting leadership for collaborative advantage: Dilemmas of ideology and pragmatism in the activities of partnership managers.' *British Journal of Management 15, 1, 39–56.*

CHAPTER 8

Collaborative Leadership: The Importance of Place-based Development

Anne Murphy

Many contemporary approaches to leadership development can be understood within the cognitive psychological tradition; a tradition that overlooks the social, historical, and cultural aspects of self, thinking and action. There are a number of problems with these assumptions, particularly in the context of *collaborative* leadership. Entrenched ideas of learning as a predominantly individual, cognitive process have meant that an effective approach to developing collective leadership capacity which connects rather than divides has received little attention. In fact, much of the literature presents leadership itself as an individual effort and by doing so underestimates the extent to which innovation, regeneration and change are products of collective activity embedded in networks. Applying generic skills or competences to a place via a person further embeds notions of heroic individual agency. By contrast, this chapter suggests an alternative model of design where place, relationships and purpose come first.

We need to understand more about the implications of this collaborative imperative and the challenges it presents to the current practice and conceptualisation of leadership and its development. Approaches to learning design should be up to the task of helping people tackle the complex interplay of stakeholders, priorities, constraints and opportunities faced by today's leaders across the increasingly blurred public, private and community boundaries. If we are to make real progress on the issues to which there are no generic, textbook answers; to make a personal difference to issues which cross organisational boundaries and traditional notions of power and hierarchy, we must equip both current and future leaders for the challenges presented by rising, multiple stakeholder influence. As working in partnership across all sectors grows in importance, so the context for learning and working together demands more attention. If we take an enquiry-led approach to learning with real action at its heart it becomes possible to build a sense of *place* and *purpose* into the process. Learning in partnership about issues which matter means asking questions, re-appraising the way things get done and taking a fresh look at personal, organisational and local or regional priorities. Leadership here is about finding appropriate solutions to the really tough problems in and between our organisations and communities. It is about connecting and making connections between people, place and future.

This chapter aims to draw practical knowledge from in-the-thick-of-it practical engagement. This experience-in-practice is drawn from a number of leadership development episodes including a formal postgraduate post experience leadership programme, a professional leadership development programme for women, a collaborative action research programme, and a development programme for young leaders.[1] What these episodes share is a an explicit focus on collaborative leadership; a strong connection with an identifiable region, city or locality; an interest in practice or theory built from practice; a desire to engage the broader community in experiencing leadership and, finally, an intent to enable (or at least encourage) a different conversation about how collaborative leadership actually happens – including who gets to lead and for what purposes.

Perceptions of collaboration and leadership

If by leadership we mean committing energy and care to a real group of people in a real place, it follows that we must also mean to tackle the challenges of multi-faceted, multi-sector collaborative practice and to ensure that any results are felt and appreciated by ordinary people living in ordinary communities. To develop the skills, expertise and collective capacity to exercise such leadership

---

1   The Post Graduate Diploma in Public Service Leadership (Collaborative Leadership for Scotland) designed, developed and delivered in partnership between Scottish Leadership Foundation and Lancaster University; 'Women on course for Leadership' (Mujeres en Dirección) designed and developed by 5F Group; the Engaged Action Learning programme supported by the Institute for Entrepreneurship and Enterprise Development at Lancaster University Management School and the Engaging Communities Foundation, a partnership research programme supported by the Centre for Urban Education, itself a partnership between Manchester City Council and Manchester Metropolitan University.

means supporting learning processes which have real relationships and real tasks at the centre.

New ways of working in the public services are demanding a different approach to leadership and management that moves away from the traditional model of 'line' accountability to one where 'authority' is not clearly related to position or status. This has led to more complex arrangements where direction, decision making and accountability cannot be described or developed in purely linear models. The demand for collective and collaborative leadership in order to deliver both government policy and meet the needs of service users and public expectations is requiring not just new skills from leaders and managers but new ways of understanding their role and the world in which they are working.

In the context of the creation of public value, collective, collaborative and community leadership are currently receiving a great deal of attention across the public services. Framed on the one hand by policy driving for improvement, and on the other by the change in focus from the service itself (health, education, social services) to the recipient (client, child, citizen) public service organisations see and are encouraged to explore 'partnership' as a way ahead.

The language of partnership is everywhere and although the words of the surface are the same, the meanings of exactly what it is hoped that collaboration will deliver are highly context specific. We must devote time and energy to understanding the nature of these differences if we are to move away from generic, superficial descriptions of competence and towards a more robust understanding of what the notions of collective and collaborative leadership mean both in practice and in context.

How we conceptualise leadership clearly influences our assumptions about how leaders can be developed. The ways in which we understand learning (when and where it occurs, what factors influence it, how we might be able to bring it about) informs the conceptual frameworks within which educators set out to design effective learning experiences. Hence how we focus our initial questions, conditions the way we define leadership development:[2]

- 'Who leaders are' – or personality-based, 'trait' theories where what matters is not the context, but the disposition, personal characteristics or personality-type of the leader. A leader is a leader, whatever the circumstances so what matters is not how to develop them but how to select them.

---

2   Categories developed by Patrick Leonard in his doctoral research entitled 'Leading Partnerships: How Do You Lead When Not in Charge?'

- 'What leaders do' – or contingency theories where the critical issue emphasises the degree of alignment between a leader and the context in which he or she operates (where both the individual leader and the context of operation are fixed and knowable). Developing leadership here is about developing self-awareness and honing analytical skills.

- 'How leaders do it' – or situational and behavioural theories where it is possible for a leader to generate a wide repertoire of styles to suit different situations and where whole behaviours can be developed to suit, for example, either a task or people centred situation.

- 'Why leaders do it' – or critical theories where the focus is on understanding the places and spaces where people get to exercise leadership. Development here is more likely to be about encouraging a different conversation about who gets to lead and for what purposes.

But what about *where* leadership occurs?

Leadership development has been founded on questions to do with the who, what, how and why of leadership; now the time has come to address the *where* so that we can make a real difference in real time in a real place.

If leadership is not an essential quality but is grounded in what Keith Grint (1997 and 2005) refers to as the 'constitutive' approaches to understanding, then questions of how such leadership is to be developed need a specific context to lend them meaning. Derived from constructivist theories in social science and taken to its most extreme form, a constitutive leadership theory rejects the idea of any kind of objectivity claiming instead that all accounts are derived from linguistic reconstructions. Language, far from being a transparent window to reality, both reflects and constitutes our world, our experiences of it, of ourselves and of each other. As language (re)presents reality, this approach suggests that what both the leader and the situation actually are is a consequence of the competing accounts and interpretations which, in effect, constitute both. According to this account then, leadership and place become part of each other.

This means that leading (and learning) in partnership is about understanding and researching the practice of leadership in a range of complex collaborative contexts – and this means finding ways of working within (and therefore talking about) the shifting expectations and perceptions of those involved in what we might loosely call 'collaborative leadership' – a leadership based on *context and perspective* rather than on *command and personality*. Below is a range of partnership contexts and perspectives mapped onto the 'Partnering Grid' (Deering and Murphy 2003)[3] which explores the different positions arising from a range of assumptions about what a partnership is all about in the first place (Figure 8.1). These shifting perspectives and perceptions are the very essence of the collaborative leadership challenge – steering the kaleidoscope of possibility away from the discussion about 'who's right' and towards the conversation about 'who's committed'.

Ambition (or in other words, the reason for partnering) is expressed on the grid as a result of the partners' views of opportunity and risk. The more the perceptions of risk rise, the lower the trust expressed. On the other hand, the greater the opportunity seen and discussed, the more open and trusting the partners become. Against this is placed the partners' views of difference itself. These can range from avoiding all differences in approach, objectives and values, to actively seeking them out in order to work with innovation and creativity. Most relationships swing unwittingly and unwillingly between these extremes, unable to get a handle on quite how to steer towards mutual benefit.

To explore the intangible elements of their working relationship, partners first need a map which enables them to describe and compare the way each sees the other and the way they interact with each other. Partnering grid positions are located by plotting each partner's view of and response to difference, against the rationale for being in partnership in the first place. The expectations, perceptions and assumptions around these dimensions are what determine success and failure and in understanding, not smoothing these differences which enable them to manage their relationship more productively.

Let's take a closer look at the hard core of these 'soft' collaborative spaces and what each means for collaboration and leadership (Figure 8.2).

Command and Control

From this perspective, all differences are potentially dangerous and should be avoided at all cost. Formal partnerships are more common than loose collaborative arrangements because up front contractual preparation is seen as crucial to overall success. The belief that everything can (and should) be planned for in advance leads to a reliance on common standards of behaviour and operating procedures. The power to get things done is usually centralised and found in a small top team where the balance of power is often weighted in favour of the

---

3   *The Partnering Imperative* (Deering and Murphy 2003) is based on original research into partnering practice carried out over a period of four years and in partnership with more than 20 public, private and voluntary sector organisations in the UK and US. The research was supported by A.T. Kearney Management Consultants between 1994 and 1998.

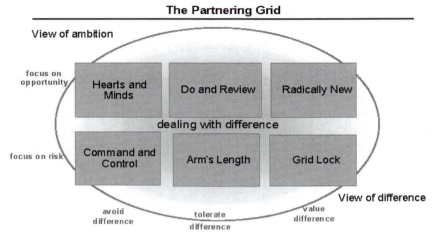

FIGURE 8.1: THE PARTNERING GRID

FIGURE 8.2: PARTNERING GRID: PERCEPTIONS OF COLLABORATION AND
LEADERSHIP

player who 'owns the customer'. As the motivation for such relationships is largely transactional in the exchange of resources (including information), the management focus is usually on minimising the risks involved rather than exploiting the opportunities. This is a perfectly sensible approach if the prevailing winds bring sudden threat. By highlighting speed and accuracy the collective energy can be focused on a single, fixed point, be that government targets, the competition, the audit or the enemy. What this approach cannot deliver however, is the sort of innovative agility required in a rapidly changing environment. In a context where power and knowledge are so concentrated in the hands of so few, the main concern of leadership tends to be to *dominate* and to do so in such a way as to bring people along in the same direction.

Hearts and Minds

'Singing from the same hymn sheet' is the motto of Hearts and Minds relationships. Here the assumption is that if everyone is working to achieve the same vision which is rooted in the same basic values, then harmony and creativity will emerge as a result. Hence vision, mission and culture change programmes are often used as core interventions to bring partners and 'cultures' together. Striving for sameness leads to a focus on alignment, not only of processes but behaviours too. Synthesis is the name of the game and the dominant leadership concern is to *integrate*. The sort of energy resulting from a compelling shared vision can mobilise people's commitment like no other message. In the right context, one of freedom and plenty, the Hearts and Minds approach can steer a steady course between the need for control and the need for creativity. The dangerous weakness is the extent to which learning is stifled. We learn to check our own assumptions when faced with ones which are different. By forcing such 'dissidence' underground, 'collaborative leaders' charged with change, may well ensure their own stagnation and downfall.

Arm's Length

Organisations with Command and Control histories discover to their initial dismay that people whose approach is borne of other cultures are by and large unchangeable. What seems at first to be insubordination becomes in time to be recognised as genuine misunderstanding. This leads to a focus on clarity of communication where meanings and implications are checked and double checked. Basic identity, however, is cherished and protected. This usually means that any move to get too close will be viewed with suspicion. Partners who share this perspective will tend to settle any imbalance by agreeing to differ on certain issues so as to give themselves the space they need to pursue other objectives. As understanding of each other's perspectives is deliberately limited to the narrow confines of the task in hand, it is common to rely on standard legal and procedural protocols for managing the interface of differences. The approach navigates a course between filling information or competence gaps on the one hand, and the need for instant independence on the other. Dependence is usually interpreted as risk and consequently avoided with passion. Only those risks which can be absolutely equally shared fall into the scope of such a relationship – and here lies the weakness: what is never on the agenda cannot be made to work. Tasked with keeping the identity boundaries of partners crisp and distinct, the concern of leadership in Arms' Length relationships is to *orchestrate*.

Do and Review

When partners seek to learn from each other's differences in approach and operations, the management focus tends to emphasise continuous process review and improvement. In a Do and Review partnership deliberate flexibility is encouraged so as to enable both parties to adapt to changing conditions and objectives, and above all to each other. Their strong process orientation and participative ethic gives rise to a shared search for improvements at the partnership interface. Learning is seen as a major management tool and most actions are reviewed to see what can be learnt. Knowledge sharing and the tracking of good practice are seen as essential to survival. Furthermore the explicit effort to understand each other's positions and priorities strengthens the durability of the relationship and widens the opportunity set for joint projects. Partners working in this space steer between change on the one hand and stability on the other by focusing energy on the virtues of adaptability and leadership priority is to *facilitate* development of the partnership and the work. This works in well-understood conditions, but can become a serious drain on entrepreneurial spirit in times of radical transformation. By stressing the quest for incremental change Do and Review partnerships may content themselves with learning to do things better at the expense of never learning to do better things (Peddler, Burgoyne and Boydell 1991).

Grid Lock

There are times in the life of all partnerships where differences between partners are both respectfully acknowledged and rigorously avoided. It would be naïve to suggest that good intentions always lead to good results, as anyone who has found it necessary to maintain the delicate balance of power in situations of extreme instability will know. Conflicts of interest and half hidden multiple agendas are to be expected where risk is high and constraints fierce. Partners here tend to vote for compromise, not by their actions but by the inertia born of their sense of powerlessness and fragmented purpose. Damage limitation (not opportunity) drives this particular dynamic as risks are often experienced as having life or death implications. Good leaders here attempt to *translate* between partners, points of view and their various purposes. Success here requires courage and integrity but the danger arises when the high level of risk disables partners from telling it as it is. The outward appearance of Grid Lock is often the result of (real or perceived) hidden agendas aimed at subtle domination of one partner over another. In such circumstances relationships deteriorate to such an extent that the only workable options are retreat, rebellion or apathy. Acknowledging and respecting differences becomes a game people play to strengthen their position in the perpetual argument about who's right. A partnership in name only, the obsession with posturing prevents partners from identifying, let alone working on, the only thing which could break the deadlock – a task which matters to everyone.

Radically New

Some collaborative groups actively seek out differences of all kinds: operational, professional and cultural *and* make it work. Often highly innovative and creative partnerships, this approach puts a premium on challenge, dialogue and democracy. By inviting and acting on the views of multiple stakeholders, partners (or more often networks of partners) are able to respond instantaneously to the changing demands of an unpredictable world. Steering a tentative course between a shared sense of direction on the one hand, and volatile unpredictability on the other requires a very pragmatic mindset – one which is rooted in what people can do together in spite of (or even because of) their differences – and it is this focus on difference which means the task of leadership is to *differentiate* perspectives and purposes before trying to reach a plan for action. This orientation works well where power, knowledge and purpose are widely distributed but there is a strong sense of place and interconnection. It is however highly unstable and steadfastly refuses to respond to plan. Solidarity is not an enforceable quality. Pinning down behaviours and working out how to make them happen ensures compliance, but it does not guarantee commitment, and this of course kills the very creativity it is intended to harness. Radically New works when something really has to change – but it can never deliver control.

Figure 8.3 sums up the perceptions of good leadership.

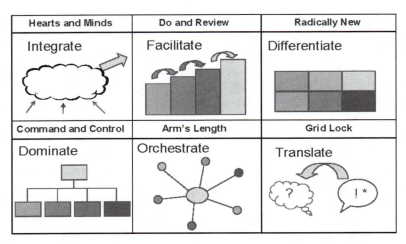

FIGURE 8.3: PERCEPTIONS OF GOOD LEADERSHIP

Perceptions of collaboration and learning

The process of collaborative leadership and learning mirrors most partnership processes – only the experience of working together over time can give people the confidence they need to establish realistic and appropriate objectives *and* the trust necessary to engage in uncompromising straight talk about expectations, opportunities and risks (Figure 8.4). There are always both – but often, partners in an immature partnership (set on establishing a 'good' relationship which is often interpreted as harmonious and uniform) tend to focus on perceived opportunities and less on perceived risks. Taking a line that it is often better to keep quiet than to rock the boat, partners run the risk of filtering objectives through the ever narrowing lens of agreement which means that, as the partnership develops, the partners are dealing more and more with appearances and less and less with shared aspirations.

Hearts and Minds	Do and Review	Radically New
We can trust you because you are the same as us	It is possible to agree to trust each other in spite of our differences	If we act to enhance trust, you will respond
Command and Control	**Arm's Length**	**Grid Lock**
We can trust you because you are different	We will find it difficult to trust each other until we really know each other	If you act to enhance trust, we will respond

FIGURE 8.4: PERCEPTIONS OF TRUST

Objectives are always multi-dimensional, change over time and can rarely be fixed for the time it takes to do the work. There is a choice here: reduce the process to that which can be expressed and measured from a single perspective, or find a way of dealing with shifting needs and expectations. Furthermore, if the participants themselves are not in some way involved in this process of negotiation, the chances are that they will come with expectations they have built up during a professional life-time of having learnt what leadership development programmes 'should' deliver. Working across organisational and sector boundaries is particularly challenging here as different individuals bring not only different expectations, but quite different definitions of what learning is and what it is for. As these notions are applied in practice in different settings (and for different purposes) they give rise to a whole host of different understandings, which in turn, lead to different actions. The key issue here is to get at the core of the constant negotiation about meaning – which meaning counts and whose definition is valid (Burgoyne and Murphy 2005). If collaborative leadership is also at the heart of the issue, then surfacing these issues is a critical task, as we cannot 'solve' the problem of collaboration by insisting on a single definition of reality. We fall into the sorts of evaluative processes whereby responsibility is clouded, mistakes 'hidden', success attributed to the powerful and experimentation disregarded as disruptive. The understanding of responsibility, power and persuasion is not to be laundered out of the evaluative process but, in this context at least, is its primary purpose. Of course taking a single 'safe' perspective enables us to prove the value of a programme by measuring how far our initial aspirations are realised, but it does not take much account of what we have learnt along the way – nor does it help us keep sight of what we are trying to do in the first place which is to *make a real difference in real time in a real place.*

The discourses of transformation, improvement and achievement, in their promise of success for all, do little to enable parties to a multi-partner collaboration to accept and articulate their individual expectations, frustrations, setbacks and disappointments in the context of what might be described as collective success. The Partnering Grid (shown in Figure 8.5) moves towards this complex and apparently paradoxical multi-stakeholder evaluation by offering a framework aiming to enable ordinary people to get some things right and others wrong so that collaboratively we might make progress on important issues.

Not so much challenge that enjoyment is compromised One programme – predict what goes on inside the participant Questions answered	Do, reflect, expreriment Change starts with the individual Improving individuals to enhance the collective	Our learning is our own responsibility but in the end, we can't do it alone Risks for all stakeholders Ambiguous. Questions not always answered
Fix objectives at the outset Simplify and control Developers take responsibility	Individuals are the locus of change Do it yourself Learners take responsibility	Multiple expectations, confusion and misunderstanding Face saving limits collective understanding Abdication of responsibility

FIGURE 8.5: PARTNERING GRID: PERCEPTIONS OF COLLABORATION AND LEARNING

Command and Control

From this perspective leadership development is a linear activity: a developer or trainer designs a programme to meet the needs of participants. These needs may be indentified by the participants themselves, or by their line managers and they are often technical in nature. Success is measured by checking that the stated objectives are said to have been met. This sort of approach when translated to leadership development tends to frame or be driven by expert content. Participants are seen as empty vessels in the need of expert knowledge and this knowledge is largely context free.

Hearts and Minds

A Hearts and Minds approach to learning is one which seeks harmony. Both developers and participants expect to enjoy the learning experience and not to be challenged too far beyond their comfort zones. If questions are brought to the learning experience (either by developers or participants) the expectation tends to be that these questions will be answered: no questions should be left hanging in the air. As difference should be smoothed over from this perspective, there is often a focus on the interior world of the participant – if people hold the 'right beliefs' collaborative leadership will be relatively straightforward. There are universal answers to the problems and challenges of collaboration.

Arm's Length

This approach steers clear of too deep or philosophical an intervention for fear of becoming too involved: learning is not an emotional affair. There may be a focus on techniques or models which are aimed at developing particular knowledge, skills or competences. The learner is expected to take responsibility for his or her own learning because the assumption is that if groups, organisations or even societies are to change, people must first make individual changes, particularly in behaviour. Developers will take the lead in design, delivery and evaluation but ultimately the responsibility for taking any learning on board lies with the learner.

Do and Review

Individuals are part of a group and developing the expertise or capabilities of one person is bound to enhance the group. From this perspective, learning is a cyclical process involving experimentation, reflection and readjustments which together lead to incremental improvements. Learning is sometimes seen as a developmental process in which different stages or levels are achieved and then surpassed. Competency approaches (Boyatzis 1982) assume a potential progression between levels on the path to more senior management and more strategic leadership – and this development can be facilitated by a developer. Collaborative leadership or learning is seen as a sum of the parts: it can be built by working on and with the individuals concerned.

Grid Lock

When people take a risk in order to provide a context for learning about something different (collaborative leadership for example) the learning experience becomes unstable and expectations about what might happen next become muddled. In this sort of situation saving face becomes very important: both for the developers and for the participants. Everyone's unspoken (maybe even unacknowledged) expectations about what leadership development 'should be' can make it very difficult to pay close attention to what is actually happening in the moment. If what is happening is *real* collaborative leadership (uncertainty, disagreement, discomfort, insecurity, improvisation, intuition and muddling through…) this may well not sit comfortably with people's view of what acceptable leadership development should feel like – and yet at the same time, it is probably the bedrock of collaborative leadership learning.

Radically New

Under similar circumstances to those described above, the Radically New approach might acknowledge the risks up front – and may even go further by acknowledging the risk posed to everyone involved. When development is linked to place there are a great many direct and indirect participants in a learning process – that's what makes it so risky. From this perspective these stakeholders should be acknowledged in design, delivery, and evaluation or even in all three (Preskill and Torres 1999). Learning about things to which we really do not know the answers is a risky business for everyone and demands that all take responsibility to ensure that the outcomes meet the expectations – even when the questions are so ambiguous as to defy rational answers.

What matters about these partnering perspectives is their descriptive (not prescriptive) power: Radically New is neither more nor less 'right' than a box on the left of the grid; Command and Control is neither more nor less useful than a box over on the other side. Rather their function is to frame and lend voice to different (but equally legitimate) points of view. The question of responsibility for learning, to take but one example, is not one which can be answered 'once and for all' because in some circumstances, the developer's willingness to take responsibility for the learning process can be the critical factor behind the success of a leadership learning experience; and in others that same willingness could rob someone else of the opportunity to lead. What matters is the space within which everyone involved gets to talk about their perspective of what makes the learning strategy work (Figure 8.6) and how that might take everyone towards a future they all desire.

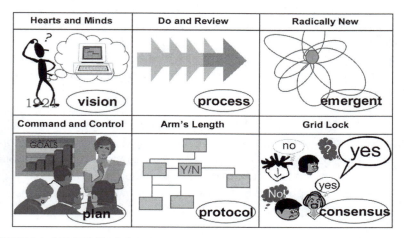

FIGURE 8.6: PERCEPTIONS OF LEARNING STRATEGY

Future directions

It is difficult, if not impossible, to teach an individual about partnering, particularly about partnering in a real context with real issues. Although popular literature would have us believe that the best way to build productive collaborative relationships is to ensure that the parties share much the same values, vision and culture, most collaborative leaders take issue with advice which can only say that sameness is good and difference is bad. Learning collectively about making such arrangements work in practice is partly about ideas and advice from outside, but it is also about addressing real issues. Critically, it is about building mutually rewarding learning experiences in partnership; experiences which enable participants from across services to work on something real and meaningful together or, in other words, build a sense of real *place, purpose* and *perspective* into the process.

In contrast, most practical learning design and development approaches focus mainly on individuals and hardly ever on the space between organisations where collaborative leadership takes place. Traditionally leadership development is directed at individuals in a controlled learning environment where 'new skills' can first be 'practised' in safety. This approach draws on cognitive assumptions where the person is divorced from their context and where mental processes can be studied in isolation from what is understood as a mechanistic universe. Cognitive approaches assume that thinking is a sequential process of problem solving followed by a series of transformations or abstract codes which represent objects or events in the real world. Learning design based on this approach tends to remove people from their everyday contexts in order for them to be taught 'new' competences and to give them space to reflect and readjust their own thinking (and hence behaviour) to new circumstances. This competency logic assumes that it is possible to develop designs for learning which are standardised, universalistic, predictable and measurable (Carroll, Levy and Richmond 2007).

So how is it possible to move learning away from the bounded certainties of time, classroom, content and cohort and instead provide rich and varied contexts where self-managed learning does precisely what it promises? Can standard management and leadership development provision wean itself away from knowing exactly what needs to be learnt with a generic framework which (more or less) guarantees predetermined outcomes? Is it possible to imagine a future where participants are seen not only as recipients of knowledge, but also as key contributors to the process of enquiry into leadership, learning and the knowledge production relationship itself? Is it realistic to conceive of learning through and in collaboration when both cognitive and competency logic emphasises the individual as the primary location of learning?

To find an alternative way of framing collaboration and learning we might look at social (rather than cognitive) learning theory and to practice (not competency) logic. Social learning theory (Lave and Wenger 1991) enables us to see that learning is about people in action in the world together and it has to do with social transformation. Learning is people's way of participating in a social practice which changes that practice. The practice turn (Chia 2004) in leadership studies also promises productive ways of framing the work of leadership development in a more situated and socially defined manner by focusing less on universal competencies and disembodied knowledge, and more on a repertoire of background dispositions and internalised know-how (Carroll *et al.* 2007). What both these ways of thinking point to is a focus on where and how the work of leadership (and learning) is actually done.

The traditional way of understanding the development of learnable traits or responses is by identifying and rectifying deficits. If however, such characteristics are not essential qualities but are instead constituted in context, in relationships and in language, then the deficit discourse makes little sense. This must be replaced by an assets based approach to leadership development which identifies and builds upon both individual and collective strengths (Murphy and Robinson 2008)

Many attempts at a social policy driven approach to increasing the practice of collaborative leadership are predicated upon a deficit understanding of communities and the people in them – there is a problem and social policy informed practice will fix the deficit, solving the problem. This thinking sits behind most diagnosis, design, development and evaluation not only of social policy and practice, but also leadership development (designed to change both leaders and organisations).

A number of elements characterise a place-based approach to developing collaborative leadership. First is to put *genuine enquiry* into a specific issue at the centre of the learning process. Stimulating ideas and frameworks are appropriate insofar as they engender a spirit of enquiry and a phase of 'finding out' answers to questions to which participants genuinely do not know the answers (Cooperrider *et al.* 2003). A second key element of sharing and building the practical know-how needed to make headway with these issues is to incorporate an element of *collective sense making* into the learning process (Reason and Bradbury 2000). How people make sense of the challenges together and develop a shared understanding of them is a key to developing new ways of working which enable collaborative leadership to be experienced and exercised. Third, for collaborative leadership to mean anything at all in context, the starting point must be the design and delivery of leadership development in *partnership* around a compelling issue of shared concern: what we should 'fix' is not the people but the task (Weisbord and Janoff 2000).

Table 8.1 below sets these elements of learning design (the important questions about leadership, collaboration and learning) against where we should look to understand their value (Robinson and Murphy 2006). The resulting questions are a useful bridge to frame design/evaluation conversations about (and in) collaboration.

TABLE 8.1: DESIGNING PLACE-BASED DEVELOPMENT

	Purpose	Perspectives	Place
Leadership Partnership	What is the activity for?	Who has a stake in the outcome?	In whose interests is it?
Learning Genuine enquiry	What are the taken for granted ways of making sense?	Whose voice is not currently being properly heard?	What's the real task?
Collaboration Sense making	How real is the learning activity?	What's the common sense knowledge?	Where should the value be felt?

It is important in all three of these learning contexts (partnership, enquiry and sense making) for leaders to gain an in-depth understanding of the political realities and differing concrete practices of the range of institutions gathering around particular issues of shared concern. A cultural change towards cross sector collaborative working is putting increasing pressure on the public services to achieve 'joined-up' service design and delivery through partnerships and collaborative working arrangements and this requires some serious thinking about the enablers and constraints arising from specific historical, political and geographic influences. While generic and sector specific development programmes have no doubt captured the public sector imagination and a significant proportion of the purse, such programmes will be unable to address the growing imperative to address public service issues across sector boundaries which are, by definition, geographically grounded. In the context of leadership learning and development this means grounding learning in reality: collaboration is meaningless if there is no task.

References

Boyatzis, R.E. (1982) *The Competent Manager: A Mode for Effective Performance*. New York: John Wiley and Sons.

Burgoyne, J.G. and Murphy, A. (2005) 'The constructiveness and destructiveness of evaluation in a complex, chaotic, multi-stakeholder and dynamic client environment for leadership development.' Paper presented to the Studying Leadership Conference, 2005, Lancaster.

Carroll, B., Levy, L. and Richmond, D. (2007) 'Leadership as practice: Challenging the competency paradigm.' Paper presented to the Studying Leadership Conference, 13 and 14 December 2007, Warwick.

Chia, R. (2004) 'Strategy-as-practice: Reflections on the research agenda.' *European Management Review 1*, 29–34.

Cooperrider, D. *et al.* (2003) *Appreciative Inquiry Handbook: The First in a Series of AI Workbooks for Leaders of Change*. San Francisco: Berrett-Koehler.

Deering, A. and Murphy, A. (2003) *The Partnering Imperative: Making Business Partnerships Work*. Chichester: Wiley.

Grint, K. (ed.) (1997) *Leadership: Classical, Contemporary, and Critical Approaches*. Oxford: Oxford University Press.

Grint, K. (2005) *Leadership: Limits and Possibilities*. New York: Palgrave MacMillan.

Lave, J. and Wenger, E. (1991) *Situated Learning: Legitimate Peripheral Participation*. Cambridge: Cambridge University Press.

Murphy, A. and Robinson, J. (2008) 'Models of leadership – Sustainable leadership for sustainable communities: Developing the next generation.' *Vestigium*, Corporación Universitaria Unitec, Bogotá, Columbia (in Spanish).

Peddler, M.J, Burgoyne, J.G. and Boydell, T.H. (1991) *The Learning Company: A Strategy for Sustainable Development*. Maidenhead: McGraw-Hill.

Preskill, H. and Torres, R.T. (1999) *Evaluative Enquiry for Learning in Organizations*. Thousand Oaks CA: Sage.

Reason, P. and Bradbury, H. (eds) (2000) *Handbook of Action Research: Participative Inquiry and Practice*. London: Sage.

Robinson, J. and Murphy, A. (2006) 'Leadership for sustainable communities: Bridging initiatives for people of the north.' Paper presented to the Studying Leadership; Knowledge into Action Conference, 14–15 December 2006, Cranfield, UK.

Weisbord, M. and Janoff, S. (2000) *Future Search: An Action Guide to Finding Common Ground in Organizations and Communities*, 2nd edn. San Francisco: Berrett-Koehler Publishers.

PART III
Leadership Development

CHAPTER 9

Leadership and Learning: The Purpose of a Continuous Learning Framework for Social Care

Carole Wilkinson

> We have an ambitious vision for the social service workforce. That is of a workforce which is competent to respond to changing needs, confident that it can make a positive difference to people's lives and valued for the contribution it makes to Scottish society. Learning and development is integral to this vision and to equipping the sector to respond to the challenges of the 21st century. (Scottish Executive 2005, p.1)

Introduction

This chapter explores the development of the Continuous Learning Framework (CLF) for the social services sector in Scotland. In describing the work, its implications and the links to leadership it begins with a description of the sector, its growing importance and the contribution social services make to the well-being of communities in Scotland. Second, it outlines the context and background leading up to the commissioning of the CLF, saying something briefly about the development of the National Workforce Strategy, the 21st Century Review of Social Work in Scotland and the policy drivers that have helped shape the framework. The chapter then introduces the framework, explains its purpose, its content, the influences that have helped shape and develop it, in particular the study of social and emotional intelligence, the role of workplace learning and the need to equip social services workers to operate in a complex and demanding environment. The chapter draws heavily on the work of Jayne Dunn, Institute for Research and Innovation in Social Services (IRISS) and Fiona Clark, Scottish Social Services Council (SSSC) and I would like to acknowledge their contributions both to this chapter and much more importantly to the development of the CLF. We have reached an important and exciting point in the work and are about to move into an implementation phase which will see SSSC and IRISS working with employees and employers to embed the CLF into practical every day use in the workplace. We are in the process of putting in place with Scottish Government support a plan to take this next phase forward. The development of a framework that provides career pathways and progression for social services workers fills an important gap and gives the workforce for the first time a recognised structure to support continuous learning and development. It brings the social service profession in line with other professionals, in particular in education and health.

Background

The social services sector in Scotland employs around 139,000 people and delivers services to over half a million people at any one time. Employers cover a range of large and small local authorities, large and small voluntary sector organisations, major private companies and hundreds of small and medium sized enterprises and individual projects.

It is an ageing workforce (with the exception of early years and childcare workers) and is predominantly female. Work is a mixture of full time, part time, casual and seasonal work with employees increasingly looking for flexible working arrangements and family friendly policies and practices. Many services are delivered 24 hours, seven days per week, with some workers and services rooted in their localities (for example childminders and care at home workers) with workers increasingly delivering services in the community and in people's homes. This context presents particular challenges for both employers and employees in supporting the learning and development of the workforce, how to offer workers access to appropriate learning opportunities whilst at the same time ensuring services continue to be delivered to vulnerable people.

One of the significant features of the sector is the growth it has witnessed in the last 10–15 years. The number of people working in the sector has risen from 97,000 in 1995 to 139,000 in 2004, a growth figure of 43 per cent compared to that of 7 per cent for the economy as a whole (Scottish Social Services Council 2007). One of the interesting features of this growth is that it is the private and voluntary sector providers who have seen the highest levels of workforce growth (Scottish Executive 2006a) particularly in care services for older people and in early years and child care provision. Social services have a significant contribution to make to economic growth and in particular to the building of a fairer, healthier, safer and stronger Scotland.

Future challenges

> Our people are our greatest economic asset. A skilled and educated workforce is essential to building our comparative advantage and to the delivery of sustainable economic growth...learning and skill development in work is also key to developing a more adaptable economy...
> (Scottish Government 2007, p.22)

There is an assumption that future demand for social services will continue with the growing elderly population and that this will be for more personalised and customer led services. The shape, growth or decline in the population has significant financial and social implications for families and governments. It raises issues about the future care needs of older people and about child care and working parents. Social policy needs to take account of living arrangements for older people and one parent households as this can be a determinant of support needs and does have implications for education, social services and health services. It is important to inject a note of caution here, as we don't yet fully understand demographic trends or know enough about the future shape of services or their means of delivery. What we do know is that governments in all four countries of the UK are developing policies that encourage service developments to support older people to maintain their independence and remain in their communities, early intervention strategies designed to assist vulnerable young children and their families to thrive and remain in their localities and support to those with disabilities and mental health problems to take control of their lives and how services are delivered for them. Government in England in December 2007 announced its 'Putting People First Programme' (Department of Health 2007b) to personalise adult care services, followed by the 'Valuing People Now' consultation (Department of Health 2007c) on the future of learning disabilities. By 2011 the Department of Health (England) wants all publicly funded users to have personal budgets (Lewis 2008). The Scottish Executive, as part of the work of the *Changing Lives* Social Work Review, commissioned a paper on Personalisation (Leadbeater 2004). The emphasis in these policies and proposals is upon service users increasingly taking control of the services they receive, becoming employers and directing their own care. This will require an extension of learning and development opportunities to those employed by services users.

People who use services have changing expectations, more people want to be supported to remain at home and maintain their independence. People are becoming more assertive in expressing their choice, and increasingly they will challenge services of poor quality and want flexibility in service delivery. The use of technology will increasingly support service delivery, assist the workforce in their day-to-day work and come to be seen as an important education and training tool. All of these pose challenges for the workforce who will increasingly have to operate in a complex and fast moving environment.

Recent developments

In 2001 Government in Scotland through the Regulation of Care (Scotland) Act 2001 introduced regulation of the social services workforce. Codes of Practice for employers and for workers in social services were first published in 2002, these set the standards for the professional conduct and practice required of social services workers. The employers' code similarly sets out the standards expected of a good employer. Both sets of codes include expectations in relation to learning and development, supporting the education and training of workers and making sure individual workers are equipped to carry out their roles and responsibilities.

> As a social services employer you must provide training and development opportunities to enable social service workers to strengthen and develop their skills and knowledge. (Scottish Social Services Council 2003a, Section 3, p.9)

> As a social service worker, you must be accountable for the quality of your work and take responsibility for maintaining and improving your knowledge and skills. (Scottish Social Services Council 2003b, Section 6, p.13)

In 2004 Government commissioned a review 'to take a fundamental look at all aspects of social work in order to strengthen its contribution to the delivery of integrated services': *Changing Lives: Report of the 21st Century Social Work Review* (Scottish Executive 2006c). The 21st Century Social Work Review in particular was asked to:

- define the role and purpose of social workers and the social work profession

- identify improvements in the organisation and delivery of social work services

- develop a strong quality improvement framework and culture, supported by robust inspection
- strengthen leadership and management giving clear direction to the service
- ensure a competent and confident workforce
- review and if necessary modernise legislation.

The Review drew three over-riding conclusions:

1. Doing more of the same won't work. Increasing demand, greater complexity and rising expectations mean that the current situation is not sustainable:

   Tomorrow's solutions will need to engage people as active participants, delivering accessible, responsive services of the highest quality and promoting well-being.

2. Social work services don't have all of the answers. They need to work closely with other universal providers in all sectors to find new ways to design and deliver services across the public sector:

   Tomorrow's solutions will involve professionals, services and agencies from across the public, private and voluntary sectors in a concerted and joined-up effort, building new capacity in individuals, families and communities and focusing on preventing problems before they damage people's life chances.

3. Social workers' skills are highly valued and increasingly relevant to the changing needs of society. Yet we are far from making the best use of these skills:

   Tomorrow's solutions will need to make the best use of skills across the public sector workforce, refocusing on the core values of social work and its mission of enabling all people to develop their full potential, enrich their lives and prevent dysfunction. Social workers will need to make effective use of therapeutic relationships and find new ways to manage risk.

(Scottish Executive 2006b, p.6)

The report of the *Changing Lives* Review identified the strengths and the challenges facing the sector and made 13 recommendations built around two key strategic themes. First, building capacity to deliver personalised services:

Personalisation is driving the shape of all public services, with a growing expectation that services will meet their needs, helping them achieve personal goals and aspirations. This may pose a particular challenge for social work, given the need also to manage growing demand and complexity as well as the need to protect the public by taking measures to control people's liberty. (Scottish Executive 2006b, p.18)

Second, building the capacity of the workforce:

We are not making the best of social work skills. Developing personalised services revitalises and refocuses services on the core values of social work. Achieving that will mean making full and effective use of the whole workforce, building capacity, developing confidence and trust and shifting the balance of power and control. (Scottish Executive 2006b, p.21)

These two strategic themes were identified as critical and the ones that could bring about significant difference. In essence delivering quality personalised services relies on a workforce supported and equipped to carry out its changing role and responsibilities.

The responses to the consultations during the *Changing Lives* Review with employers, managers and front line workers recognised the need to do more to ensure front line workers had the right skills and knowledge, that there was the right balance between professional accountability, scope to practice autonomously and support and supervision. There were strong messages about the need to develop new career pathways and a structure for continuous learning and development.

These findings echo the key messages in the *National Strategy for the Development of Social Service Workforce*, published in 2005. The strategy argued the need for recognition of the existing skills in the workforce, the need to develop flexible routes to learning, to change attitudes so that learning is valued in every workplace and the importance of offering learning and development opportunities at every level and throughout the working life (Figure 9.1).

Prior Learning	Induction	Initial Qualification	Employee Development

FIGURE 9.1: LIFELONG LEARNING FOR LIFE-CHANGING WORK
SOURCE: SCOTTISH EXECUTIVE 2005, P.23

Importantly the strategy 'makes clear links between policy, working practices and workforce development' (Scottish Executive 2005, p.7). There is a tendency in the social services sector to separate supporting and developing the workforce from other organisational activity and not to recognise the linkages and the contribution a well-motivated and supported workforce makes to delivering the organisation's objectives and better outcomes for service users and carers.

Concept of leadership

Another interesting feature of both the strategy and the 21st Century Review is the discussion of the concept of leadership as something not just residing in senior managers or executives but as an expectation of all workers at all levels.

'The construct of leadership that has been delivered goes beyond the concept of the individual named as "leader" in any organisation and looks to the development of a concept of leadership that encapsulates those individuals, their organisations and whole profession of social work and social care services' (Van Zwanenberg 2008, p.4). It also means to go beyond organisational boundaries so that it supports partnership and inter-professional working. The 21st Century Review describes a national framework for leadership that encompasses professional and practice leadership, operational management, academic leadership and citizen leadership. This envisages opportunities at all levels to develop and create solutions and to contribute to service design and delivery. The goal is one of empowering and stimulating a supportive and creative environment.

One of the interesting developments arising from the *Changing Lives* Implementation Plan has been the work on citizen leadership developed by the User and Carer Forum. The Forum began to meet in 2006, it had a key role in informing and influencing the work of all the Change Programmes and under the auspices of the Practice Governance Change Programme produced the Principles and Standards of Citizen Leadership. This defines citizen leadership as: 'An activity...it happens when citizens have power and influence and responsibility to make decisions. Citizen leadership happens when individuals have some control over their own services. It also happens when citizens take action for the benefit of other citizens.' People who use services and carers are citizens who they argue should have a say, get information, take part in decisions and make things happen. 'A leader influences and enables others to make a contribution and so helps to make it happen' (Scottish Executive 2008, pp.4–5). There is an assumption that everyone has leadership potential but that this needs to be developed through learning and by being given opportunities to practice.

Continuous Learning Framework (CLF)

Following on from the development of the National Workforce Development Strategy (Scottish Executive 2005), the introduction of Regulation of the Workforce, Codes of Practice and the *Changing Lives* Review, work was commissioned to develop the Continuous Learning Framework. The overarching aim of the framework is to improve the quality of outcomes for people who use social services by supporting those who deliver services to be the best they can be. The framework aims to do this by producing a structure which focuses on three important areas, learning and development, career pathways and progression and post registration and advanced practice standards. It sets out what people in the social services workforce need in order to be able to do their job well now and in the future. It also outlines what their employer can do to support them to do this (Clark and Dunn 2006 and 2008). This, as has been noted by those contributing to the development, is complex and groundbreaking work. It is attempting to develop a framework for the whole sector, one that supports the care at home worker, early years worker, residential care manager, social worker, middle and senior managers and ultimately those working as personal assistants in self-directed care. It is for everyone working in the public, private and voluntary sectors. There has, therefore, to be scope for flexible use and compromise in order to achieve relevance and practical application. It also needs to be capable of adaptation to meet current and future needs.

The CLF is then 'a seamless vertical and horizontal continuum of learning and development in the social services workforce which spans the career dimensions from registration through to advance practitioner' (Clark and Dunn 2008, p.3). Career progression 'is the provision of clear information and guidance on routes and tools to assist employees and employers with career planning' (p.3). Standards are defined 'as a level of competence that an individual worker is expected to demonstrate' (p.3).

The work has been shaped by basing the development upon:

- National Occupational Standards
- standards in social work education
- Scottish Credit and Qualifications Framework
- Codes of Practice
- Sector Learning Strategy Sector Skills Agreement
- Regulatory Framework and Registration Requirements.

The framework as developed is focused around three key areas. These together describe the attributes a person needs to undertake any role in social services and the support they need from their employer (Clark and Dunn 2006).

1. Knowledge, skills, values and understanding/qualifications and training

These are described in the National Occupational Standards, Codes of Practice and the standards underpinning specific qualifications and awards. They include the qualifications required for registration with the Scottish Social Services Council (SSSC) and the range of training and learning developed and supported by employers and often delivered in the workplace. The CLF draws, therefore, upon what is already in place and cites these as examples of good practice. The two areas that form the first part of the CLF are already well developed. The SSSC as part of putting together the Sector Skills Agreement (SSA) was able to demonstrate the range of qualifications and training provision available. Feedback from the sector indicated that the provision was largely relevant and comprehensive though there was scope to refine and perhaps relook at some long established qualifications. More significant were issues of capacity and delivery in more remote and rural areas of Scotland.

2. Personal capabilities

This area focuses on being able to consistently apply knowledge, skills, value and understanding, what are sometimes known as 'soft skills' or social and emotional intelligence (ESI). The notions of social and emotional intelligence have been developed over the past 35 years, but put simply this describes how people handle themselves and their relationships (Goleman, Boyatzis and McKee 2002). There is growing research evidence to suggest that the majority of competencies linked to superior performance are social and emotional in nature (Cherniss 2000; Dulewicz and Higgs 2000; Goleman 1995) so it makes sense not just to invest in developing the knowledge, skills and understanding as described through standards but to build upon the social and emotional capabilities across the workforce. Emotional and social intelligence bring together a range of interrelated skill sets, self-awareness, self-management and social awareness and relationship management. Whilst these have been researched and identified as leadership qualities they have only recently been brought together. Importantly and very helpfully evidence supports the conclusion that ESI competencies can be developed and sustained (Seal, Boyatzis and Bailey 2006). This is pertinent to a profession that works with people and relies heavily upon building relationships as part of promoting change. There are a number of activities: assessment, advocacy, mediation, crisis management and capacity building, that form key parts of the role of front line workers. However, relationship skills go beyond front line practitioners and are required of supervisors, administrators, leaders and managers (Morrison 2007). Morrison argues:

> It might be suggested that the future health of social work rests, in part, on restoring a sense of dynamic connectedness with both its task and those who social work seek to assist. It is, therefore, precisely at a time of professional and occupational turbulence that an understanding of relationship based practice and the contribution of emotional intelligence to social work can make their most important contribution. (2007, p.249)

In developing the CLF we have recognised that personal capabilities add value to the qualifications, knowledge and skills that people have gained and therefore add quality to the services provided. Seventeen personal capabilities have been developed:

Managing self	**Managing relationships**
Self-confidence	Developing others
Accurate self-assessment	Working with others across organisational boundaries
Awareness of impact on others	Motivating and leading others
Flexibility	Managing conflict
Judgement	Teamwork
Managing workloads	Organisational awareness
Lifelong learning	A focus on service users and carers
Initiative	Empathy

(Clark and Dunn 2006, p.3)

Interestingly, debates are taking place in England (Mickel 2008, pp.14–15) about promoting and measuring compassion. This article argues that the use of compassion can transform care and improve experiences for service users and patients. Measurement of compassion is to be included in the quality framework for the NHS workforce as part of Lord Darzi's Review of the NHS for the Government in England (2007–2008).

3. Organisational capabilities

Increasingly the role of the organisation and the support offered through political and executive leadership are being recognised as crucial to enabling individuals to realise their potential and in the case of social services deliver quality services. Organisational capabilities describe the culture and conditions in the workplace which allows workers to develop and thrive. In the CLF the organisational capabilities aim to show the shared commitment required by both the individual and the organisation so that the employee can learn and develop. Six capabilities are described:

- access to good feedback
- access to quality learning and development
- a planned approach to learning and development
- being part of an organisation that values learning
- being part of an organisation which is open and inclusive
- being part of an organisation which values health and well-being.

Beth Taylor in her newspaper article 'The elusive delights of learning' (2001) describes the changing relationship between employer and employee. The paternalistic approach, she argues, is being replaced by one where both employer and employee take responsibility for personal development, an approach reflected in the Codes of Practice for social service workers and their employers. However, this change is not easy to embrace and does not just simply happen, there needs to be a desire to learn. In her article Beth Taylor discusses the barriers: apathy, fear, time and poor previous educational experiences, that prevent employees trying out the new experience of learning. What is essential is the shift in responsibility for learning so that employers create the climate for their employees to learn and develop and employees embrace the desire and delights of learning.

Rona Beattie undertook a piece of research (2006) to study the interface between the workplace and line managers and the role managers play in supporting the learning and development of their staff in the voluntary sector. Managers who embraced and supported learning were shown in this small study to create a culture in which staff responded positively to learning. Managers put learning on the agenda during supervision and were seen to have a critical role to play in workplace learning.

The CLF, therefore, can be used in three different ways, to support learning and development, to provide a path for career progression and to support standards-based applications. Its aim is to add value and not to replace systems or processes that employers already have in place (for example appraisal, performance review) and throughout the consultation process care has been taken and opportunities used to test it against existing systems and to try out its practical application.

The *National Strategy for the Development of the Social Service Workforce* (Scottish Executive 2005) emphasised the importance of enabling leadership and effective management skills as important drivers for the delivery of quality services. The CLF as developed is intended to create the space and the opportunities for leadership at all levels to develop. At the heart of the Workforce Strategy, the *Changing Lives* Review and the establishment of the SSSC with its responsibilities for registering and regulating the workforce, is the objective of developing a competent, confident and valued workforce. Staff need to be and feel competent in carrying out the functions and tasks associated with their roles and responsibilities and in their ability to respond to the changing needs of service users and carers. They need to feel confident in their abilities, in their professional knowledge and skills and that they can make a difference to the lives of vulnerable people. Staff also need to feel valued by their employer, their organisation and their colleagues and by the service users. They also need to be valued by the wider community and recognised for the contribution they can make to Scottish society. In addition we increasingly need workers who can operate across the different sectors, voluntary, private and public, and work with other professions and disciplines. Competent, confident workers should be able to make the transition to this way of working more seamlessly than those less competent and confident.

The *Changing Lives* Review (Scottish Executive 2006c) argued strongly, based on consultation and feedback from the social services sector, that there was a need within the sector for a framework that provided for career progression and development. It was needed to help a diverse workforce to operate in a challenging environment, to work with other professions and in integrated services and to be sufficiently flexible to recognise the range and complexity of the roles and functions of social service workers. The CLF is a tool to support learning and development across the sector, it helps to support and develop leadership at all levels and fits well with the frameworks developed for leadership and management, practice governance and performance improvement. The challenge now is to move from development to embedding the framework across all social service sectors in Scotland and in doing so to strengthen and develop leadership at all levels.

References

Beattie, R.S. (2006) 'Line managers and workplace learning: Learning from the voluntary sector.' *Human Resources International 9*, 1, 99–119.

Cherniss, C. (2000) 'Social and Emotional Intelligence in the Workforce.' In. Seal, C.R. Boyatzis, R.E. and Bailey, J. (2006) 'Fostering Emotional and Social Intelligence in Organisations.' *Organisational Management Journal.* Linking Theory and Practice. EAM White Paper Series *3*, 3, 190–209.

Clark, F. and Dunn, J. (2006, 2008) *Continuous Learning Framework..* SSSC and IRISS.

Clark, F. and Dunn, J. (2008) *Continuous Learning Framework, Advanced Practice Standards and Career Progression: Working Papers,* p.3. SSSC and IRISS.

Department of Health (2007a) *Our NHS Our Future: NHS Next Stage Review Interim Report.* London: Department of Health.

Department of Health (2007b) *Putting People First Programme.* London: Department of Health.

Department of Health (2007c) *Valuing People Now.* Consultation Paper. London: Department of Health.

Dulewicz, V. and Higgs, M. (2000) 'Emotional intelligence – A review and an evaluation study.' *Journal of Managerial Psychology 15*, 4341.

Goleman, D. (1995) *Emotional Intelligence: Why It Can Matter More than the IQ.* New York: Bantam Books.

Goleman, D., Boyatzis, R.E. and McKee, A. (2002) *Leadership and Emotional Intelligence.* Boston: Harvard Business School Press.

Leadbeater, C. (2004) *Personalisation Through Participation.* Demos.

Lewis, I. (2008) 'Ivan Lewis Interviewed.' *Community Care*, 4–5.

Mickel, A. (2008) 'Compassion: More than just chemistry?' *Community Care*, July 2008, 14–15.

Morrison, T. (2007) 'Emotional intelligence, emotion and social work: Context, characteristics, complications and contributions.' *British Journal of Social Work 37*, 245–263.

Scottish Executive (2005) *National Strategy for the Development of the Social Service Workforce in Scotland.* Edinburgh: Scottish Executive.

Scottish Executive (2006a) *National Workforce Group: Scotland's Social Services Labour Market: 2nd Report.* Edinburgh: Scottish Executive.

Scottish Executive (2006b) *Summary Report of the 21st Century Social Work Review.* Edinburgh: Scottish Executive.

Scottish Executive (2006c) *Changing Lives: Report of the 21st Century Social Work Review.* Edinburgh: Scottish Executive.

Scottish Executive (2008) *Citizen Leadership.* Edinburgh: Scottish Executive.

Scottish Government (2007) *Government Economic Strategy.* Edinburgh: Scottish Government.

Scottish Social Services Council (2003a) *Codes of Practice for Employers of Social Services Workers.* Dundee: Scottish Social Services Council.

Scottish Social Services Council (2003b) *Codes of Practice for Social Service Workers.* Dundee: Scottish Social Services Council.

Scottish Social Services Council (2007) *Sector Skills Agreement Stages 1 and 2.* Dundee: Scottish Social Services Council.

Seal, C.R., Boyatzis, R.E. and Bailey, J.R. (2006) 'Fostering emotional and social intelligence in organisations.' *Organisation Management Journal.* Linking Theory and Practice: EAM White Paper Series 3, 3, 190–209.

Taylor, B. (2001) 'The elusive delights of learning.' *Financial Times*, 14 May, 3.

Van Zwanenberg, Z. (2008) *Changing Lives Analytical Review. Report for Chairs of Change Programmes.* Unpublished paper.

CHAPTER 10

Social Work Leadership and Management Development: Comparable Approaches

Richard H. Beinecke

The state of social work leadership and management training

Social work educators have long recognized the challenge of training social work administrators, the limitations of schools in doing so, and the issue of what management content to include in the social work curriculum. During the latter part of the twentieth century the macro skills of community organizing, social planning and political advocacy have become less important as more students choose clinical training (Rank and Hutchison 2000). For three decades there has been a decline in the number of social workers identifying themselves as administrators. Only 3 percent of students in social work schools are in administration concentrations and interest of social work students is very low. Yet over 50 percent of social workers do some form of administration (Patti 2003; Wuenschel 2006). While 96 percent of social workers in the United States report that they work in direct services and 61 percent say that they spend over 20 hours per week in it, 69 percent spend some time in administration and management (20% over 20 hours per week), 67 percent in planning, and 30 percent in policy development (NASW Center for Workforce Studies 2006, p.9).

A growing number of agencies are run by administrators trained in fields other than social work (Nesoff 2007). The debate about which degree, the MSW, MPA or MBA, is best for managing human service agencies continues, is not resolved and will probably never be agreed upon (Faherty 1987; Hoefer

2003; Nesoff 2007). While many argue that social work graduate programs are weak in management training, each degree program has its own strengths and weaknesses, and social work training brings many assets to an administrator or policy maker. However, it is very difficult for a social work program to fit in as much management training as degrees whose prime focus is in this area.

Little attention has been given in the social work literature to concepts of leadership and management. While it is a theme in the literature of many other disciplines, it is not part of the professional foundation for social work education (Gellis 2001; Rank and Hutchison 2000). While the National Association of Social Workers (NASW) has conducted many studies of social workers in clinical positions, they have never conducted any studies of social workers in management positions (Whitaker 2008). Within NASW there is no management or leadership speciality section and only a link on its website to the National Network for Social Work Managers. Of the 152 continuing education courses listed on NASW's website on 16 April 2008, only one appeared to be about leadership or management. NASW's Leadership Academy only lasted from 1994 to 1997 (Rank and Hutchison 2000). As a look at the references for this chapter show, only one journal, *Administration in Social Work*, is focused on social work management, while many are concerned about clinical issues. Lucas (2005) and others report how uncomfortable their students felt going into the business section of libraries looking for books on management, since there were few in the social work section, and students often had the view that management or business were not appropriate areas for social work practice. In a study of three social work schools Ezell, Chernesky and Healy (2004) found that clinical students are often critical of peers who select administration as a concentration or career, majorities of students expressed anti-management attitudes and courses did not provide adequate administrative training. This mirrors the ambivalence with which society views social work and social work administrators in particular (Rank and Hutchison 2000).

Perlmutter (2006) met with 14 CEOs of social service organizations. They agreed that many social workers have little status in society, that many are not respected as administrators, that the focus of most students entering the field is on clinical skills not management, that many graduates of social work schools do not have the necessary communication and analytical skills and that many social workers have parochial views about management and leadership. Thus, she raises the questions: is the need to educate practitioners in direct service and in leadership incompatible? Should social workers be trained in management and leadership?

The answer is definitely yes, whether in social work degree programs, in additional management degrees or in continuing education. We face a looming crisis in nonprofit management as many leaders are on the verge of retirement, few potential leaders are poised to take over, and few organizations are investing in management and leadership training (Nesoff 2007). This mirrors the crisis throughout public administration. In the United States and many other countries, as many as 40 percent of senior managers at all levels of government, health, local agencies and advocacy organizations will retire within the next five years (Wamunya 2003). We are not doing an adequate job of training the next generation of leaders.

The Annapolis Coalition, a not-for-profit organization focused on improving workforce development in the behavioral health field in the United States, concludes that 'leadership development, as a strategic goal, offers high potential to transform behavioral health'. To achieve this strategic goal,

> the competencies necessary for leadership roles in behavioral health must be identified. Particular attention must be given to developing core leadership competencies that can be adapted to the different sectors of this field... Available curricula for leadership development must be identified and further developed to ensure that the core competencies are adequately addressed. Increased support should be allocated to the formal, continuous development of emerging leaders in the field. (Annapolis Coalition 2007, pp.19–20)

Leadership challenges facing social workers

Social work leadership has become increasingly important as the field and profession have changed. Complex social, cultural, economic, political and demographic factors are creating changes in human service delivery systems. 'Globalization, managed care, computerization, the Internet, welfare reform, privatization, diversity, and the increasing gap between the rich and the poor are just some of the macro forces currently affecting social work practice' (Rank and Hutchison 2000, pp.487–488).

Persons in mental health and social workers in particular face many challenges. According to the Scottish *Summary Report of the 21st Century Social Work Review: Changing Lives*, they include changing needs, opportunities, society and expectations. Doing more of the same won't work. Increasing demand, greater complexity and rising expectations mean that 'tomorrow's solutions will need to engage people as active participants, delivering accessible, responsive services of the highest quality'. Social work does not have all the answers and will need to work with other providers and professionals to find new ways to design and deliver services across the public sector. Social workers' skills are highly valued yet they are far from making the best use of them. In many countries they need to much more actively involve those who use services and their carers in every aspect of care, policy and research (Scottish Executive 2005).

Leadership and management challenges include:

- the diminished role of social workers in leadership/management and the stigma of social workers in management

- the Peter Principle of most social workers moving up into management and leadership from practitioner positions without any training or even supervision in administration

- competition from other degrees such as the MBA and MPA for training of human service managers

- limited management and leadership skills and training in social work schools, continuing education and agencies.

A personal story

In the early 1970s I was a clinical social worker in a community mental health center in Vermont, seeing clients and responsible for managing the adult and emergency services of the agency and supervising clinical and management students from the SUNY-Albany School of Social Work. A few years earlier I had completed my MA in Social Service Administration at the University of Chicago, double majoring in family practice and community organizing. As often happens, I began work seeing clients and, within a couple of years, without any additional management training, moved up to my leadership positions. In my new management role I quickly realized that my clinical students needed to understand administration to operate effectively even as line staff, while my management students needed first hand experience with those that they served so that they could understand their needs and be empathetic to their concerns. Therefore, I required my clinical students to take on certain administrative tasks and my administrative students to see at least two clients. In addition to individual supervision, we shared our experiences in weekly group meetings.

Since that time the people who have most impressed me in mental health are those who combine clinical and management/policy training and experiences, in many cases continuing to see clients while serving in high level leadership positions. In my case, as a 'social worker who does weird things', I have served in a variety of clinical, management and academic positions, at the local, state and federal levels, and in business as well as non-profit organizations. For the past 15 years, while self-identifying as a social worker, I have taught and conducted research in a public administration department located within a business school.

Throughout this 35-year career I have always found that social workers at any level need to be good managers and leaders. I agree with Veronica Coulshed (Coulshed *et al.* 2006, p.2) 'that all social workers are managers. Their circles of activity ripple outwards from managing themselves, at the core, to managing others, and onwards again to managing systems.' The core skills needed for this are the same wherever one practices, though the need for certain skills may vary depending upon one's level of practice and the particular policy area or setting that one is working in. My recent research, in which I have studied the leadership and management literature and identified mental health, health and public administration training programs and skill sets in eight English speaking countries (Beinecke and Spencer 2007), further confirms this view and demonstrates that the competencies are essentially the same at least in developed countries (we are now expanding the research into developing countries to see what similarities and differences are present).

The *21st Century Social Work* report emphasized that we need enabling leadership and effective management to be developed at all levels – professional and practice leadership, political leadership, strategic leadership, operational management, academic leadership and citizen (user and carer) leadership. 'Our goal is to empower workers, people who can use services and managers to promote partnership and provide a supportive environment where creative solutions can be developed to meet people's needs. Developing both services and workers will require visionary, creative leadership and effective, supportive management' (Scottish Executive 2005, p.25).

Management needs to create a culture and climate for change. 'The shift needed is in leadership and management style to embrace a partnership approach that empowers staff, users, and managers to participate in developing creative solutions, developing positive, supportive behaviors and environments to sustain leadership and management development in social work services' (Leadership and Management Sub-Group 2005, p.5).

Leadership and management

Some authors consider leadership and management to be the same, while others say that they are distinct but overlapping (see Kanji and Moura E Sa 2001 for an excellent review of this debate). Kotter (1990) considers them to be very distinct. However, both are needed if an organization is to prosper

(Beinecke and Spencer 2007). A leader motivates and inspires; a manager controls and problem solves. A leader produces change, and a manager produces efficiency (Alban-Metcalfe and Alimo-Metcalfe 2000).

Others feel that these are not separate functions or roles but are dimensions that all leaders share and utilize differently depending upon their position or task. The authors of 'What Is Leadership' (Leadership Development Centre 2007) believe that a good manager needs to be a good leader. Management is a role which underpins an organization's ability to perform, while leadership is a behavior that breathes life into organizational performance. Together they communicate vision, shape an organization's culture, build a high performing workforce, promote diversity, apply sound management practices and business operations, create networks of external relationships and apply functional and technical knowledge.

Packard (2004, p.12) conceptualizes a social work administration curriculum that includes both management (program design, financial management, information systems, human resource management, program evaluation, project management, diversity) and leadership (visioning, change management, strategy development, organization design, culture management, community collaboration, ethics and values, political advocacy).

Transactional and transformative leadership

Burns (1978, p.4) distinguishes between transactional and transformational leadership. 'The relations of most leaders and followers are transactional – leaders approach followers with an eye to exchanging one thing for another.' They accept and work within the system as it is. Transactional leadership is the most common style in organizations. Someone who is a strong transactional leader stresses efficiency, planning and goal setting, competency, structure and maintaining the organization. He or she may be more reactive and supportive of the status quo.

The transforming leader, by contrast, 'looks for potential motives in followers, seeks to satisfy higher needs, and engages the full person of the follower. The result of transforming leadership is a relationship of mutual stimulation and elevation that converts followers and leaders and may convert leaders into moral agents' (Burns 1978, p.4).

Both types of leadership are needed. 'The overriding function of management has been to provide order and consistency to organizations – transactional skills. Leadership is most often construed as seeking adaptive and constructive change – transformational skills' (Leadership and Management Sub-Group 2005, p.4). 'Management is about continuity as well as change.

Managers may be urged by new public management to do things differently, but they still have to keep things running' (Harris 2007, p.19).

Based on a survey of a sample of social workers in hospitals, Gellis (2001) concluded that transformational leadership did have significant and substantial add-on effects to transactional leadership in the prediction of perceived effectiveness and satisfaction with the leader. Transformational leadership adds to group performance over and above transactional leadership. Mary (2005) found that social work leaders were more transformational than transactional in their leadership style, and that there is a strong relationship between perceived transformational leadership style of the leader and positive leadership outcomes and success.

All writers agree that leadership is necessary at all levels of the organization, not just the top:

> Leadership is also not the preserve of a few people at 'the top.' It needs to permeate each ward team, community team, functional team etc. and support frontline leaders to deliver improvements... Leadership needs to be visible across the whole organization and wherever social work services are delivered and to articulate the vision of that organization and how it will go about fulfilling that vision... Thus, what is required is both empowering, enabling leadership and effective management.' Leadership and management should inspire staff, promote and meet service aims, develop joint working partnerships, empower staff and users, value people and recognise potential, provide an environment and time in which to develop reflective practice, and take responsibility for professional development. (Leadership and Management Sub-Group 2005, pp.4, 6)

Leadership and management competencies

Competencies are 'individual characteristics which must be demonstrated to provide evidence of superior or effective performance in a job... The complete competency set or model for an individual role identifies all the knowledge, skills, experiences, and attributes a person should display in their behaviour when they are doing the job well' (Mackay 1997).

Beinecke and Spencer (2007) conducted an extensive review of the leadership and management literature in mental health, health and public administration. We then reviewed mental health, health, and public administration training programs in eight English-speaking countries (Australia, Canada, Ireland, Northern Ireland, New Zealand, Scotland, United Kingdom and the United States), identified the leadership and management models and competencies in each, and analyzed which competencies were the ones that were most taught in these training programs. On this basis we created the Leadership and Management Skill Set, five areas that nearly all of the mental health, health and public administration articles, books, reports and programs that we reviewed covered, whether in one course or in a group of courses. Our five leadership competency areas (Figure 10.1; see the report for a full listing of the competencies in each) are:

- personal skills and knowledge
- interpersonal (people) skills
- transactional (execution, management) skills
- transformational skills
- policy and program knowledge.

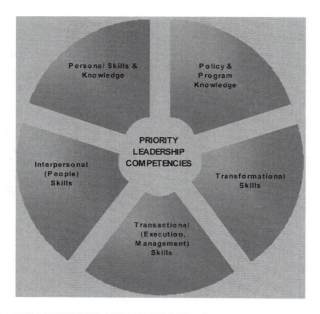

FIGURE 10.1: THE LEADERSHIP AND MANAGEMENT SKILL SET

A wide variety of transactional skills are taught in the studied programs. The most common are quality management and assessment, human resource management, finance and budgeting, organizational theory and design, information systems and project planning and management. Transactional skills are the ones most being taught in training programs. Many managers move up into leadership and management programs from clinical and lower level positions, and these skills are not part of their training or experience. Other skills such as quality improvement and performance management and information systems have only recently become important in our fields and thus need to be learned by many managers and leaders.

Interpersonal skills are honed in many of the studied programs. Written and verbal communicating, teamwork, coaching and enabling others, and negotiating and facilitating are particularly important. Working with people of other cultures and with stakeholders and empowering others are also viewed as valuable skills.

Visioning and strategic planning are emphasized in many of the programs. Other frequently offered transformational training is in catalyzing change and innovation and goal setting.

The personal skills that programs indicate they foster are emotional intelligence (self-awareness), values and beliefs and ethical behavior.

Relatively few programs teach policy and program knowledge. This may be an artefact of their descriptions; these areas are core subjects in training but are not explicitly listed in program descriptions. Alternatively, the field may believe that experienced people already know much about the mental health or health field or that teaching basic transferable skills is more important than learning about particular policies.

We found that the first four leadership competencies for mental health were not different from those in health or public administration and that these competencies did not differ depending upon the country in which they were used. Core leadership competencies are universal. On the other hand, the knowledge needed of policies and programs are different for mental health than for health and vary depending upon the country or locality where they are applied.

The capable practitioner

The Training and Practice Development Section of the Sainsbury Centre for Mental Health described 'The Capable Practitioner'.

> Practitioners require more than a prescribed set of competencies. They need to be capable of providing the benefits of both effective and reflective practice. This requires an underpinning framework of values, attitudes and knowledge in addition to competencies along with an ability to apply those in practice, across a range of clinical contexts. (Sainsbury Centre 2001, p.5)

Capability includes a performance component, an ethical component, a component that emphasizes reflective practice in action (see Schon 1983), the capability to effectively implement evidence-based interventions, and a responsibility for lifelong learning. The Framework for Capable Practice includes five related areas: ethical practice (values and attitudes), knowledge of mental health and mental health services, process of care (capabilities to work effectively with users, carers, families, team members and other agencies), interventions and their applications to specific service settings (Sainsbury Centre 2001, p.8). The detailed descriptions of each of these areas are important complements to needed competencies, whether one is a clinician, manager or policy maker.

Differences in use in management levels and settings

While the core leadership and management competencies are the same for all, there are differences in their use depending upon the levels of management and between different sectors that one is working in. The Scottish Leadership Foundation (van Zwanenberg 2003, pp.10, 22–23) surveyed chief social work officers, senior managers and first/middle managers on their use and training in change management and complex change, partnership and cross organizational working, multi-professional teams, negotiating skills and leadership. Clear differences were found between different levels of management and these were very significant compared to the critical challenges experienced and predicted by these managers. They also were different depending upon whether one was working in the statutory or voluntary sectors. The Sainsbury Centre (2001), having described 'the broad brush of capabilities not specific to any setting or to professional level,' then addressed 'the specific applications required for each of these areas, that are distinct from the essential capabilities'. Each of the ten settings required use of certain sometimes different management, interpersonal and leadership skills. Lewis *et al.* (2001, p.10) considered the three types of management skills to be technical, human (people) and conceptual. While all managers use these skills, technical is used more by supervisory than middle or top management, human is used equally by all and conceptual is needed primarily by top management.

Hoefer (2003) surveyed nonprofit agency administrators, government administrators, social work educators and public administration educators at entry, middle and top levels on what skills are most important for managers. The most important for nearly all respondents, whatever the area or level, were commitment to clients, professionalism, oral and written communication, leadership and decision making. In all groups people skills were considered to be the most important. In every case respondents wanted more skill in each area as one moved from entry to middle to top level management. Thus, the need may not be for different skills, but more of each the higher one moves up the management ladder.

Human service and social work competencies

The limited literature on what human service and social work leaders do includes many of these competencies. Rank and Hutchison (2000) surveyed deans and directors from social work programs and executive directors and presidents of NASW chapters. Nine essential leadership skills were identified: community development, communication and interpersonal skills, analysis of social, political and cultural events, technological, political, visioning, ethical reasoning, risk taking, and cultural competence/diversity.

Menefee and Thompson (1994) defined human service administrator roles as leadership, interactional and analytic tasks. Using this typology Austin and Kruzich (2004) analyzed the most common skills taught in human service management textbooks from 1994 to 2002 – organizer (leadership), communicator, supervisor, and facilitator (interactional), and resource manager and evaluator (analytic). Innovator, advocate and policy practitioner were the three skills least covered in these texts. Lewis *et al.* (2001) considered the functions of human service management, whether programs provide direct or indirect services and whether they are housed in public or private agencies to be planning, designing, developing human resources, supervising, managing finances, monitoring and developing. 'The force that binds together and energizes these processes is leadership: working with employees to articulate a vision, manage the external environment, oversee the design of organizational processes, link elements of the systems together, create a supportive organizational culture, and manage change' (p.11).

The National Network of Social Work Managers (NNSWM) promulgated a list of ten competencies required for successful human service management: contemporary social and public policy issues, advocacy, public/community relations and marketing, governance, planning, program development, financial development, evaluation, human resource management and staff development. These competencies are the core of the Certified Social Work Management credential (Nesoff 2007; Wimpfheimer 2004). Four sets of standards are used to assess applicants: substantive knowledge, personal skills, ethical standards and technical skills (Packard 2004).

Skidmore (1995) listed the ways in which competent social administrators act: accepting, caring, creating, democratizing, trusting, approving, maintaining personal equilibrium and balance, planning, organizing, setting priorities, delegating, interacting with the community and professions, decision making, facilitating, communicating, timing, building and motivating. His chapters cover ethical conduct, the planning process, decision making, financial management, accountability and evaluation, organizing, committee and board operation, leadership, teamwork, motivation, communicating, community relations, staffing and supervision and staff development. In an ideal world a competent leader should be strong in all of these areas. Given the reality of who we are, that is usually not possible. We all have our strengths and areas of weaknesses.

One solution is for a leader to support and surround him or herself with team members with complementary skills. Another is to strengthen one's capabilities through continuing learning, training and introspection – self-renewal (Gardner 1965, 1990).

Uniqueness of administration in human service organizations

The debate over whether management in social work agencies requires different skills than for public administration or business continues. Patti (2000) and Wuenschel (2006) argue that these managers must possess unique skills, including addressing difficult moral choices, accommodating the expectations of external constituents, advocating for stigmatized populations, collaborating with other agencies and relying on front line professional personnel. Their primary goal is individual and community service, not profit, a commonly heard argument. More than 77 percent of those interviewed by Rank and Hutchison (2000) thought that leadership for social work was different than that for other professions. They defined five common elements of leadership for the social work profession: proaction, values and ethics, empowerment, vision and communication. The themes of the differences were: commitment to the NASW Code of Ethics, a systemic perspective, a participatory leadership style, altruism and concern about the public image of the profession. While these are certainly important skills, are they really unique to social service agency management or ones that are present in many settings but may need to be emphasized more here?

Social workers may be particularly suited to be administrators. Their values may be especially important for successful leadership. Many practitioner skills in social work are also managerial ones that social workers are especially well trained in. They include management of people, team leadership, systemic thinking, bargaining, negotiating and advocacy, working with limited resources, meeting required standards and procedures and contributing to change and innovation. In many ways social workers are 'practitioner-managers' (Coulshed *et al.* 2006).

> Managerial functions are closely allied with the skills of helping. Social work and counseling degree programs in particular emphasize effective communications skills such as active listening, giving and receiving feedback, group dynamics and facilitation, and positive regard for all individuals. All these skills are important for managers as they design systems and lead staff in accomplishing organizational goals. (Lewis *et al.* 2001, p.19)

According to Statham *et al.* (in Scottish Executive 2005) social workers have three main functions: to intervene between the state and the citizen, to maximize the capacity of people using services and to contribute to policies and practice that support social and personal well-being. Social workers are especially equipped to make successful interventions because of their empathy, respect and warmth, their ability to establish positive relationships and their person centered and collaborative approach). 'Social work services have built on values such as choice and self-determination to develop practice that is person-centred and emphasises social inclusion, advocacy, engagement and partnership with service users' (Leadership and Management Sub-Group 2005, p.6). These values need to be elevated into management decision making. When a practitioner moves into management, they have not left social work, but have brought the strengths of social work into it (Maslyn 2002).

Globalization and the need to add global knowledge and skills to any curriculum or training

We live in a globalized world with many interconnected social problems that know no boundaries and that are becoming more important. Poverty, armed conflicts and natural disasters, health epidemics such as HIV/AIDS and chronic illnesses, children and women's issues, migration, war, global warming – the list goes on and on. Mental health accounts for four of the top ten causes of disability in the world, yet it is largely ignored as a global concern. Most social work training does not address these issues or give students the skills needed to practice, manage and lead the changes that need to take place in the millennium (Dominelli 2007). Only a few schools such as the Boston College School of Social Work have programs on global health or HIV/AIDS. We are all impacted by these issues, whether we work in our own country or abroad. Students need to learn about these issues and how to apply leadership and management skills appropriately to them.

Conclusion: We need more management and leadership training

Beinecke and Spencer (2007, p.61) found that 'in most countries that we have studied, the United States being a prime example, leadership training is scattered and only partially covers many of these areas. It is not well organized or coordinated. Program availability varies greatly depending upon where one lives. There is no central site to find such programs.'

This more detailed look at social work and human service literature and programs shows that this problem is even more common in these areas. The need for effective managers and leaders is high. The competencies that social work managers and leaders should have are clear. We must do much more to develop social work degree concentrations and continuing education programs in this area and, as this book hopes to do, bring this knowledge to the people who are the carers of many people in the world.

References

Alban-Metcalfe, R.J. and Alimo-Metcalfe, B. (2000) 'An analysis of the convergent and discriminant validity of the transformational leadership questionnaire.' *International Journal of Selection and Assessment 8*, 3, 158–175.

Annapolis Coalition (2007) *An Action Plan for Behavioral Health Workforce Development: A Framework for Discussion: Executive Summary.* Available at www.annapoliscoalition.org, accessed 11 May 2009.

Austin, M.J. and Kruzich, J.M. (2004) 'Assessing recent textbooks and casebooks in human service administration: Implications and future directions.' *Administration in Social Work 28*, 1, 115–129.

Beinecke, R.H. and Spencer, J. (2007) *Leadership Training Programs and Competencies for Mental Health, Substance, Use, Health, and Public Administration in Eight Countries. International Initiative for Mental Health Leadership.* Available at www.iimhl.com, accessed 11 May 2009.

Burns, J.M. (1978) *Leadership.* New York: Harper and Row.

Coulshed, V., Mullender, A., Jones, D.N. and Thompson, N. (2006) *Management in Social Work*, 3rd edn. New York: Palgrave Macmillan.

Dominelli, L. (2007) 'Contemporary challenges to social work education in England.' *Australian Social Work 60*, 1, 29–45.

Ezell, M., Chernesky, R.H. and Healy, L.M. (2004) 'The learning climate for administration students.' *Administration in Social Work 28*, 1, 57–76.

Faherty, V.E. (1987) 'The battle of the ms: the mba, mpa, mph, and msw.' *Administration in Social Work 11*, 2, 33–43.

Gardner, J.W. (1965) *Self-Renewal: The Individual and the Innovative Society.* New York: Harper and Row.

Gardner, J.W. (1990) *On Leadership.* New York: The Free Press.

Gellis, Z.D. (2001) 'Social work perceptions of transformational and transactional leadership in health care.' *Social Work Research 25*, 1, 17–25.

Harris, J. (2007) 'Looking backward, looking forward: Current trends in human services management.' In J. Aldgate, L. Healy, B. Malcolm, B. Pine, W. Rose and J. Seden (eds) *Enhancing Social Work Management: Theory and Best Practice from the UK and USA.* London: Jessica Kingsley Publishers.

Hoefer, R. (2003) 'Administrative skills and degrees: The "best place" debate rages on.' *Administration in Social Work 27,* 1, 25–46.

Kanji, G.K. and Moura E Sa, P. (2001) 'Measuring leadership excellence.' *Total Quality Management 12,* 6, 701–718.

Kotter, J.P. (1990) *A Force for Change: How Leadership Differs from Management.* New York: The Free Press.

Leadership and Management Sub-Group (September 2005) *21st Century Social Work: Strengthening Leadership and Management Capacity Across Social Work Services.* Available at www.SocialworkScotland.org.uk/resources/Cp-Im/Leadershipand ManagementSubGroupReport.pdf, accessed 11 May 2009.

Leadership Development Centre (2007) 'What is leadership.' Available at www.ldc.govt.nz/?/resources/whatisleadership, accessed 11 May 2009.

Lewis, J.A., Lewis, M.D., Packard, T. and Souflee, Jr. F. (2001) *Management of Human Service Programs,* 3rd edn. Boston: Brooks/Cole.

Lucas, G.I. (2005) 'The emerging sophistication in human service management: A welcome and essential evolution.' *Journal of Community Practice 13,* 3, 107–114.

Mackay, P. (January 1997) *Competencies and Competence: What are They and What Part do They Play.* Available at www.ldc.govt.nz/?/information/publications, accessed 11 May 2009.

Mary, N. L (2005) 'Transformational leadership in human service organizations.' *Administration in Social Work 29,* 2, 105–118.

Maslyn, R.T (2002) 'Why I founded the national network for social work managers.' Available at www.socialworkmanager.org/articles.php?id=article03, accessed 11 May 2009.

Menefee, D.T. and Thompson, J.J. (1994) 'Identifying and comparing competencies for social work management: a practice-driven approach.' *Administration in Social Work 18,* 3, 1–25.

NASW Center for Workforce Studies (2006) *Assuring the Sufficiency of a Frontline Workforce: A National Study of Licensed Social Workers.* Washington, DC: National Association of Social Workers.

Nesoff, I. (2007) 'The importance of revitalizing management education for social workers.' *Social Work 52,* 3, 283–285.

Packard, T. (2004) 'Issues in designing and adapting an administration concentration.' *Administration in Social Work 28,* 1, 5–20.

Patti, R.J. (2000) 'The landscape of social welfare management.' In R.J. Patti (ed.) *The Handbook of Social Welfare Management.* Thousand Oaks, CA: Sage Publications.

Patti, R.J. (2003) 'Reflections on the state of management in social work.' *Administration in Social Work 27,* 2, 1–11.

Perlmutter, F.D. (2006) 'Guest editorial: Ensuring social work administration.' *Administration in Social Work 30,* 2, 3–10.

Rank, M.G. and Hutchison, W.S. (2000) 'An analysis of leadership within the social work profession.' *Journal of Social Work Education 36,* 3, 487–502.

Sainsbury Centre for Mental Health, Training and Practice Development Section (April 2001) *The Capable Practitioner: A Framework and List of the Practitioner Capabilities Required to Implement The National Service Framework for Mental Health.* Available at www.scmh.org.uk/publications/capable_practitioner.aspx?ID=552, accessed 11 May 2009.

Schon, D.A. (1983) *The Reflective Practitioner: How Professionals Think in Action.* London: TempleSmith.

Scottish Executive (2005) *Summary Report of the 21st Century Social Work Review: Changing Lives.* Available at www.socialworkScotland.org.uk/resources/pub/ChangingLivesSummary Report.pdf, accessed 11 May 2009.

Skidmore, R.A. (1995) *Social Work Administration: Dynamic Management and Human Relationships,* 3rd edn. Boston: Allyn and Bacon.

Van Zwanenberg, Z. (2003) *Leadership and Management Development in Social Work Services.* Available at www.socialworkscotland.org.uk/resources/Cp-Im/Leadershipand ManagementDevinSocialServOrgs.pdf, accessed 11 May 2009.

Wamunya, W. (2003) 'Uncle Sam wants…workers; Retirements to cause employee shortage.' *Boston Herald,* 10 March, 37.

Whitaker, T. (2008) Personal communication. Washington, DC: National Association of Social Workers Center for Workforce Studies.

Wimpfheimer, S. (2004) 'Leadership and management competencies defined by practicing social work managers: An overview of standards developed by the national network for social work managers.' *Administration in Social Work 28,* 1, 45–56.

Wuenschel, P. (2006) 'The diminishing role of social work administrators in social service agencies: Issues for consideration.' *Administration in Social Work 30,* 4, 5–18.

CHAPTER 11

Lessons from Health Leadership

Graham Dickson

Health leadership in Canada

In Canada, as in many other jurisdictions across the globe, the construct of leadership has gained significant attention in the last ten years (Goodwin 2005; House *et al.* 2004; International Initiative for Mental Health Leadership 2007; Scottish Leadership Foundation 2007; Weiss and Molinaro 2005). Why all this attention on 'leadership'? One answer is that leadership is vital to the success of change and quality improvement in the health and/or social service sectors (Boaden 2005; Degeling and Carr 2004; Philippon 2007; Rowlands 2007). The churn in all social enterprises occasioned by the growth of technology, global economics and communications, climate change and environmental sensitivity has created a pace of change that demands new and better leadership to respond to and shape that change. A second answer is that health organizations and systems 'are an ideal setting for the application of complexity science due to the diversity of organizational forms and interactions' (Begun, Zimmerman and Dooley 2003, p.252). A third answer is that there is a growing sense of urgency that leadership of change is needed. As the 2008 *Getting Our Money's Worth* report on health care in the province of Quebec states: 'Everyone is aware of the difficulties of the health system, yet the situation is not changing quickly enough' (Gouvernement du Québec 2008). This chapter highlights recent efforts in Canada to define and develop leadership as a means of improving the health sector, highlighting three initiatives that are pushing the boundaries of our knowledge and expertise in understanding and developing leadership in the Canadian health sector. It is hoped that these examples may be helpful to people with the same intentions in other countries.

Context: The Canadian health system

Canada is a federation. A federation is 'a form of government in which powers and functions are divided between a central government and a number of political subdivisions that have a significant degree of political autonomy' (Outline of American Geography 2008). Canada divides constitutional responsibility for delivery of health services between a central government (capital Ottawa) and provincial or territorial governments in each singular jurisdiction. British Columbia is the westernmost province and is one of ten provinces and three territories in Canada.[1]

Provincial and territorial governments are responsible for the management, organization and delivery of health services for their residents under the jurisdiction of the federal Canadian Health Act (CHA) (British North America Act 1867; Department of Justice Canada 2008).[2] The CHA specifies universal health care and guarantees that the full cost of health service delivery will be borne by the Canadian taxpayer for specific services that are medically necessary (mainly hospital, physician services and extended care, although the latter is *not* fully publicly funded) (Department of Justice Canada 2008). Each province has a Ministry of Health (MOH) (or similar entity) that oversees funding and stewardship of a provincial health system. For example, in British Columbia (BC), a province of approximately 4.5 million people, the BC MOH has further delegated responsibility for service delivery to five regional health authorities and one provincial region (responsible for delivery of services that are only efficient when coordinated or delivered on a provincial

---

1   There are 18 large health systems in Canada. The 13 provinces, the First Nations, the Military, Veterans, the federal prison system and the Royal Canadian Mounted Police.

2   The British North America Act of 1867 gave provinces jurisdiction over 'The Establishment, Maintenance, and Management of Hospitals, Asylums, Charities, and Eleemosynary Institutions in and for the Province, other than Marine Hospitals'. Subsequent legislation on health insurance and medicare qualified these provisions. The Canada Health Act 1984 modernized the relationships by approving federal spending intervention as a legitimate option for healthcare. The Act includes this statement 'Although the federal government is not responsible for health-care administration, organization or delivery, it can exert considerable influence on provincial health-care policies by using the political and financial leverage afforded by the spending power. In fact, by setting the requirements for providing federal funding, the *Canada Health Act* has to a large extent shaped provincial health-care insurance plans throughout the country' (Department of Justice Canada 2008).

scale).[3] Recently, in British Columbia, and also across Canada, there has been a growing demand for focused investment and planning to address a perceived 'leadership gap' in the Canadian health system (Canadian Health Leadership Network 2008; Dickson, Norman and Shoop 2007; Leeb, Zelmer and Taylor 2005; Leatt and Porter 2003; Penney 2007).

Health leadership in Canada

In Canada the health-care system is constantly being exposed to significant public scrutiny. The media acts as the public's spokesperson: there are ongoing news stories about lengthy wait lists; regular anecdotes about how a senior's care was botched or neglected and constant political turmoil about where the money is going to come from as a population ages and demands for services outstrips both the capacity of the government to pay for them as well as the taxpayer's willingness to foot the bill (see Figure 11.1: Gouvernement du Québec 2008).

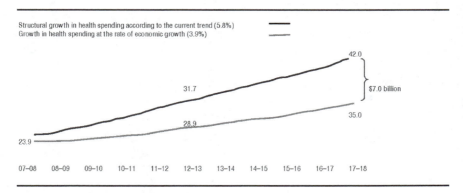

FIGURE 11.1: PROJECTED PUBLIC SPENDING ON HEALTH 2007–08 TO 2017–18 (BILLIONS OF DOLLARS)
SOURCE: MINISTÈRE DES FINANCES DU QUÉBEC

---

3   BC is highlighted here because a case study for that province is included in this chapter. The provinces of Canada are, west to east: British Columbia; Alberta; Saskatchewan; Manitoba; Ontario; Quebec; New Brunswick; Nova Scotia; Newfoundland and Labrador, and Prince Edward Island. The two territories are Iqualit (former Northwest Territories) and the Yukon.

In this context Stephen Lewis (2007) and Roy Romanow (2007),[4] two well-known health experts, have stated that improved leadership is key to making the changes that are necessary (for example waitlist management, fiscal sustainability, primary care reform, end-of-life care [Ward 2007]). It seems that many health Chief Executive Officers agree with them: in May 2008 150 CEOs from across Canada's health system recently attended an executive forum focused on the topic of *transformational leadership in health care* — strategies for and examples of how to lead meaningful change in service delivery at the unit, organization or provincial level (Canadian College of Health Service Executives 2008).

At the core of these issues is either a direct or an indirect criticism of health care's current leadership. What is the vision of the Canadian health system (Carver 2008; Canadian Union of Public Employees 2008)? Who's going to 'take charge' and implement change, rather than simply study these issues? And what kind of leadership is needed to resolve these problems, problems that no western society really has ever experienced before?

The changing face of leadership in Canadian health care

As the world changes, so must practices of leadership change. In Canada, there appears to be a growing conviction that the kind of leadership that created the health system of today is not the leadership that will take us into the future (Leaders for Life 2008; Lewis 2007; Philippon 2007). Health system changes in Canada include medical and communications innovations, a trend to integrating small health authorities into bigger ones, and the expansion of professional health associations; this accelerating pace has created health authorities of increasingly larger size and complexity (for example moving from nine health authorities in Alberta to only one: Alberta 2008). These dynamics create a demand for leaders who need sophisticated leadership skills. It is therefore not surprising that health leaders and educators have found the principles of complexity science and chaos theory helpful in informing the nature and challenges of leadership needed for the future (Begun, Zimmerman and Dooley 2003; Plsek and Greenhalgh 2001).

Within Canada, efforts on a provincial scale to develop health leadership have been pursued in Alberta (Johnson 2006), British Columbia (Leaders for Life 2008), and Ontario (Philippon 2008). Professional development and graduate leadership education programs specialized to the health sector within

---

4   Roy Romanow is a former premier of Saskatchewan who was commissioned in 2002 to
     conduct a Royal Commission on the state of the health care system in Canada. See
     Government of Canada 2002.

the post-secondary community in Canada are also evolving to meet the contemporary demands for leadership. Some examples include the Dorothy M.
Wylie Leadership Institute in Ontario (Simpson *et al.* 2002), the Master of Arts
in Leadership Program (Health specialization) at Royal Roads University
(Royal Roads University 2006), executive programs at the University of
Toronto (Rotman School of Management 2008) and the new Executive MBA
in Health at the University of British Columbia (Sauder School of Business
2008) have aimed at addressing the leadership gap. Nationally the Canadian
Health Leadership Network (Canadian Health Leadership Network 2008) was
established in 2007 to enhance the quality of leadership needed in a complex,
modern health system.

This paper highlights three of those examples. The first is the efforts of
Royal Roads University (RRU) to engage with the health sector regarding
health systems leadership (Royal Roads University 2006). This example was
chosen because of the uniqueness of the approach within the post-secondary
community in Canada, and its reach into the health industry – somewhat
surprising, given RRU does not have any clinical programs for health
professions. The second is a major provincial project called the Leaders for Life
Program in British Columbia (Leaders for Life 2008) that is building on and
extending the work done in the United Kingdom under the stewardship of the
National Health Service (Clark 2008; NHS Institute for Innovation and
Improvement 2008).[5] It has been chosen because of the scope, reach and level
of success of this project across a province in Canada. Leaders for Life is also
tangentially connected to the growth and development of the third national
example: the Canadian Health Leadership Network (CHLNet) initiative in
Canada (Canadian Health Leadership Network 2008).[6] CHLNet was chosen
because it is the only initiative that is aiming at coalescing leadership resources
in health at a national level. This chapter will focus primarily on 'lessons
learned' through the author's active engagement and involvement in these
three projects.

---

5   The other two provincial examples – Alberta and Ontario – are still at very early stages of
        development. Indeed, the Alberta project may well not proceed as a consequence of the recent
        restructuring of Alberta's health authorities into one provincial authority (Alberta 2008).
6   CHLNet is tangentially connected to Leaders for Life in that the individual who initiated the
        original meeting of CHLNet, Mr William Tholl, General Secretary of the Canadian Medical
        Association, did so after presenting at a symposium in British Columbia. At that session he met
        Mr Geoff Rowlands, the Executive Director of HCLABC, who tirelessly lobbied other
        organizations in BC over the next year to generate the initial $3.0 million funding received by
        Leaders for Life from the provincial government. Mr Tholl has stated on numerous occasions
        that it was knowledge of the success in BC that inspired him to initiate the first meeting of
        CHLNet (William Tholl, personal communication, 10 November 2007). Mr Rowlands remains
        on the Steering Committee for the CHLNet initiative.

Health leadership initiatives at Royal Roads University

Royal Roads University was established in 1996. It makes the claim to be the only public university in Canada with a mandate to exclusively offer applied and professional programs (Directory of Canadian Universities 2008). RRU programs are in the fields of applied sciences (leadership, environmental management, conflict resolution, human security and peace-building, applied communications, and information and society); management and business and tourism. All of these programs are designed for adult learners, enabling them to remain in their jobs while completing their education. RRU uses a unique 'blended learning' model, which combines intensive face-to-face residencies with a sophisticated on-line learning system so that learners attend short intensive residencies (usually 1–3 weeks) on campus, but continue their learning while back at work (on-line).

RRU's Master of Arts in Leadership program (MAL) has had the greatest ongoing enrolment of RRU's program offerings since its inception in 1996. In the autumn of 1997 a MAL learner wrote her major project chronicling the design and delivery of the first dedicated health leadership program at RRU called *Creative Leadership in Health Care* (Cikaliuk 1998). Two years later RRU launched the MA Leadership with a specialization in health. Numerous health agencies within Canada sponsor learners into this program (Royal Roads University 2008a). In 2006 RRU launched two new health leadership initiatives: the Centre for Health Leadership and Research, dedicated to developing 'exceptional health systems leadership in Canada' (Royal Roads University 2008b) and the Graduate Certificate in Health Systems Leadership, developed in partnership with the Canadian Health Services Research Foundation's EXTRA program and the Canadian College of Health Service Executives (Royal Roads University 2008b; Canadian Health Services Research Foundation 2008).[7]

Royal Roads University's programs are unique in Canada for three reasons. First, the degree, certificate, and professional development programs are *competency-based programs* that emphasize leadership capabilities including personal mastery, emotional intelligence, teamwork, relationship-building,

---

7   The Canadian Health Services Research Foundation EXTRA program (Executive Training for
     Research Application) program contributed curriculum content for the RRU Health Systems
     Leadership program and assists in its marketing. Its web address can be found at
     www.chsrf.ca/extra, accessed on 12 May 2009. The Canadian College of Health Service
     Executives (CCHSE) was involved in the design of the program, and its members provide
     executive coaching services to participants in the program. Its web address can be found at
     www.cchse.org/default1.asp?active_page_id=1andlang=English, accessed on 12 May 2009.
     In addition, the Health Care Leaders Association of BC's Leaders for Life program provided
     funding for both of these initiatives in 2007–08.

creativity, evidence-based decision making, vision-setting, strategic planning, organizational change and systems thinking. These complement but are distinct from an emphasis on management and administrative knowledge. The program also features a complexity theory-based view of organizational systems. Assessment is based on demonstrated performance and intellectual comprehension of competencies by a leader (Master of Arts in Leadership: Residency 1 2008).

A second notable element of RRU programs is the belief that leadership competencies are best developed by practice. Programs are designed (Dickson and Hamilton 2006) to integrate theory and practice by linking the classroom and the workplace. The worksite becomes a 'laboratory' for the study of leadership (Fenwick 2002). The instructors require participants to set personal goals in the context of one's real-life leadership role during the on-line component of the program, and in the residencies to use real-life leadership challenges™ as vehicles for learning. Leadership challenges™ are current, unresolved and real-time examples of leadership dilemmas faced by people in leadership positions.[8] (Centre for Health Leadership and Research 2008b).

Learners must also do 'applied research' employing action research methodology. As leaders, they are to implement a change in their work setting simultaneously gathering data about the efficacy of their initiative. Action research is also the form of research undertaken by the Centre for Health Leadership and Research (CHLR). For example, it recently partnered with the BC Ministry of Health, the Canadian Medical Association and the Canadian Council on Learning to do action research in the field of self-directed learning for leadership development (Dickson, Norman and Shoop 2007). It has also worked with the Health Care Leaders' Association of BC in developing leadership competency or capability frameworks for organizations within the BC health sector (Health Care Leaders' Association of BC 2007a).

A third element that distinguishes Royal Roads University's approach to Canadian health leadership is its emphasis on a 'systems' view of leadership and change. This takes form in the conceptualization of the leadership competencies themselves that underpin its programs, but also in the framing of strategic leadership:

---

8   The term Leadership Challenge is trademarked at RRU. Leadership challenges are current, unresolved and real-time examples of leadership dilemmas faced by people in leadership positions. An example of a recent leadership challenge used in the Graduate Certificate in Health Systems Leadership was entitled 'Measuring Success: The Act Now BC Challenge'. Act Now is a province-wide policy to improve wellness in BC (Graduate Certificate in Health Systems Leadership 2007).

a leader who does not recognize the living dynamics of…systems is poorly equipped to orchestrate change… Leaders must use *transactional* leadership methods (i.e., changes in structure, legislation, and/or rules) as well as *transformational* methods (i.e., knowledge mobilization, value imperatives, and meaning making) to orchestrate change. The former approach changes the rules of the game; the latter approach intends to engage people in wanting to play the game within those rules, and giving them the skills to do so. (Dickson and White 2006, p.38)

The BC Leaders for Life Program

The second case that provides insights into Canadian health leadership is the BC Leaders for Life Program. Launched in January 2006, the Leaders for Life Program consists of a range of activities and opportunities aimed at growing the broader talent level of leadership in health care across the province of BC (Leaders for Life 2008). Leaders for Life is an initiative designed and supported by the Health Care Leaders' Association of British Columbia (HCLABC), in partnership with representatives of BC's health employers, post-secondary education system, selected organizations in the corporate sector and the Ministry of Health. Leaders for Life was given a start-up grant of $3.0 million with the mandate to prove that a viable, effective and first-class program of leadership development in BC's health sector can be created through facilitating alliances and partnerships amongst all the above-mentioned institutions (Rowlands 2007).

Leaders for Life claims originality in three ways. First, it is currently successful in generating buy-in and active support from the regional authorities, contracted agencies and individual leaders that comprise the health system in BC (Cikaliuk 2008). In British Columbia leadership development has traditionally been a responsibility of each health organization in the provincial system. Rarely did these organizations exchange ideas and collaborate on programs. A competitive ethos existed – not deliberately in most cases, or even overtly – but fostered by the natural 'silo-ing' of effort within different regional infrastructures. The developers of Leaders for Life came on the scene determined *not* to be a competing organization, *not* to be an additional administrative infrastructure and *not* to be a top-down program imposed by the provincial government (Rowlands 2007). Instead, it adopted a practice of building coalitions and alliances as a means of expanding leadership development capacity in BC. Support for the principles and vision of Leaders for Life amongst the various provincial organizations grew because it built on existing strengths within the province, leveraging existing quality wherever it could be found, and because it resorted to provincial solutions only where individual solutions were not possible (for example where critical mass was lacking).[9]

The second noteworthy contribution of Leaders for Life is that it has developed a system-wide set of leadership capabilities: 'The LEADS framework represents the key skills, abilities and knowledge required to lead at all levels of the health system. It aligns and consolidates the competency frameworks of individual health employers, professional associations and other progressive organizations into a common strategy' (Health Care Leaders' Association of BC 2007a). The LEADS framework is a simple and easy to use schema that is a key component of a Leaders for Life strategy to align provincial and local resources behind one model of leadership that represents the capabilities that are required for a system to actually work as a coherent system (see Figure 11.2).

Each of the five LEADS domains has sub-domains to give further clarity to them (Health Care Leaders' Association of BC 2007a). Self assessments and 360 assessments against the framework provide the necessary information for career planning and professional development.

Leads self

    Engages others

        Achieves results

            Develops coalitions

                Systems transformation

FIGURE 11.2: THE LEADS HEALTH SYSTEM LEADERSHIP CAPABILITIES FRAMEWORK

---

9   Leaders for Life's 12 for 12 program is dedicated to the development of future CEOs in BC's health sector. It was developed by Leaders for Life because no individual health authority was able to develop a truly comprehensive and meaningful program for one or two aspiring CEOs. However, Leaders for Life could develop a meaningful program for 16–20 people, a critical mass that can provide a program that is rich in content and provincial in scope.

A third unique strength of Leaders for life is the overall structure and composi-
tion of its learning design. Rather than utilize only one method of leadership
development (for example mentoring or executive programs) it has built a
broad suite of learning opportunities including: scholarships to graduate
programs that focus on developing the LEADS capabilities; a 360-degree assessment instrument informed by LEADS, combined with an executive
coaching function and individual professional development programs that
emphasize action learning linked to the ever-evolving real-life challenges
facing the health system in BC. For example, one such program, Leadership at
the Pulse, partnered physician medical officers and administrative officers
from health authorities to develop LEADS capabilities in their place of employment (Learning Strategies Group 2007). Another is an on-line
self-directed learning program that utilizes work experience opportunities to
expand knowledge of the health system (still in development). In addition, it is
in the process of building a state-of-the-art on-line learning 'talent management' schema that will support all of the above programs (Cikaliuk and
Fenwick 2008).

The LEADS framework has been adopted by a number of health
authorities and the BC Ministry of Health (BC MOH). Three new professional
development programs have been developed and supported by health
authorities and the BC MOH, and three new post-secondary credit programs
have been developed.[10] Three post-secondary institutions have begun to
conduct applied research and knowledge mobilization in support of the
Leaders for Life program.[11] The BC MOH has contributed an additional $2
million to extend the Leaders for Life program for an additional year, and
health authorities are discussing how collaborative action across the
authorities will secure Leaders for Life's future.

---

10   In terms of professional development programs RRU has developed the Art of Leadership
     program aimed at mid-managers and the 12 for 12 program, and Simon Fraser University the
     Leadership at the Pulse program, all mentioned earlier in the paper. In 'for credit'
     programming Leaders for Life has sponsored developmental work and scholarships to help
     launch a new MBA Health program at the University of BC and a Certificate in Health
     Systems Leadership at Royal Roads University. With the support of Leaders for Life RRU is
     also collaborating with the BC Institute of Technology Health Sciences faculty to create an
     entry level Master of Arts in Health Leadership and Management.
11   The Centre for Health Care Management (Sauder Business School) at the University of British
     Columbia, the Learning Strategies Group at Simon Fraser University (Segal School of
     Business), and the Centre for Health Leadership and the Centre for Applied Leadership and
     Management at Royal Roads University have contributed significant components to the
     Leaders for Life learning infrastructure.

The Canadian Health Leadership Network (CHLNet)

The Canadian Health Leadership Network is a coalition of individuals and organizations formed to stimulate the development of an enriched community of leaders and managers in Canada (Canadian Health Leadership Network 2008). CHLNet is encouraging health organizations and agencies in Canada to collaborate on succession planning, coalesce resources for leadership development and recruitment, and attract greater resources and energy to leadership development and leadership research across the country. Impetus for its formation is described in a statement from the Canadian College of Health Service Executives:

> Issues relating to aging of the leadership cohort, burnout, lack of succession planning and appropriate training, mentoring the next generation of leaders, and difficulty in persuading up and coming leaders and managers to take on more demanding roles in an ever-changing, increasingly complex health care environment are all worrisome signs that a leadership crisis is looming if not already here. (BC Health Leadership Capacity Project 2006, p.4)

CHLNet wishes to address the leadership gap in the health system by attracting more people to leadership positions and assisting those leaders to acquire the capabilities required to do the work expected of them. CHLNet recognizes that there are a number of organizations, public or private, which offer leadership training and development opportunities. It seeks to provide rapid access to the palette of leading practices in health leadership development found in the health sector in Canada. As stated in an original working paper, 'The goal is not to replicate or subsume existing leadership development strategies, but rather to create a "community of champions" whose common focus is increasing leadership capacity across the country' (Canadian Health Leadership Network 2008).

Currently CHLNet is in its fledgling stage of development. It has a steering committee; created a secretariat to steward its developmental work agenda; developed a three year business plan; gathered financial support from a variety of different organizational sources; commissioned (in partnership with the Canadian Health Services Research Foundation) a report on qualities of leadership called the Pan-Canadian Health Systems Leadership Capabilities Framework; and developed a web-portal for its partners to share knowledge and progress (Canadian Health Leadership Network 2008).[12]

There are three notable contributions of CHLNet to Canadian health care leadership. First, it has begun to coalesce interest amongst a diverse group of

---

12   The web portal for CHLNet can be found at: www.chlnet.ca, accessed 12 May 2009.

national agencies and individual senior leaders around efforts to create a leadership framework that they could all endorse. As stated in the Pan Canadian Leadership Report:

A clear model of exceptional leadership, endorsed by all agencies in Canada, can assist aspiring leaders to answer the following questions:

- What kind of leadership (in the form of capabilities) is required to steward the Canadian health system into the future?

- How might these leadership capabilities take shape in my organization?

- What expectations or definitions of 'best practice' do they suggest for me and my organization?

- What do these leadership capabilities look like in my specific role or in the context in which I work, and what guidance do they give me in setting direction for my career growth, and/or my professional growth?

- What programs can be designed and delivered to ensure efficient and effective capacity building in leadership within the Canadian health sector?

(Dickson *et al.* 2007, p.6)

The second significant contribution was to propose a model of exceptional leadership that would be acceptable to potential CHLNet members. In seeking to answer the above questions, a proposed framework was developed based on a literature review, data from interviews and focus groups conducted across the country, and analysis of existing leadership/management frameworks in health authorities, national organizations and international jurisdictions. The result was what is called the *Pan-Canadian Framework: CHAMPIONS caring; CULTIVATES self and others; CONNECTS with others; CREATES results; and CHANGES systems* (Canadian Health Leadership Network 2008). This framework is gaining acceptance within CHLNet and is currently being used in leadership development efforts within the Catholic Health Association (Catholic Health Leadership Project Working Committee 2007) and the Capital Health Region in Halifax, Nova Scotia (Capital Health Region 2008).

The third key contribution of CHLNet is that it has gained support and a national presence without any formal authority or budget. CHLNet is a 'coalition of the willing' (Philippon 2007) and has managed to gain adherence from organizations and individuals who are willing to invest – albeit conservatively – in the vision of a national approach to defining and developing health systems leadership. It promotes the concept of 'leadership without ownership' (Tholl 2004) as an approach to inviting individuals to put aside their traditional organizational affiliations and to collaborate in pursuit of a national strategy for health systems leadership development.

Lessons learned

There are six lessons regarding health leadership and leadership development that can be derived from these three examples.

First is that strategic organizational leadership is a relatively new concept within the Canadian health sector. Traditionally health leaders have focused primarily on clinical management and administration in an operational perspective. This lesson is derived from triangulating the literature reviews done in the Leaders for Life and CHLNet capability projects, existing leadership and management competency frameworks in the health sector, and the priorities expressed by leaders articulated in the interviews and focus groups (Briscoe and Romilly 2006; Romilly 2007). As one colleague stated: 'I would suggest it (the health sector) is in "catch up" mode because of the crisis it finds itself in. Older models…[of leadership]…are not working anymore in this more complex environment – and at a time when external factors have much more influence than in the past' (Briscoe 2008). Similarly, most existing frameworks in the health sector emphasize administrative/management competencies (Romilly 2007). Yet in the interviews and focus groups leadership terms and concepts consistent with the leadership literature search were mentioned more often than management constructs (Briscoe and Romilly 2006). It appears that there is a latent energy pertinent to leadership emerging in the health sector.

A second lesson from these three cases is that there appears to be growing appreciation and understanding of leadership, and its significance within the context of the destabilized and uncertain Canadian health care environment. It is the responsibility of leaders to adapt, change or transform our social systems in response to new and before-unseen challenges that the future presents (Lewis 2007; Penney 2007; Romanow 2007; Ward 2007), while it is the role of management to generate stability once the direction of change – and the energy for it – has been created. Both are vital to the future success of the Canadian health system. If the rate of change is accelerating, then leadership becomes paramount. Currently, the growth of technology, demographic patterns, global economics and communications, climate change and environmental sensitivity has created such a pace of change that new and better leadership is needed to respond and shape that change. As one councilor on the Board of the Canadian Health Council stated recently, 'I think one of the most challenging issues for all of us is *influencing* system change. I think this is an issue that is bigger than just the health system (Juzwishin 2008: my emphasis).[13]

A third lesson is that there is an emerging consensus as to what quality health systems leadership is in Canada. The work done to define leadership in these three cases is common and consistent enough to suggest a definition of leadership: *Leadership is the capacity to influence others to work together to envision and achieve a constructive future for the health system in Canada.* Implicit in this definition is influence in its many forms; not just positional influence but also influence of personality, experience, expertise, character, knowledge or wisdom that comes from an authentic place of serving others. Leadership might well be construed as individual or collective potential or kinetic energy that can be utilized when it is needed. This energy derives from believing in and sharing with others a vision of an optimistic future – a moral, constructive future – aimed at improving the lives of those being led. Leadership appears to be the force that gives the health enterprise meaning, purpose, cohesion, direction and energy.

A fourth lesson is that health care has aspects to leadership that are unique to the health sector. One aspect – emphasized in all projects, and that grounds leadership in the identity of the health system – is the concept that leaders care for themselves and others and therefore are dedicated to constantly improving services to Canadian citizens. For example, the Pan Canadian framework states that a leader 'Inspires and encourages a commitment to health' and 'Leads change consistent with vision, values and a commitment to health' (Dickson *et al.* 2007). In the LEADS framework, leaders 'take responsibility for their own performance and health' and 'actively contribute to change processes that improve health service delivery' (Health Care Leaders' Association of BC 2007a). Another major 'emerging' feature about health care leadership in Canada is a recognition of the complexity of the health system and the need for leadership to be conceptualized in that context. For example, the 'Connects others' (CHLNet) and the 'Develops coalitions' (LEADS) capabilities were identified and raised to a level of prominence not found in competency/capability frameworks in other sectors (Briscoe and Romilly 2006; Dickson *et al.* 2007). These capabilities emphasize the leadership imperative of aligning individuals and groups from a complex number of professional bodies, interest and stakeholder groups, and members of the public, to create a quality health system (Gouvernement du Québec 2008). Other qualities of modern Canadian health leadership are that leaders 'hold themselves accountable for results', and 'mobilize knowledge to challenge processes and guide change' (Briscoe and

---

13   Dr Donald W.M. Juzwishin, former Chief Executive Officer of the Health Council of Canada.

Romilly 2006; Dickson *et al.* 2007). As health systems change and become more complex, and as society changes around them, then the qualities of leadership required to lead them appear also to need to change.

The fifth lesson derived from the cases relates to methods employed to develop leadership. One insight is that leadership development programming must respect and reflect the 'risk' implicit in the construct of leadership. Programs should not be managed so as to eliminate the context of ambiguity that distinguishes leadership from management. Also, efforts to use the real-life experiences of leaders to grow their capacity, rather than relying on traditional 'pull-out' learning models to do so, have promise. The proper mix of learning tactics such as mentoring (Bicego 2006), executive coaching (Turner 2003), action learning (Pedler and Abbott 2008), utilizing real-life issues of health system change to create relevance (Dickson and Hamilton 2006), self-directed learning methods (Centre for Health Leadership and Research 2008a) and competency assessment (Master of Arts in Leadership: Residency 1 2008) need to be investigated and defined.

A final lesson derived from the three case studies is that defining leadership for developmental purposes in large systems is best done as a memorable (i.e., simple but research-based; conceptually linked) set of capabilities that define the qualities of exceptional health systems leadership (Dickson *et al.* 2007; Pawar and Eastman 1997). For example, the LEADS framework provides guidance to chief executive officers, mid-managers, community leaders or, indeed, anyone whose goal is to exercise effective health leadership on behalf of system change (Leaders for Life 2008). How those capabilities play out in an individual's behavior is a function of that person's position, level of knowledge and skill development, personality, character and talents. The LEADS framework is a set of guidelines for individuals to use to guide individual and organizational growth and development rather than a set of standards by which all people's leadership should be judged (Health Care Leaders' Association of BC 2007b). It is not a detailed enough framework to take away an individual or an organization's right to be more definitive about what standards they wish to set for themselves for developmental purposes, but is definitive enough to ensure that everyone is viewing leadership from a common conceptual and practical perspective.

Conclusion

Significant forces for change within the health sector suggest major transformation of the current Canadian model. To do this, a different leadership is needed. To fill that gap, significant efforts are being made in Canada to define the quality of leadership required, and to coalesce the resources needed to stimulate its development. Three such efforts – Royal Roads University, the BC Leaders for Life program and CHLNet – have generated a number of lessons pertaining to effective leadership and leadership development. Leadership in the health sector is seen to be a caring, quality health-service driven enterprise in which concepts such as accountability, systems thinking and constant learning are the currency of effective change. Leadership development opportunities that are grounded in real-life experience, that take a systems approach, that demand leadership in their design, and that are customized to the needs of the individual participant appear to have significant promise. It is hoped that these lessons from the Canadian health system have relevance and meaning to other jurisdictions grappling with many of the same issues as Canada, and that seek the best health care for their citizens.

References

Alberta (2008) 'One provincial board to govern Alberta's health system.' News release, 15 May. Available at www.alberta.ca/acn/200805/23523ED9498C0-0827-451C-E98A0B8430DC1879.html, accessed 12 May 2009.

BC Health Leadership Capacity Project (2006) 'Phase 1: A competency framework for healthcare leadership.' Unpublished working paper (August). Victoria: Health Care Leaders' Association of BC.

Begun, J.W., Zimmerman, B. and Dooley, K. (2003) 'Health Care Organizations as Complex Adaptive Systems.' In S.M. Mick and M. Wyttenbach (eds) *Advances in Health Care Organization Theory.* San Francisco: Jossey-Bass.

Bicego, M. (2006) 'Mentoring: Bridging the gap between learning and leadership development.' Master of Arts thesis in Leadership and Training, Royal Roads University, Victoria, BC, Canada.

British North America Act (1867) *British North America Act 1867.* Available at www.solon.org/Constitutions/Canada/English/ca_1867.html, accessed 16 June 2009.

Boaden, R. (2005) 'Leadership development: Does it make a difference?' *Leadership and Organization Development Journal 27,* 1, 5–27.

Briscoe, D. (2008) Director, Office of Leadership in Medicine at the Canadian Medical Association, Personal communication, 10 August.

Briscoe, D. and Romilly, L. (2006) 'A competency framework for BC health system leadership: A literature review.' Unpublished working paper. Royal Roads University, Victoria, BC, Canada.

Canadian College of Health Service Executives (2008) 'Executive forum on transformational leadership.' Unpublished summary report. Ottawa, ON: Canadian College of Health Service Executives.

Canadian Health Leadership Network (2008) *CHLNet Purpose.* Available at www.chlnet.ca, accessed 12 May 2009.

Canadian Health Services Research Foundation (2008) *Statement of Institutional Purpose.* Available at www.chsrf.ca/about/do_statement_purpose_e.php, accessed 12 May 2009.

Canadian Union of Public Employees (CUPE) (2008) 'The Chaoulli Supreme Court of Canada Decision, 9 June 2005.' *On the Front Line.* Available at http://cupe.ca/updir/Chaouilli_Backgrounder_rev.pdf, accessed 16 June 2009.

Capital Health Region (2008) *My Leadership*. Draft for discussion, 6 June 2008. Halifax: Capital Health.

Carver, P. (2008) 'Comment on Chaouilli v. Quebec.' *Law and Governance*. Toronto, ON: Longwoods Publishing. Available at www.longwoods.com/product.php?productid=17191, accessed 12 May 2009.

Catholic Health Leadership Project Working Committee (2007) *Being, Caring and Doing: Leadership Development in the Catholic Tradition of Providing Health Care*. Recommended RFP for joint associations and PJP sponsors group, prepared by the Catholic Health Leadership Development Project Working Committee. Ottawa: Canadian Catholic Health Association.

Centre for Health Leadership and Research (2008a) *Stage Two: Self-Directed Learning as a Strategy to Improve Health Literacy and Health Human Resource Professional Development*. A research study for the Canadian Council on Learning. Victoria, BC: Royal Roads University.

Centre for Health Leadership and Research (2008b) 'Business plan April 2008.' Unpublished document. Victoria, BC: Royal Roads University.

Cikaliuk, M.L. (1998) 'The leadership crisis in health care: The development, implementation and evaluation of a quality solution.' Master of Arts thesis in Leadership and Training, Royal Roads University, Victoria, BC, Canada.

Cikaliuk, M. (2008) 'Learning while innovating in a strategic alliance: Learning strategies for public–private alliances.' Paper presented at the Multi-Organizational Partnerships, Alliances, and Networks 15th International Conference, June, Boston: Suffolk University.

Cikaliuk, M. and Fenwick, S. (2008) Contractors, Learning design and learning management system, Leaders for Life program, personal communication, 6 June.

Clark, J. (2008) Director, International programs, Institute for Innovation and Improvement, personal communication, 29 April.

Degeling, P. and Carr, A. (2004) 'Leadership for the systemization of health care: The unaddressed issue in health care reform.' *Journal of Health Organization and Management* *18*, 6, 399–414.

Department of Justice Canada (2008) *Canada Health Act*. Available at http://laws.justice.gc.ca/en/showtdm/cs/C-6, accessed 12 May 2009.

Dickson, G., Briscoe, D., Fenwick, S., Romilly, L. and MacLeod, Z. (2007) *The Pan-Canadian Health Leadership Capability Framework Project: A Collaborative Research Initiative to Develop a Leadership Capability Framework for Healthcare in Canada*. A final report submitted to Canadian Health Services Research Foundation, Ottawa, ON. Available at www.chsrf.ca/pdf/Health_Leadership_Framework_E.pdf, accessed 12 May 2009.

Dickson, G. and Hamilton, D. (2006) 'Twenty-first century leadership development.' *B.C. School Leadership e-journal*. 5 May. Vancouver: UBC Faculty of Education.

Dickson, G., Norman, P. and Shoop, M. (2007) *Self-Directed Learning as a Strategy for Improved Health Literacy and Health Human Resource Continuing Professional Education*. A research study for the Canadian Council on Learning. Victoria, BC: Centre for Health Leadership and Research.

Dickson, G. and White, F. (2006) *Linking Leadership to Healthy Living: Policy Implementation Strategies*. Paper commissioned by the Ministry of Tourism, Sport and the Arts (October).

Directory of Canadian Universities (2008) 'Royal Roads University.' Available at www.aucc.ca/can_uni/our_universities/royal_roads_e.html, accessed 12 May 2009.

Fenwick, T. (2002) 'Problem-based learning, group process and the mid-career professional: Implications for graduate education.' *Higher Education Research and Development 21*, 1, 5–21.

Goodwin, N. (2005) *Leadership in Health Care: A European Perspective.* London: Routledge.

Gouvernement du Québec (2008) *Getting Our Money's Worth.* Summary report of the task force on the funding of the health system, February. Available at http://greatdivide.typepad.com/across_the_great_divide/files/SommaireENG_Finance mentSante.pdf, accessed 12 May 2009.

Government of Canada (2002) *Building on Values: The Future of Health Care in Canada.* Final report of the Commission on the Future of Health Care in Canada. Ottawa, ON.

Graduate Certificate in Health Systems Leadership (2007) 'Measuring success: The act now BC challenge.' Unpublished working paper. Victoria, BC: Royal Roads University.

Health Care Leaders' Association of BC (2007a) *Health Leadership Capabilities Framework. Leaders for Life Program.* Victoria: BC. Available at www.leadersforlife.ca/resources, accessed 12 May 2009.

Health Care Leaders' Association of BC (2007b) *Health Leadership Capabilities Framework for Senior Executives. Leaders for Life Program.* Victoria: BC. Available at www.leadersforlife.ca/ resources, accessed 12 May 2009.

House, R.J., Hanges, P.J., Javidan, M., Dorfman, P.W. and Gupta, V. (eds) (2004) *Culture, Leadership and Organizations. The GLOBE Study of 62 Societies.* London: Sage.

International Initiative for Mental Health Leadership (2007) *Leadership Training Programs and Competencies for Mental Health, Substance Use, Health, and Public Administration in Eight Countries.* Boston, MA: Suffolk University.

Johnson, M. (2006) Teleconference with representatives of the Alberta Leadership Capacity Building Initiative, personal communication, 5 May.

Juzwishin, D. (2008) Chair, Health Council of Canada, personal communication, 18 July.

Leaders for Life (2008) *Shaping Health with Vision.* Available at www.leadersforlife.ca, accessed 12 May 2009.

Learning Strategies Group (2007) 'The Leadership at the Pulse program.' Unpublished working document. Vancouver: Simon Fraser University.

Leatt, P. and Porter, J. (2003) 'Where are the healthcare leaders? The need for investment in leadership development.' *Healthcare Papers 4*, 1, 14–31.

Leeb, K., Zelmer, J. and Taylor, B. (2005) 'CIHI survey: Canada's health system: Transitions in leadership.' *Healthcare Quarterly 8*, 1, 33–34.

Lewis, S. (2007) 'Learning from the best and learning from the worst: What the world can teach BC about improving health and health care.' Presentation at the International Symposium on Health Innovation, British Columbia Conversation on Health, June, Vancouver.

Master of Arts in Leadership: Residency 1 (2008) 'Basic learning principles and assessment of learner progress.' Unpublished document for learners. Victoria, BC: Royal Roads University.

NHS Institute for Innovation and Improvement (2008) *Medical Leadership Competency Framework – Homepage.* Available at www.institute.nhs.uk/assessment_tool/general/ medical_leadership_competency_framework_-_homepage.html, accessed 12 May 2009.

Outline of American Geography (2008) *Glossary.* Available at http://odur.let.rug.nl/~usa/ GEO/glossary.htm#sectF, accessed 12 May 2009.

Pawar, B.S. and Eastman, K.K. (1997) 'The nature and implications of contextual influences on transformational leadership: A conceptual examination.' *Academy of Management Review 22*, 1, 80–109.

Pedler, M. and Abbott, C. (2008) 'Am I doing it right? Facilitating action learning for service improvement.' *Leadership in Health Services 21*, 3, 185–199.

Penney, C. (2007) *Report of the Canadian Health Leadership Network (CHLNet) Summit.* Ottawa: Canadian Health Services Research Foundation. Available at www.chsrf.ca/research_themes/pdf/CHLNet_Summit_Report_2007_e.pdf, accessed 12 May 2009.

Philippon, D. (2007) 'Addressing challenges and renewal in the Canadian Health System: The leadership imperative.' A presentation to the University of Alberta, November.

Philippon, D. (2008) Teleconference, personal communication, 31 May.

Plsek, P. and Greenhalgh, T. (2001) 'The challenge of complexity in health care.' *Complexity science, British Medical Journal 15*, 323, 7313, 625–628.

Romanow, R. (2007) 'Canada's health temperature.' Justice Emmet Hall Memorial Lecture, presentation to the National Healthcare Leadership Conference, Toronto, ON.

Romilly, L. (2007) 'Literature review, Health leadership competencies.' National Health Leadership Competency Project. An unpublished working paper. Victoria, BC: Royal Roads University.

Rotman School of Management (2008) *Executive Programs.* University of Toronto. Available at http://ep.rotman.utoronto.ca/faculty/faculty_list.asp?show=Programandpid=9&wcid=55, accessed 12 May 2009.

Royal Roads University (2006) *Royal Roads University Strategic Plan 2006–2010*, 9 July. Victoria, BC: Royal Roads University. Available at www.royalroads.ca/NR/rdonlyres/43C025D8-D6B7-4B21-BC7D-9EA9200A8B52/0/RRU_StrategicPlan_200610_3.pdf, accessed 12 May 2009.

Royal Roads University (2008a) *The Master of Arts in Leadership Program.* Available at www.royalroads.ca/programs/faculties-schools-centres/faculty-social-applied-sciences/leadership-studies/ldrship-ma, accessed 12 May 2009.

Royal Roads University (2008b) *Centre for Health Leadership and Research.* Available at www.royalroads.ca/programs/faculties-schools-centres/centre-health-leadership-research, accessed 12 May 2009.

Rowlands, G. (2007) 'Leaders for Life: Shaping health with vision.' A presentation at the Health Care Leaders of BC Annual Conference, Vancouver, BC, October.

Sauder School of Business (2008) *UBC Executive MBA in Healthcare*, University of British Columbia. Available at www.chcm.ubc.ca/documents/EMBAbrochure.pdf, accessed 12 May 2009.

Scottish Leadership Foundation (2007) *Leadership and Management Framework.* Discussion paper. Edinburgh: Scottish Leadership Foundation.

Simpson, B., Skelton-Green, J., Scott, J. and O'Brien-Pallas, L. (2002) 'Building capacity in nursing: Creating a leadership institute.' *Canadian Journal of Nursing Leadership 15*, 3, 22–27.

Tholl W. (2004) 'Leadership without ownership.' Presentation at the Symposium on Strategic Leadership in Health Care, Victoria, BC: Royal Roads University.

Turner, C.E. (2003) 'Executive coaching as a leadership development strategy.' *Dissertation Abstracts International 64*, 4, 1332.

Ward, T. (2007) 'A background and commentary to the Conversations on Health.' An unpublished paper prepared for The Centre for Health Leadership and Research, Royal Roads University, Victoria, BC, October.

Weiss, D.S. and Molinaro, V. (2005) *The Leadership Gap. Building Leadership Capacity for a Competitive Advantage.* Mississauga, ON: Wiley and Sons.

Further reading

Boyatzis, R. and McKee, A. (2005) *Resonant Leadership.* Boston, MA: Harvard Business School Press.

Currie, G. and Lockett, A. (2007) 'A critique of transformational leadership: Moral, professional and contingent dimensions of leadership within public services organizations.' *Human Relations 60*, 2, 341–370.

Griffiths, M. and Hewison, A. (2006) 'Leadership development in health care.' *Journal of Health Organization and Management 18*, 6, 464–473.

Polyani, M. (1967) *The Tacit Dimension.* Garden City, NY: Anchor Books.

CHAPTER 12

Learning from Current Trends in Leadership Development in Scotland

Dennis Tourish and Ashly Pinnington

Introduction

Interest in leadership is now intense in many organisations – and not always for good reason. It is sometimes touted as a panacea for deeply embedded problems, with Government in particular urging the universal application of models drawn from the private sector, on the assumption that they will be effective (Currie and Lockett 2007). One might paraphrase this policy rationale as: 'What works in Texas, works in Tooting.' There has also been far too much stress on larger than life 'hero' figures, such as General Electric's Jack Welch. Like the front cover of *Vogue* magazine, their blemishes have been airbrushed out of the picture (Amernic, Craig and Tourish 2007), projecting such an exaggerated impression of leadership prowess that most people mistakenly conclude genuine leadership is beyond them (Conger 2004). Few of us perform miracles twice daily, and walk on water before 5.00 p.m. If leaders are expected to combine the saintliness of Gandhi, the forgiveness of Mandela, the compassion of Mother Theresa, the rhetorical skills of Martin Luther King, the vision of John F. Kennedy and the inspirational abilities of Winston Churchill, then we can only conclude that almost all of our organisations are in deep trouble.

Yet it is undeniable that effective leadership, more modestly defined, is important for organisational success, including within the social care sector (Yoo and Brooks 2005). Various reports (Audit Scotland 2005; Scottish Executive 2005; Hexagon Consulting 2006) have all drawn attention to the need for effective leadership in the public sector and emphasised how good practice in leadership development will improve effectiveness. The challenge is to have a workable vision of what we mean by leadership, and then devise some form of development to help as many people as possible put into practice the leadership talents they possess. Such talents are rarely in full bloom at birth: leaders are born *and* made. It is clear that much of this 'making' has to happen when people are at work in organisations rather than before employment. A UK survey by the Chartered Institute of Personnel Development (2008) found 66 per cent of organisations reporting that new employees lacked sufficient management and leadership skills. To remedy this, huge sums of money are now spent on leadership development – at least $50 billion worldwide by 2004 (Raelin 2004).

The question arises as to how effective this spending is, and what organisations aiming to develop their pool of leadership talent should do to achieve best results. The answers aren't immediately obvious. As Blackler and Kennedy (2004, p.181) have noted, there is surprisingly 'little consensus about appropriate approaches for leader development in the public sector'. In this chapter we attempt to shed some light on these issues by drawing on an extensive survey that we conducted on leadership development practices in Scottish organisations. We examine a number of methods that are most commonly employed to develop people. Whereas none of them are necessarily superior to the others, they show the range of options available, so that social care organisations can select whichever ones are most appropriate to their needs and resources. We describe how organisations generally evaluate the impact of their activities in leadership development, and discuss the most common obstacles to effective practice. While there are no magic wands that will wave away all prospects of stormy weather, it is our hope that this approach will assist social care organisations with improving their leadership development processes. Tentatively, we therefore recommend some steps that can be taken, and present some questions that should be routinely asked, when leadership development strategies are being developed.

The nature of leadership

It is useful to begin by specifying what we mean by 'leadership,' since it is difficult to 'develop' what you have not defined. Despite this, as previous researchers have found, the concept of leadership is poorly thought through in many organisations (Alimo-Metcalfe and Lawler 2001). In particular, leaders in social care are often required to take on a leadership role 'in situations where many of the key players and the resources are not under their direct control' (van Zwanenberg 2003, p.14). Command and control views of leadership are not only inappropriate, they are likely to be counter productive. We would therefore commend the perspective of Northouse (2003, p.3), who asserts that 'Leadership is a process whereby an individual influences a group of individuals to achieve a common goal.' We would only add that leadership is a *reciprocal* process. Followers influence leaders just as much as the other way round, or need to, if rounded individuals are to assume leadership roles and proceed to lead effective organisations. As Mintzberg (2004, p.141) has wisely noted: 'We are now inundated with heroic leaders who are dragging their organizations down amidst their own hubris.' Genuine leaders are those who are open to feedback from others, including when it is critical of organisational strategy or the leader's own performance (Tourish 2005). Leadership development, then, must seek to cultivate an attitude of self-confidence that is always balanced by the recognition that no one person has all of the answers, and instead one is engaged in a quest to build staff commitment, engagement and participation in the achievement of the organisation's goals. It follows that leadership development should seek to encourage people into leadership roles and processes, while recognising that this will encompass those with both formal and informal authority (Day 2000).

Forms of leadership development

Normally, leadership development assumes seven main forms.

1. *Development programmes and courses*
   These may be internally or externally provided and usually involve attendance off-the-job. These vary hugely in their quality, duration, location, credibility and impact. On completion, they may or may not be followed by evaluation reviews, appraisal reports and participants obtaining various certificates, awards and qualifications.

2. *360-degree performance feedback*
   This describes a variety of survey methods used to collect feedback on an individual's performance from a wide range of relevant viewpoints. Typically, this would include their peers, subordinates and superiors. Its key claim is to produce a more thorough and accurate picture of individual performance, thereby controlling for the biases that can arise from either an individual feedback source or from feedback drawn from only one vantage point in the organisational hierarchy (Becton and Schraeder 2004). Its use has grown to such an extent that some writers have described its

adoption as 'perhaps the most notable management innovation of the 1990s' (Atwater and Waldman 1998).

3. *Coaching*

    This describes practical, goal-focused, ongoing and one-to-one learning and behavioural change. The emphasis is generally on improving individual rather than unit or team performance, although some coaching efforts also address performance at team level (LeMay and Ellis 2007). In view of the cost implications, most coaching initiatives are short term.

4. *Mentoring*

    This aims to help people in their development through creating a relationship between a relatively inexperienced leader and a more experienced counterpart. While informal and unplanned mentoring is common, it is also often formalised, with senior figures rewarded for engaging in mentoring relationships. There is some evidence that it is particularly effective as a form of development, since 'the opportunity to observe and interact with members of senior management…helps develop a more sophisticated and strategic perspective on the organisation' (Day 2000, p.594). Clearly, it can absorb considerable time on the part of those involved, although one of its most frequent shortcomings is unproductive relationships occurring due to poor communication and too few meetings being held between mentor and mentee.

5. *Networking*

    This seeks to break down barriers between functional areas to foster wider individual networks, create a greater business literacy and more in-depth organisational knowledge. For example, groups of managers can be brought together on a regular basis to engage in dialogue and share experiences. In some cases, this can be accomplished electronically. It seeks to provide leaders with knowledge about not just what they should do, but with whom they can connect with to make it happen. Thus, the peer relationships that are so often critical for long-term leadership success are developed (Ragins and Cotton 1999).

6. *Job assignments*

    This provides people with challenging job assignments, which seek to develop leaders by providing new roles, tasks and responsibilities. Job assignments are particularly helpful in teaching people how to build teams, become better strategic thinkers, and improve their influencing and persuasion skills (McCall, Lombardo and Morrison 1988). Thus, some organisations transfer their managers between divisions or countries to gain requisite experience, while others perform more locally based and modest versions of such assignments.

7. *Action learning*

This assumes that people learn most by getting things done, and in particular by working on real organisational problems (Stein and Farmer 2004). Typically, participants meet to identify issues or problems, and then develop and implement recommendations designed to address them. A common approach is for a special team to be created for a few weeks or months that reports to a senior manager or the executive board. This 'action learning set' (Revans 1983) normally consists of a group of people with different backgrounds, positions in the organisation and work experience. Its purpose is to create and implement innovative solutions to complex organisational challenges. The development goal for participants is to reflect and learn from both their own actions and those of others.

Leadership development in Scotland – our research

The research reported here was designed to investigate what organisations in Scotland are doing on these varied fronts (Tourish *et al.* 2007). It covered the private, public and not-for-profit sectors.

Our primary objectives were to identify:

- how much leadership development takes place at present in Scotland

- what forms it assumes

- how organisations evaluate their leadership development activities, and which forms of evaluation they find to be the most effective

- the obstacles that prevent effective leadership development taking place

- what needs to be done to improve leadership development throughout Scotland.

To achieve this, a comprehensive questionnaire survey was sent to a broad range of organisations to gather both quantitative and qualitative data. This was complemented by a series of semi-structured interviews carried out with a selection of organisations who responded to the initial survey. The survey was issued to just over 1500 organisations, via post or email to named contacts in the organisations. Where possible, it was sent to those at chief executive level who had indicated a willingness to respond, or to a senior human resources figure who had been identified as having a particular interest in or responsibility for leadership development. After a reminder letter, 192 organisations responded to the survey, giving an overall response rate of 13 per cent. A series of semi-structured interviews were also held. These were carried out with a broad range of participants, selected from organisations who had responded to the initial survey.

The interviews therefore covered the three main employment sectors (private, public and not for profit) and organisation sizes (small, medium and large). A total of 47 face-to-face interviews were held across 13 organisations, in which 2–5 participants at various levels throughout the organisations were interviewed. Here, we will focus on some of the main findings that we anticipate have particular relevance for social care organisations.

Main findings

We were surprised to find that just under half of the organisations surveyed had a clear statement about how they expected their leaders to behave. This suggests considerable vagueness about the formal organisational expectation for leadership. In this case, there were significant differences between sectors, with 19 per cent of organisations in the not-for-profit sector having such a statement, compared with 65 per cent in the public sector and 42 per cent in the private sector. In our view, this is a first base requirement for effective leadership development. Vagueness surrounding what leadership is makes it harder for organisations to design interventions geared towards producing well-balanced, effective and insightful leaders. It also means that evaluating the impact of leadership development is considerably more difficult, since there is little in the way of clear criteria to guide it.

Leadership development courses

Participants were asked to describe major course initiatives for developing leaders. Just over half (58%) said that they provided such opportunities. Over half (54%) of those responding to this question (N=111), sent people to externally provided courses. Almost a third of the people (30%) so involved were senior managers, 13 per cent were board members and 16 per cent were middle and junior managers.

A similar number of organisations (54%) said they ran courses internally to develop leaders. Again, these were provided for people from board level right through to middle and junior manager levels. The majority were, however, geared for senior managers (53%), a small proportion were for the board (12%) and just over a third for middle/junior level managers (35%).

What is most interesting here is that very large numbers of organisations offer their people *no* opportunities for development through attending courses of any kind. While we would not suggest that they are an automatic panacea, and acknowledge that their quality varies widely, there are nevertheless many excellent development programmes capable of giving people a different perspective on how to lead their organisations. But a common problem arising from our research is that people find it difficult to differentiate between initiatives that are useful and those that are useless. While five people we talked to were positive about leadership development programmes they had experienced, the rest were not. Critical comments often focused on the feeling that the programmes were not relevant or appropriate for the target audience, or were too fragmented or inconsistently applied in their organisations. As one interviewee commented: 'They tend to be stop start. They'll start a programme and it will run for maybe a few sessions and then it comes to an end and there is no sort of continuation.'

Beyond this, a great many people, including those at the top, simply appear to be too busy running the organisations to reflect on new ideas, and draw inspiration from some of the best thinking on leadership that is readily available. It may therefore be that many leaders are recycling a limited amount of personal experience across their entire career, and are unaware of the many changes in thinking on management and leadership that would benefit them. A clear challenge flowing from this is to create some institutional mechanism for the provision of indisputably world class leadership development programmes to which people could look with confidence.

Leadership practices

We now focus on our findings that explored six specific formal and informal leadership development practices commonly referred to in the leadership literature (Day 2000), and which we outlined at the beginning of this chapter. The overall picture is of huge variations in practice, not always driven by conscious choice and strategic intent.

Figure 12.1 shows the overall percentage of organisations currently implementing these practices.

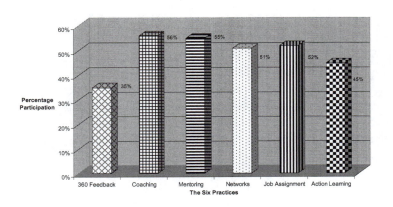

FIGURE 12.1: PARTICIPATION IN THE SIX PRACTICES

Four of the practices are currently implemented in just over half of the organisations. The feedback received at leadership and talent management conferences from audiences in Europe and Asia is that this is felt to be too low for competitive human resource development of any nation's workforce. These data confirm that coaching, closely followed by mentoring, is the most widely used leadership development activity undertaken by Scottish organisations. It is also clear that many organisations use many of these techniques in combination with each other, although only 9 per cent implemented all six practices. The majority of these (14 out of 18) were large organisations with over 250 employees. Conversely, 10 per cent of organisations implemented *none* and the majority of them were from the private sector (13 out of the 20). This is a fundamental problem. As Hartley and Hinksman (2003, p.39) noted: 'Leadership and leadership development is still a field of inquiry high on exhortation and low on evaluation.' There is much that could be done, but which clearly isn't.

Furthermore, it is likely that many of these methods are employed on a very informal basis – for example, that mentoring relationships are frequently informal, voluntary and subject to limited evaluation. In this chapter we will focus attention on two of these practices where we think our data reveals that opportunities are being missed: 360-degree feedback and job assignments.

360-DEGREE FEEDBACK

This practice was most commonly employed in public sector organisations, where 50 per cent used it to at least some extent (see Figure 12.2). On the other hand, only 10 per cent of not-for-profit organisations did so, and 33 per cent of private sector organisations. Organisational size is clearly a factor in this. A significantly higher percentage of larger organisations used 360-degree feedback (46%) compared to their medium (23%) and small (17%) sized counterparts. It may be that 360-degree feedback is viewed as being most appropriate in larger organisations, where more varied management levels and occupational groups are to be found. However, the basic techniques of 360-degree feedback are widely applicable, and one possible concern from these data is that the not-for-profit sector in particular is missing out on a key leadership development tool, despite the potential benefits it offers.

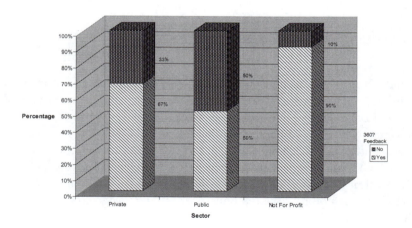

FIGURE 12.2: PERCENTAGE OF 360-DEGREE FEEDBACK BREAKDOWN BY SECTOR

JOB ASSIGNMENTS

Higher amounts of private and not-for-profit sector organisations participated in job assignments than did organisations in the public sector. Public sector organisations (46%) tended to use job assignments for leadership development slightly less often than their private (57%) and not-for-profit (52%) counterparts (see Figure 12.3). As with many of the techniques discussed here, job assignments can be an effective development tool, and in general they appear to be under-utilised by Scottish organisations.

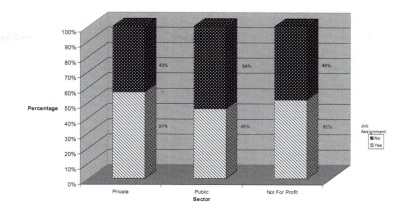

FIGURE 12.3: PERCENTAGE OF JOB ASSIGNMENTS BY SECTOR

Evaluation of leadership development

How leadership development is evaluated is a critical question. As we noted earlier, huge sums are spent on it, directly and indirectly. Few organisations would spend such money on capital projects without considering its wider business impact. Yet our data suggests that this is precisely what often happens when the issue is leadership development.

Participants were asked how leadership development was periodically evaluated in their organisation. Kirkpatrick's (1994) influential levels of evaluation were used to facilitate the categorisation of responses in this instance. This proposes four key dimensions against which development can be evaluated (see Table 12.1).

TABLE 12.1: KIRKPATRICK'S FOUR LEVELS OF EVALUATION

Reactions	How participants react to it
Learning	Extent to which participants have advanced in areas such as: competencies, skills, knowledge and attitudes
Transfer	Extent to which learning from a programme has transferred to behaviour at work
Results	Extent to which the programme has improved performance, including return on investment, higher profits, increased sales, improved quality, decreased costs

Only 15 per cent of organisations in our survey evaluated their leadership development activities at all Kirkpatrick's four levels (see Table 12.2 below). The majority of these (22 out of the 29 organisations) were large, with over 250 employees, with more tending to come from the private sector (17 out of the 29).

TABLE 12.2: PERCENTAGE OF ORGANISATIONS THAT
EVALUATED LEADERSHIP DEVELOPMENT AT EACH LEVEL

Level of evaluation	% of organisations evaluating leadership development at these levels
Reactions	54%
Learning	55%
Transfer	49%
Results	32%

Leadership development tended to be evaluated quite equally across the first three levels, except for evaluation by results, which was carried out to a much lesser extent across the three sectors. What is most striking in this data is that, overall, evaluation is limited. Over a quarter (26%) of organisations did not evaluate at any one of the levels and half of these were from the public sector (28 out of the 50). Each one of Kirkpatrick's levels of evaluation is crucial. Yet almost half of organisations appear to accord them little importance, with the last category – results – receiving especially low attention. These data suggest that either the need for evaluation is little recognised, or that the task is perceived as too difficult to grapple with. In either eventuality, our data suggests that increased evaluation is a key priority in order to review and subsequently improve the effectiveness of leadership development. Most interestingly, private sector organisations had a significantly higher percentage of organisations who evaluated for results (45%) compared to their public (21%) and not-for-profit (11%) counterparts (see Figure 12.4 below).

Overall, the focus of organisations on this level of evaluation is disappointingly low. There does not appear to be enough emphasis on combining leadership development activities with sufficiently rigorous measures of its impact on organisational performance.

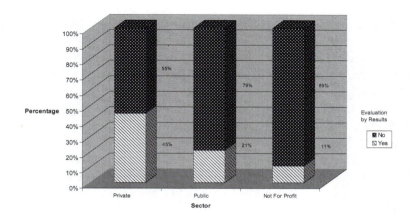

FIGURE 12.4: PERCENTAGE EVALUATION – RESULTS BY SECTOR

Barriers

We also explored the main barriers to implementing leadership development. From our review of the literature, we identified seven common barriers. Respondents then rated on a five-point scale the extent to which these were a barrier for them, ranging from 'always' a barrier to 'never'.

TABLE 12.3: PERCENTAGE OF ORGANISATIONS RATING
BARRIERS TO EFFECTIVE LEADERSHIP DEVELOPMENT

Barrier	% rated it 'always/often/sometimes'
Inability to prove direct impact of activities	79
Organisational culture	74
Lack of support/commitment from senior managers	68
Lack of interest of those taking part	64
Lack of financial support	62
Not linked to business or HR strategy	61
Lack of knowledge, expertise and experience to deliver leadership development	60

An overall percentage was taken of each of the barriers based upon the extent to which they 'always', 'often' and 'sometimes' prevented effective leadership development taking place in the participants' organisations. These are shown in Table 12.3.

'Inability to prove direct impact' was the most common barrier and the least was 'lack of ability or knowledge to deliver'. Clearly, our findings on evaluation are linked to the barriers that people perceive in implementing and then sustaining leadership development. In particular, it would appear that those who advocate it are challenged to prove that it will benefit the bottom line. Many of them do not know how to do this.

But the barriers are not limited to debates on the organisational outcomes of leadership development and the benefits to be gained from evaluating it. Participants were asked to outline any other barriers or obstacles to leadership development that they encountered. One third responded to this (33%), and sample comments are as follows:

- 'Time, pace of change, other work commitments.'

- 'Time constraints on individual managers. No spare staff to cover.'

- 'Shortage of finance. Running a very tight ship means leaders can only be spared from their posts for a limited time.'

- 'Programmes too expensive, poor value for money, unsure as to how to assess benefits and outcomes.'

- 'Main barriers are time and money.'

- 'Capacity to free staff to participate.'

- 'Day-to-day pressures. Sometimes people don't understand the need to take an overview and train for something that will impact them and the business in the future when they have deadlines to meet this week.'

These data reveal a perceived lack of time for leadership development, whatever form it takes. Clearly, this is a huge issue for organisations of all kinds. As Kerr (2004, p.118) has noted: 'nothing is more vexing to organizational leaders than attempting to ensure that the generation of leaders that follows them will actually be able to lead'. Most organisations therefore know that they must accord it attention. But many managers simultaneously feel that time constraints render leadership development virtually impossible. We suspect that, paradoxically, one reason for this inadequacy is an insufficient minimum of activity in leadership development. Such development would embed strategic dialogue at deeper levels of the organisation, draw more people into important decision making roles, address the problem of 'delegation upwards' and ease the demands made on top managers. It may be that part of the reason people feel they have problems in seriously addressing this issue is that they are busy frantically 'fire-fighting' – and fighting fires that often arise because the leadership talents of key people have not been sufficiently developed. An unfortunate consequence of sustained periods of fire-fighting is that the drama of it all becomes regarded as 'real' work, and it may then be presumed that such embattled activity constitutes the essence of the leadership role.

In our view this reflects some serious misconceptions about the function of leaders. As part of our research, we asked people how much management and leadership literature they read. The responses were worrying. Many managers reported that that they read very little, other than the occasional newspaper and magazine articles. Few read management books on a regular basis. One senior oil executive that we spoke with told the following illuminating story: 'I was at my desk the other day and just glancing at the business pages of the local newspaper. Two colleagues walked past, and I heard one say to the other: "X hasn't got much to do, has he, sitting just reading the paper." [Pause] I won't be doing that again.'

On the contrary, we would argue that this is precisely what leaders should be encouraged to do as part of their development and as part of their leadership role. Leaders bring in new perspectives, ideas and challenges – or they ought to. Thinking is a critical part of the job description. But it appears that anything which resembles thinking risks being ridiculed and dismissed, thereby ensuring that less of it occurs. Perhaps we could suggest, tongue in cheek, that if many people in leadership roles were offered the choice between being caught thinking or shoplifting they would unhesitatingly choose the latter, feeling that there is less disgrace in it.

Our suggestion here is that while the problem of 'a lack of time' for leadership development undoubtedly arises in part from everyday operational pressures, it also reflects a limited mindset about how leaders should spend their time. It is critical that this view is challenged and more time allocated to leadership development and its evaluation.

Main lessons and conclusions

There are a number of important lessons that we believe social care organisations can draw from our research. The first might be: don't assume that other sectors are doing this already, are doing it well, and that copies of what they are doing can easily be imported. Our data shows huge variations in practice, significant obstacles across all sectors, general conceptual confusion about both leadership and leadership development, and few ready-made models that can be straightforwardly transported to social care situations.

That said, there are some general points on good practice in leadership development. We recommend that all organisations should be clear about what they mean by leadership, and provide an unambiguous statement on how they expect their leaders to behave. As we have shown, most do not. Such reluctance makes it difficult to design well-focused programmes, and renders evaluation much more problematic. A clear statement by itself changes nothing, unless its intentions are genuinely pursued. But, in its absence, we doubt that organisations will be sufficiently motivated or focused to develop the leaders that they need.

We have also highlighted the problem of time. Most leaders read and study far too little, about either management or leadership. An analogy might be useful. Patients facing open heart surgery would expect their surgeon to be using the most up-to-date surgical techniques. They would not be reassured if, in response to a query, the surgeon barked back: 'Don't bother me with that stuff. I've been too busy operating to key up to date with the literature.' It should be equally unheard of for those who lead our organisations to have terminated serious study on graduation from formal programmes, relatively early in their career. A first start is for leaders to cast aside whatever inhibitions they have about the 'thoughtful' side of their role. This means banishing macho images of the leader as fire-fighter, dashing from crisis to crisis, while occasionally donning a Superman outfit. Key questions that should be asked to assist with this change of focus include:

- How much do you read?

- How can you free up time to read more widely?

- How much time do you spend on strategic thinking?

- How much time do your colleagues spend on this?

- How much time do you put into it, collectively as well as individually?

- What *precisely* can you change in order to spend more time on strategic thinking?

- How, *precisely*, can you get your colleagues to do likewise?

Without change on this front, at an individual, team, organisational and systemic level, no prolonged leadership development will really occur. It follows that leadership and leadership development should be declared a priority, a clear vision of what leadership means needs to be developed, and clear statements made articulating how social care organisations expect their leaders to behave. In turn, this should be linked to appropriate forms of leadership development, aimed at producing the kinds of leaders and behaviours that the organisation needs to achieve its goals.

We also believe that more information about best practice in leadership development needs to be disseminated. Our study found, repeatedly, that many organisations had very little idea of what other organisations were doing and what good practices they had developed that could be usefully applied and then improved upon. In many organisations the process whereby people are selected for leadership development opportunities is haphazard. Contrast this with the approach of the Bank of America (Conger and Fishel 2007). There, 360-degree appraisal processes are employed to identify those most suited for leadership roles. The following are just some of the questions employed in this process:

1. Would you personally trust your career to this person?

2. Do you see yourself learning from them?

3. Is this person capable of putting enterprise objectives ahead of their own goals?

4. Would this person complement the direct team s/he would be a part of?

5. Would this person be able to accept, process, and apply candid coaching and feedback in order to continuously improve?

6. Do they have the drive and passion to be part of a winning team?

7. Can you see this person leading from and living the company's core values? Would they fit our culture?

8. Does the person have the potential to assume greater responsibility in the future?

(Conger and Fishel 2007, p.447)

Obviously, the precise questions that should inform such a process will vary from sector to sector. But the principle identified here could be widely used. It has the advantage of compelling senior leaders to be unambiguous and precise in what they are looking for in future leaders. It is a clarity that could also be advantageous in the social care sector.

More widely, there is significant evidence that the best forms of leadership development create opportunities for people to learn from their experiences, and then apply it to solving real and pressing problems in their organisations (McCall 2004; Thomas 2008). This suggests that although organisations should employ leadership development programmes they must take care to ensure that such programmes focus people's attention on those issues they are experiencing at work, draw out appropriate lessons and equip them to make a real difference on their return. Often, 'the lessons learned from traditional classroom development programs do not last much beyond the end of the program. Soon after the course ends, people slip back into their previous behavioural patterns, and little lasting change or developmental progress is achieved' (Day 2000, p.601). Formal programmes should therefore be supplemented by mentoring, coaching and other interventions designed to sustain deep reflection and ongoing learning in the real world of work. In short, there is no silver bullet, and leadership development will never achieve its potential as a tool of organisational development if it is outsourced to a provider in order to absolve senior managers from their responsibilities in this area.

Finally, there are particular challenges in the area of evaluation. Our study shows that most organisations are failing to do this well, where they attempt it at all. In particular, too few gauge the effect of leadership development by assessing its impact on organisational performance – a more important measure of success than the 'happy sheets' which those attending leadership development courses routinely complete. This is a key challenge in the field, and one where much can be done. For example, Hannum, Martineau and Reinelt (2007) suggest that organisations intent on good evaluation should:

- involve all stakeholders to consider multiple needs and perspectives
- design evaluation before the initiative is implemented
- clarify desired outcomes with stakeholders
- discuss the purpose of evaluation and how it will be used beforehand
- use multiple measures to get information about complex or vague outcomes.

(Hannum *et al.* 2007, p. 565)

As part of improving activities in evaluation and review, we propose that social care organisations should first identify the barriers, problems and opportunities that designated leaders are expected to address, and then evaluate the effectiveness of leadership development by the extent to which these challenges are met. This approach will enable them to create an environment in which people are compelled to confront their experiences, address real organisational problems and learn from both their successes and setbacks. If nothing of significance changes as a result then this means that the development has failed, and another strategy is required.

None of what we propose is easy, and all of it demands resources. However, if leadership is genuinely important for social care organisations these are the kinds of challenges which must be addressed. Ultimately, people are the most important determinant of any organisation's future. It is time their development as leaders is recognised and given much greater priority than it has had in the past.

References

Alimo-Metcalfe, B. and Lawler, J. (2001) 'Leadership development in UK companies at the beginning of the twenty-first century: Lessons for the NHS?' *Journal of Management in Medicine 15*, 387–404.

Amernic, J., Craig, R. and Tourish, D. (2007) 'The charismatic leader as pedagogue, physician, architect, commander, and saint: Five master metaphors in Jack Welch's letters to stockholders of General Electric.' *Human Relations 60*, 1839–1872.

Atwater, L. and Waldman, D. (1998) '360 degree feedback and leadership development.' *Leadership Quarterly 9*, 423–426.

Audit Scotland (2005) *Leadership Development. How Government Works.* Edinburgh: Audit Scotland.

Becton, J. and Schraeder, M. (2004) 'Participant input into rater selection: Potential effects on the quality and acceptance of ratings in the context of 360-degree feedback.' *Public Personnel Management 33*, 23–32.

Blackler, F. and Kennedy, A. (2004) 'The design and evaluation of a leadership programme for experienced chief executives from the public sector.' *Management Learning 35*, 181–203.

Chartered Institute of Personnel Development (2008) *Annual Survey Report: Learning and Development.* London: Chartered Institute of Personnel Development.

Conger, J. (2004) 'Developing leadership capability: What's inside the black box?' *Academy of Management Executive 18*, 136–139.

Conger, J. and Fishel, B. (2007) 'Accelerating leadership performance at the top: Lessons from the Bank of America's executive on-boarding process.' *Human Resource Management Review 17*, 442–454.

Currie, G. and Lockett, A. (2007) 'A critique of transformational leadership: Moral, professional and contingent dimensions of leadership within public sector organisations.' *Human Relations 60*, 341–370.

Day, D.V. (2000) 'Leadership development: A review in context.' *Leadership Quarterly 11*, 581–613.

Hannum, K., Martineau, J. and Reinelt, C. (2007) 'Afterword: Future directions for leadership development evaluation.' In K. Hannum, J. Martineau and C. Reinelt (eds) *The Handbook of Leadership Development Evaluation.* San Francisco: Jossey-Bass.

Hartley, J. and Hinksman, B. (2003) *Leadership Development: A Systematic Review of the Literature.* Warwick: Warwick Institute of Governance and Public Management, Warwick University.

Hexagon Consulting (2006) *Leadership and Management Development in Scottish Local Government.* A report for the Improvement Service. West Lothian: Improvement Service.

Kerr, S. (2004) 'Introduction: Preparing people to lead.' *Academy of Management Executive 18,* 118–120.

Kirkpatrick, D. (1994) *Evaluating Training Programmes: The Four Levels.* San Francisco: Berrett-Koehler.

LeMay, N. and Ellis, A. (2007) 'Evaluating leadership development and organizational performance.' In K. Hannum, J. Martineau and C. Reinelt (eds) *The Handbook of Leadership Development Evaluation.* San Francisco: Jossey-Bass.

McCall, M. (2004) 'Leadership development through experience.' *Academy of Management Executive 18,* 127–130.

McCall, M., Lombardo, M. and Morrison, A. (1988) *The Lessons Of Experience: How Successful Executives Develop On The Job.* Lexington, MA: Lexington Books.

Mintzberg, H. (2004) 'Leadership and management development: An afterword.' *Academy of Management Executive 18,* 140–142.

Northouse, P. (2003) *Leadership: Theory and Practice,* 3rd edn. London: Sage.

Raelin, J. (2004) 'Don't bother putting leadership into people.' *Academy of Management Executive 18,* 131–135.

Ragins, B. and Cotton, J. (1999) 'Mentor functions and outcomes: A comparison of men and women in formal and informal mentoring relationships.' *Journal of Applied Psychology 84,* 529–550.

Revans, R. (1983) *The ABC of Action Learning.* London: Chartwell-Bratt.

Scottish Executive (2005) *Delivery through Leadership: Leadership Development.* Edinburgh: Scottish Executive.

Stein, S. and Farmer, S. (eds) (2004) *Connotative Learning: The Trainer's Guide to Learning Theories and Their Practical Application to Training Design.* New York: Kendall Hunt.

Thomas, R. (2008) *Crucibles of Leadership: How to Learn from Experience to Become a Great Leader.* Boston: Harvard Business School Press.

Tourish, D. (2005) 'Critical upward communication: Ten commandments for improving strategy and decision making.' *Long Range Planning 38,* 485–503.

Tourish, D., Pinnington, A. and Braithwaite-Anderson, S. (2007) *Evaluating Leadership Development in Scotland.* Aberdeen: Robert Gordon University.

van Zwanenberg, Z. (2003) *Leadership and Management Development in Social Work Services.* Edinburgh: Scottish Leadership Foundation.

Yoo, J. and Brooks, D. (2005) 'The role of organizational variables in predicting service effectiveness: An analysis of a multilevel model.' *Research on Social Work Practice 15,* 267–277.

CHAPTER 13

Leading Flourishing Organisations: Lessons from Positive Psychology

Angus Skinner

What is positive psychology and why does it matter for social work services?

Positive psychology is the scientific study of what enables individuals and communities to thrive. A balanced focus on strengths is central to its development and the applications of its findings.

Positive psychology was launched in 2000 as the American Psychological Association's millennium contribution to the perception (held by many and by no means just by psychologists) that there was an urgent need to shift away from the dominant deficit model of behavioural sciences – a focus on what is wrong with people. Whilst much had been achieved over the post-war decades by social sciences focused on people's problems and difficulties a rebalancing was required. This perception was already shared by many social workers both in academia, in practice and in management. For instance, the first edition of Dennis Saleebey's *The Strengths Perspective in Social Work Practice* was published in 1992 (reprinted 2005) and this reflected earlier work by Saleebey and others which emphasised people's environment and the importance of humanistic and social psychology. Indeed social work can take pride in a long-established duality of approach that incorporates strengths as well as problems.

So why should social work now take more cognisance of changes in other disciplines? First, and mainly, because it can; because these add insights and new approaches and because the modern world demands a more holistic and joined-up approach to services, organisations and leadership. As these changes in requirements are essentially driven by the revolution in information and its availability they are highly unlikely to be reversed and indeed are set to grow and accelerate as policies evolve to fulfil them. Second, and importantly, because these developments have a much stronger scientific base.

The launch of positive psychology in 2000 was led by Martin Seligman and Mihaly Csikszentmihalyi. Both eminent psychologists, Seligman was President of the American Psychological Association (APA) that year. Over several decades both Seligman and Csikszentmihalyi had pursued work that ran against the grain of much behaviourist psychology. Dominated by B.F. Skinner, behaviourism seemed to leave little room for the efficacy of human effort or the reality of human choice of attitude. The influence of behaviourism of course spread much further than psychology and included for a time behaviourist schools of social work education and practice.

Seligman's famous early work was on 'learned helplessness' which demonstrated that animals and humans could 'learn' a pessimism, a sense of not being able to achieve something even when the objective facts refuted this. Of itself this alone was and is an important finding for social work services to take on board. Seligman devoted his work and life to finding pathways to learn how to understand this, and in time how to learn optimism.

Csikszentmihalyi had led work on 'flow', on the engagement with skill and challenge to just the right level to achieve both task and satisfaction. Perhaps far too few social care and social work staff experience flow in their work. And perhaps if they are really to make the joined-up, creative and constructive contribution that they can in the future then many jobs may have to be re-crafted to provide more opportunities for them to do so.

Seligman went on to publish two further highly influential books: *What You Can Change and What You Can't* and *The Optimistic Child*. In *The Optimistic Child* Seligman sets out a strong case against aspects of the 'self-esteem' movements as practised by some in the US and the UK. In both books Seligman takes a balanced view of positive and negative emotions and realistic views on how we may approach these whether in self-regulation or in helping others. Positive psychology is not at all to be equated with positive thinking; it is an effort to rebalance the frameworks of behavioural science so that strengths and positive emotions are recognised as vital in solving problems, in personal development throughout life, and in organisational life and performance.

Approaching the millennium launch of this rebalancing Seligman and his colleagues knew that a major gap was the absence of anything on character strengths and positive emotions to set beside the recently published fourth edition of the *Diagnostic and Statistical Manual of Mental Disorders* (DSM-IV, there is a UN version ICD10 which some UK references relate to). Rather than adding anything on strengths the DSM-IV had extended by a further hundred pages its definitions of disorders. So Seligman and his colleagues set about creating a manual of strengths. And who else was arguing the case for this in 1999? None other, of course, than Dennis Saleebey, Professor of Social Welfare. Indeed part of Saleebey's argument is headed 'Where's the rest of me? Missing Virtues'.

The work on producing a classification of *Character Strengths and Virtues* (2004) was led by Professor Chris Peterson of Michigan Univeristy in conjunction with Seligman. It involved an impressive range of researchers (including historians). Saleebey's work was referenced and acknowledged. Perhaps in the more joined-up interdisciplinary emerging world the contributions of social work researchers to future revisions will be stronger. The social work profession is certainly well placed to further help develop a balanced view.

It is important to note that the development of positive psychology has had significant impacts on other social sciences. In particular, aspects of this new approach have been taken up by influential economists.

The foremost of these in the UK has been Lord Richard Layard, Emeritus Professor at the London School of Economics, who published *Happiness: Lessons from a New Science* in 2005. Like many other economists Layard is in part responding to the broad sweep of Gregg Easterbrook's analysis in *The Progress Paradox* (2003) that whilst almost all aspects of Western life have materially improved over the last hundred years 'most men and women feel less happy than in previous generations'. This important paradox gives rise to a multitude of policy questions and both Easterbrook and Layard present their own answers.

Easterbrook argues for widespread changes in attitudes, values and behaviour ('Waking up from the American dream' as he calls it). Layard (at least to an extent) looks rather more to specifically meeting the needs of those in mental distress. Andrew Oswald (Professor of Economics at Warwick University) considers that European economists have now taken the lead in 'happiness' economics, even though much of the initial work was led by Richard Easterlin at Harvard University. Easterlin's influence remains evident not least in the fact that Harvard has the world's first undergraduate course on positive psychology (and it is the most popular course at Harvard).

Other social scientists, health disciplines and professions and educationalists all demonstrate different ways in which they are adapting to this major shift across social science and public policy. It is vital that social work services also do so.

Is positive psychology just a fad?

From its beginning positive psychology took full account of the negative, of the inevitability of negative feelings and above all of the adversities and challenges that all people face, and especially of the problems caused by increasing divisions between the rich and the poor. There is no doubt that the launch of positive psychology is not just an important contribution but has influenced developments not only across Europe and the US in particular but also globally – economically and socially. Importantly the commitment to social justice was clear from the beginning.

In their 'Introduction to Positive Psychology' Seligman and Csikszentmihalyi make a clarion call for a new turn.

> Entering a new millennium, we face an historical choice. Left alone on the pinnacle of economic and political leadership, the United States can continue to increase its material wealth while ignoring the human needs of its people and that of the rest of the planet. Such a course is likely to lead to increasing selfishness, alienation between the more and the less fortunate, and eventually to chaos and despair. At this juncture the social and behavioral sciences can play an enormously important role. (Seligman and Csikszentmihalyi 2000, p.5)

They call for developments at three levels:

- individual
- group/families/communities
- systems and institutions.

If the new science of positive psychology is to help play the historic role called for by Seligman and Csikszentmihalyi then it must do so across the globe, applicable across cultures; it must identify that which is universal, whilst still allowing the diversity of cultural differences.

This is a big ask. But if illness has global dimensions, as it does, then why should not human strengths? And crucially it must work with other disciplines and in other fields. Social work services in any country have much of value to learn from and to contribute to these developments.

The economic dimensions

The economic dimensions to these changes are vital drivers (social work services in the UK alone are a multi-billion pound industry) but they are highly complex. By and large economists deal with models of measurable variables. Economists (especially since the introduction oddly of 'positive' economics: 'positive' as opposed to normative, Marxist, Keynesian etc, have been focused on predictive models. And, as in all science, the speed of publication and its effects on careers has perhaps over-emphasised the measurable.

Many social work service professionals will be familiar with the work of Richard Titmuss who founded the academic discipline of social administration (or social policy) and whose work at the London School of Economics led much of the development of modern social work services. One of Titmuss's most influential books, *The Gift Relationship* (1997), reported studies of blood donation systems in the UK (voluntary) and the US (some voluntary some bought). His finding that voluntary donation systems provided better quality and reliability had a profound effect on policy in relation to blood donor systems (not just in the UK, though there it probably saved the service from privatisation). The work was influential much more widely across social policy and indeed social work services. The idea of a 'gift relationship' then seemed central to social care – to fostering, to care for older people, to kinship care – across the whole range.

Titmuss was describing one aspect of the interchanges between social and economic aspects of life and societies. One of his main predecessors in this was Adam Smith, the great Scottish moral philosopher and founder of modern economics. Known across the world for his hugely influential *The Wealth of Nations* Smith spent the last years of his life revising his earlier (and to his mind more important) book, *The Theory of Moral Sentiments*. Like Titmuss, Smith knew it was essential to see the intersections, linkages and optimal functioning of both economic and social systems. This is particularly crucial in social work services, in social care. Social policy depends on understanding these intersections, and so too does leading social work services. Yet the underlying challenges are social, about relationships. The future development of this policy field depends wholly on understanding the interrelationships between:

1. the personal (gift) relationships that are inevitably a pervasive feature of social care

2. state financial support for income such as pensions and benefits, and

3. the costs and financing of state-funded service provision.

At a policy level the implications can be illustrated by reference to Scotland's policy of free personal care. There was considerable controversy in the establishment of this policy. Many argued that it was regressive in that it provided more benefits for the rich than for the poor; others that it corrected a diagnostic deficit. Care provided through the NHS was free but not care provided through local authorities. The UK Treasury argued that it was not affordable, at least in the longer term.

Implementing the policy has been fraught with financial difficulties. Often the attempt has been to resolve these through bureaucratic mechanisms. Should the preparation of food be 'free personal care' or charged for? Why, if one elderly spouse (say a husband, though more often the other way round) is happy to lovingly feed his life-time companion but cannot clean the windows so she can enjoy the view that has been central to their lives for years, should the one be provided but not the other? Or whilst some stranger (in some cases contracted to report in 15-minute slots for the time they spend delivering a contract) prepares food for or even feeds his wife must he hobble painfully over to clean the windows? Is that the best care?

It is not easy to resolve these issues by agency boundary definitions of functions, though a lot of management and other resources have been devoted to attempting to do so. Such boundary issues have been problematic in community care services for decades, ever since the famous debates around whether assisting someone to have a bath was a social (and thus chargeable) or health (and thus free) service in the early 1990s.

The solution to these issues does not and never has lain in telephone-book sized specifications of contracts. The flaw is not in the contracts but in the concept. Social care is profoundly about engagement with social systems; it can never be sustained or indeed successfully separated out from these.

By far the biggest amount of care for older people is provided by family, mainly indeed by equally elderly spouses. Little policy debate or action has focused on the implications of this. I once suggested, with all seriousness, that social care statistics should be reconfigured so that they reported mainly on so called 'informal care' (care by families, friends, communities) and then reported on state-funded care as a contribution to this much wider picture. What we have is some support for carers as a 'separate client group'. This is a very top-down picture shot. National statistics report mainly on what the state does (locally or centrally). This monocular view does not help leadership.

The role of voluntary organisations is crucial to understanding not only ways forward but how the overall social system works at all. In this Scotland has an exceptional record of voluntary contribution. NGOs (Non-Governmental Organisations) play crucial roles but are by no means immune from delay in adapting to new approaches. Social policy, as indeed exemplified in the creation of the free personal care policy, often enough attends only to the costs and financing of state provision. This inadequate focus is often driven by reference to 'protecting the public pound', the need to account for public expenditure. This in itself is driven by the dominance of the deficit model.

This is a complex matter but paring it down the basic model, if person A, either through taxation or through insurance, is going to pay person B to help person C with their problems then person A (the taxpayer) wants certain reassurances. He/she wants to know that person B (the service provider) can effectively help person C (the service user), and to know that they will do so efficiently. He/she also wants to know that person C's problems really require and merit help in the first place; that they meet an entitlement barrier. These work out as complicated reassurances to provide. The entitlement criteria are hard to specify and to apply consistently even across one organisation let alone across the multitude of organisations that operate in a nation. The effectiveness of the services (is the money well spent?) is hard to measure, requires complicated audit trails and costly investigation through research or inspection. To provide these reassurances local and national agencies and authorities devote major parts of their financial, human and intellectual resources. From my experience at least half of most organisations' resources are deployed to provide these reassurances. Sometimes this seems to become almost their main business; that's crazy, but I don't blame them. Moreover, and not least because of this complicatedness, most countries have burgeoning external regulatory systems and bodies, many of which at least partially duplicate each others' efforts.

All of this is problematic enough. How much of the public pound should be spent 'protecting' the public pound? How much of the financial, human and intellectual resources devoted to social work services should be spent on accounting for social work services? Yet there is a bigger problem. Because the audit systems focus so much on entitlement they drive the deficit model. This is the big challenge.

Sitting in the Scottish Executive in 1997 I couldn't see what the sustainable way forward was. More money was being provided (tripling most budgets) and this helped to stem what otherwise might have seemed an overwhelming tide of demand. But the main difficulty was human, not financial, resources. Staff were in short supply to meet the increased demand and provision; staff were being recruited from other nations, which I thought unsustainable (and in respect of under-developed nations unethical at least in the long term). Importantly many staff were clearly under-trained and the social work services training sector seemed too often bogged down in processes (not through any fault of the many excellent folk involved).

But most importantly morale was frighteningly poor. People whose sole motivation was to help others were finding their energies sapped by bureaucratic practices that prevented their engagement with people, their creative time with service users. Looked-after children complained they hardly ever saw their social worker; social workers complained they were so tied down to processes that they had barely a day a week to actually do their main job, with looked-after children or other service users. In adult services and in criminal justice the stories were much the same. The problem clearly was systemic. And most public services – education, the police and health – showed similar signs of malaise.

I looked around not for alternatives but for new pathways. In re-reading Titmuss and Adam Smith I became convinced that two things were necessary. First, to set all public services in their strategic context, that is the whole of the society they sought to serve. Second, to end the dominance of the Poor Law deficit model of social care.

Leadership is about engagement with these real world systems, facilitating professional and all staff engagement with these systems. And it is not easy. Moreover, since no rules can provide for this then inevitably it is sometimes about breaking the rules, weathering as best as possible the turbulence and delivering for communities.

Strategic leadership is about relating the organisation to its external context, situated over time. Whether in respect of older people, of children, of people with learning disabilities or sensory impairment, or in criminal justice this is the crucial strategic leadership task. The external context for social work services is the social and economic exchanges, the infrastructure of social life, of those they seek to help.

The principal external context for leaders in social work services is carers, families and communities and, above all, the person's life experience. The focus on people's experience at the centre of Scotland's National Care Standards was hard fought, by all involved. But it still survives the tests of time.

Strategic leadership requires understanding the intersections of the social and economic exchanges not principally of the organisation that is led, though that is important, but of those it seeks to serve. Positive psychology, by re-centring social science on human strengths and capabilities and on the centrality of relationships in establishing meaning, provides a framework for reasserting much that was at the heart of social work in its formation.

The financial dimensions are vital, like the blood through the body. But they are not in charge; nor should your leadership be. And they are not the main coursing of the rivers; emotions are – and so, since you are reading this, that is where your attentions are. How do people in your organisation feel about their work? How much does low morale cost (not just in sickness days)? How much could be gained by helping them flourish?

Positive psychology is not a fad. It provides a scientific basis for developments such as positive organisational scholarship, for appreciative inquiry and for much else. This is a major shift, a paradigm shift if you will – though let us never throw out the value of what has gone before. Providing leadership in these changing times will require resilience, efficacy in managing yourself as well as others, optimism – and optimism to share with others, and hope. There is no one on Mars dictating that things, even in social work services, have to be the way they are. Leadership is about finding new pathways and, as Ghandi said 'You must be the change you want to see in the world.'

Developing well all through life

Much of positive psychology is drawn from work on how some people live happily and successfully into a ripe old age. Indeed some of the most important studies have been about the ways in which an optimistic and hopeful attitude is a good predictor of longer life. In the famous Nuns Study (Danner *et al.* 2001) for instance it was found that those nuns who on entering the order (aged around 18) wrote optimistically about their lives and future lived longer. The nuns' writings were analysed retrospectively and rated by researchers who did not know how long they lived. Of the 25 per cent writing most optimistically when novitiates 90 per cent were still alive at the age of 85 whilst only 34 per cent (of those 25%) writing least optimistically were still alive. Similarly 54 per cent of the most cheerful were still alive at 95 whilst only 11 per cent of the least cheerful were. This study showed the longevity of optimism and of thinking. And whilst it is no cure it stands evident that it counts. On the whole nuns who in their noviatate letters 60 years earlier had written most positively tended to live longer (by 8–10 years, other factors being controlled for).

Many social work staff will have some familiarity with the work of Erik Erikson (an artist, anthropologist and psychoanalyst) who charted life's social development through various stages, essentially an ever-widening social engagement. Issues had to be resolved at each stage. These are 'Basic Trust versus Mistrust' (for the early years), 'Autonomy versus Shame' (for adolescence and early adulthood), 'Initiative versus Guilt' and 'Industry versus Inferiority' for middle years. Erikson partly drew on Freud (and also the work by Anna Freud on mechanisms of defence). In his classic *Childhood and Society* Erikson was essentially the first social scientist to conceptualise adult development as progress, not decline. Through a sequence of stages he believed adults participated in life within a widening social radius and whilst the ambit of the later stages might in some ways be more restricted the progress could continue through generativity (guiding the next generation) and integrity.

Erikson's framework underpinned much social work teaching and practice in regard to human growth and development. It also underpinned the analysis by the positive psychologist (and medic) George Vaillant of the *Harvard Study of Adult Development*. The Harvard Study is the largest prospective longitudinal study of physical and mental health in the world. It had three cohorts: 268 socially advantaged Harvard graduates born in 1920, 456 socially disadvantaged inner city men born about 1930, and 90 middle-class intellectually gifted women born about 1910. It is not only remarkable for its size (and longevity!) but also because it deliberately (an even rarer thing when it started than now) set out to study the lives of the well and learn not just from studying the sick.

In this approach George Vaillant is also following the urgings of Robin Skynner who has also been very influential in social work education and practice, especially in work with families. A family therapist (and psychiatrist), Robin Skynner also became known to the wider public through a series of books he wrote with John Cleese (who suffered from depression) notably, *Life and How to Survive It*. Skynner was constantly urging social scientists to learn from the positive. Late in life he learnt to ski and said in a TV interview, 'We do not expect to learn to ski or play golf by watching videos of people who aren't very good. We learn by watching videos of the best.'

The Harvard Study gave rise to an enormous amount of valuable knowledge about human development, health and happiness, about the importance of marriage, the impact of divorce, the role of play and creativity, the vital benefits of friendships and forming new social networks and the importance of curiosity and life-long learning. Many of its findings influenced the seminal classification of *Character Strengths and Virtues* by Peterson and Seligman.

But the study (and George Vaillant's writing on it) does not nor ever could have avoided what is difficult. Life has adversities and not infrequently we create them. It deals with issues like disability, mental illness, alcoholism and the inevitable physical effects of ageing. But it draws its lessons from those who handle these things successfully.

This whole approach of positive psychology has an important implication that is often missed. One of its central messages is that responsibility does not generally lie elsewhere. As Vaillant writes 'Whether we live to a vigourous old age lies not so much in our stars or our genes as in ourselves.' So positive ageing (at whatever age) is not something that can be achieved by someone else on your behalf. It depends centrally on responsibility being taken by the individual. Social workers cannot expect or be expected to 'fix' people whatever their age. But this also is the central message of *Changing Lives* (Scottish Executive 2006). Social work and social care services for the twenty-first century have to depend on models of co-production where service users, including children, young people, adults in whatever circumstances and older people all have a greater say, but also more responsibility.

This applies in all fields of social work services, be it learning disabilities, mental health, work with families, communities, offenders, older people, children and young people. Many new techniques and methods are being developed. Social work service staff could bring enormous knowledge of critical life situations to bear on these developments. However bruised, these are resilient professionals, thinking always holistically and open to creative approaches. They know that generally relationships matter most in life and in organisations.

'Be not solitary, be not idle'

This is the introductory advice of Democritus to the reader in Robert Burton's famous seventeenth century *Anatomy of Melancholy*. It is also the main message not just from the Harvard Study but from the whole field of positive psychology. Relationships are what matter most to people. Andrew Oswald (Professor of Economics at Warwick) stood in front of an audience of 300 and said 'I never dreamed as an economist for 30 years that I would stand in front of you today and say "relationships are the most important thing in life." But rigorous social science in economics and in psychology shows that to be true.' Like many insights it seems obvious looking back. Many social work service leaders will rightly proclaim they have been arguing this for decades. This is a great time to add that voice and those experiences in collaborations across this new field. But there will be challenges in doing so.

Whilst in several fields social work services have lost the centrality of direct work with people (often because staff are burdened by responsibilities of risk assessment and case management) the heart of social work and of social care remains direct work, not just commissioning services from others or managing cases. Positive psychology offers a rich field to draw on in the development of skills essential for working directly with people, helping them set realisable goals, identify how to achieve these and supporting them in the effort required.

Changing Lives is about setting a new direction. One which has real hope for future improvements; for building a more sustainable co-productive, collaborative future for social services working with others. Putting relationships at the centre will be crucial to the success of this new direction.

Leadership courses through organisations, engaging them with reality. Yet it is not often obvious. Social work services staff and organisations are at the forefront of new more holistic and variable organisational forms. In responding to *Getting It Right for Every Child* (Scottish Government 2005), *Joint Future* (Scottish Government 2000), *Changing Lives* (Scottish Executive 2006) and the creation of new Community Criminal Justice Authorities, social work services in Scotland are having to let go of established organisational forms and methods.

Letting go is never easy. But the future is a myriad of organisational forms. Health, education, police and all other public services face a future of letting go of organisational forms and practices made out-moded by two unstoppable drivers. These are the information revolution and the exponential growth of science. Why do these impact so much on social work services, which after all is not a high-technology industry, it is a people industry?

Is it because of the development of new information systems, working across agencies, struggling with data definitions and key data protection? Is it because of the development of new diagnoses, treatments and procedures? Is it because of the increase in internet access and availability? In part. Do all three together add up to the major reason for these developments to be so significant for social work services? Not in my view.

The key point is that the information is about real people. It is not about people as they are defined within closed systems: e.g. a child is a child, not a pupil, case or patient. When an older person trips because they cannot see the edge of the step, breaks a bone, ends up in hospital and needs care afterwards the leadership required is to recognise the importance of tackling sensory impairment as we age, providing visual aids and support. We all do age, in doing so lets maximise wisdom and flamboyance and minimise risk and service silos.

Engaging with new realities requires different skills: courage in accepting uncertainty, openness to new pathways as well as new ideas, maintaining hope during adversity. It requires different attitudes: learning rather than knowing.

Marty Seligman argues, and I agree with him, that much of positive psychology can be traced back to the Scottish Enlightenment. The Scottish Enlightenment of the eighteenth century was very different from the French and indeed from the English, marked in particular by the work of Adam Smith and his friend and mentor David Hume, who broke with much by asserting 'Reason is and ever should be the servant of the passions.'

Social work has always had the passion, for individuals and for social justice. Too often it has lacked the science. E.O. Wilson (1998) argues that the twenty-first century will see a consilience: a jumping together of the arts and science not seen since the Scottish Enlightenment. Hume, and indeed social work, are right – reason is and only ever should be the servant of the passions; but reason is a great servant, and always should be attended to.

Bringing the science of positive psychology together with social work services could be uniquely beneficial. Not easy, but more than worthwhile and: 'be not solitary, be not idle'.

References

Danner, D., Snowden, D. and Friesen, W. (2001) 'Positive emotions in early life and longevity: Findings from the nun study.' *Journal of Personality and Social Psychology 80*, 804–813.

Easterbrook, G. (2003) *The Progress Paradox: How Life Gets Better While People Feel Worse.* New York: Random House.

Erikson, E.H. (1950, 1963) *Childhood and Society.* 2nd edn. New York: Norton.

Layard, R. (2005) *Happiness: Lessons from a New Science.* London: Allen Lane.

Peterson, C. and Seligman, M.E.P. (2004) *Character Strength and Virtues.* New York: OUP.

Saleebey, D. (1992) *The Strengths Perspective in Social Work Practice.* New York: Allyn and Bacon.

Scottish Executive (2006) *Changing Lives: Report of the 21st Century Social Work Review.* Edinburgh: Scottish Executive. Available at www.socialworkscotland.org.uk, accessed 9 August 2009.

Scottish Government (2000) *Joint Future.* Available at www.scotland.gov.uk/TopicsHealth/care/JointFuture, accessed 9 August 2009.

Scottish Government (2005) *Getting it Right for Every Child.* Available at www.scotland.gov.uk/Topics/People/Young-People/childrenservices/girfec, accessed 9 August 2009.

Seligman, M.E.P. (2007a) *What You Can Change and What You Can't.* New York: Nicholas Brealy Publishing.

Seligman, M.E.P. (2007b) *The Optimistic Child.* New York: US Imports reprint.

Seligman, M.E.P. and Csikszentmihalyi, M. (2000) 'Positive psychology: an introduction.' *American Psychologist 55*, 1, 5–14

Skynner, R. and Cleese, J. (1993) *Life and How to Survive It.* New York: Oxford University Press.

Smith, A. (1759/1976) *The Theory of Moral Sentiments.* Oxford: Clarendon Press.

Titmuss, R. (1997) *The Gift Relationship: From Human Blood to Social Policy.* London: New Press.

Vaillant, G.E. (2002) *Aging Well.* Boston, MA: Little Brown and Company.

Wilson, E.O. (1998) *Consilience – The Unity of Knowledge.* London: Little Brown and Company.

The Contributors

Zoë van Zwanenberg is Director of Zwan Consulting and Project Coordinator for the Centre for Confidence and Well-Being, working on issues of personal and organisational leadership and change. Zoë was the Chief Executive of the Scottish Leadership Foundation from its creation in 2001 to its closure in 2008. The Foundation was dedicated to the development of leadership capacity and capability across all of Scotland's public services. Prior to this she led the Strategic Change Unit for the National Health Service in Scotland focusing on leadership and change across the whole health system in Scotland. Zoë's career has been mainly focused in the public services, including roles as a Chief Executive, General Manager, HR Director and Organisational Change advisor. She has worked in organisations as diverse as the Railways, the Police, the National Health Service and the Environment Agency. Throughout all of these roles she has been concerned with leadership, change and the development of individuals and teams.

Richard H. Beinecke is Associate Professor in the Departments of Public Management and Healthcare at Suffolk University. For over ten years, he was the principle evaluator of the Massachusetts Behavioral Health Program. He has served in clinical and management positions in several community mental health centers and at Harvard Community Health Plan. His current research is on implementation of evidence-based practices, comparative mental health and health systems, and global leadership competencies and workforce concerns.

Anne Cullen is a registered social worker with more than 30 years' experience as a practitioner and manager, chiefly in services for children, young people and families. She became interested in the relationship between social work and leadership while working as Director of Social Work Development for Skills for Care, the English social care workforce development organisation. Anne is currently employed as manager of psychosocial and spiritual care at Princess Alice Hospice in Esher, Surrey.

Graham Dickson is Director of the Centre for Health Leadership and Research and a Professor of Leadership at Royal Roads University. Dr Dickson has been instrumental in the establishment of the *MA in Health Leadership* at RRU and the *BC Leaders for Life* program, a leadership and succession planning initiative for the BC health sector. He also spearheaded the development of the *Pan-Canadian Health Systems Leadership Capabilities Framework* for the Canadian Health Services Research Foundation.

Chris Huxham is Professor of Management and Head of the Department of Management in the University of Strathclyde Business School. She has worked for almost 20 years with people of all sectors involved in networks, partnerships and alliances and has written many articles in this area, three of which have received awards from the Academy of Management. Her books include, *Managing to Collaborate: The Theory and Practice of Collaborative Advantage* (co-author Siv Vangen; Routledge, 2005).

Patrick Leonard is Director of Riverside in Carlisle, one of the largest housing associations in England which provides 6000 affordable homes in the city. He was previously Chief Executive of Allerdale Borough Council. His chapter is drawn from his PhD research which was based on an empirical study of a group of Scottish public service managers, participants in a postgraduate diploma at Lancaster University, under the auspices of the Scottish Leadership Foundation.

Anne Murphy is an educator, researcher and consultant. She has experience in learning and development work spanning more than 30 years across a wide range of educational and organisational settings both in Europe and the Americas. She specialises in researching, designing and leading collaborative learning processes aimed at supporting equality, democracy and transformation.

Sonia Ospina is an Associate Professor in the Wagner Graduate School of Public Service and Faculty Director of the Research Center for Leadership in Action at New York University. A sociologist by training, her academic interests include leadership, engaged scholarship, and democratic governance. She is the author of *Illusions of Opportunity: Employee Expectations and Work place Inequality* (Cornell 1996).

Professor Ashly Pinnington is the Head of the Faculty of Business at The British University in Dubai. Most of his research work is on Knowledge Management and Human Resource Management and he has published articles in academic journals such as the *Journal of Management Studies, Organization Studies and Human Relations*. His current research interests are leadership development, professional competence and the internationalisation of knowledge intensive firms.

Angel Saz-Carranza is the coordinator of PARTNERS Program in Public-Private Cooperation and a post-doctoral research fellow for the Institute of Public Governance and Management at ESADE Business School in Barcelona. He has been an Associate Professor at the Catalan Polytechnic University (Barcelona) and a Visiting Scholar at

Wagner School of Public Service (New York University). His public management research focuses on interorganizational relations and performance management.

Angus Skinner is the former Chief Social Work Inspector and Chief Social Work Adviser to Scottish Ministers. He has authored many strategic reports on current issues in social care and his vision for Scottish social work services extends from the two room black house in Skye where his mother was born to the complex needs of modern urban society. He is currently a Visiting Professor at the University of Strathclyde.

Kate Skinner is an independent consultant in health and social care. She spent a number of years working in local authority social work services in England and Scotland before moving to the University of Stirling. From 2007 Kate was Institute Lead for Research, Development and Application at the Institute for Research and Innovation in Social Services. Her research focuses on how people learn and aims to maximise learning transfer from training into practice.

Harry Stevenson is Executive Director of Social Work Resources for South Lanarkshire Council. Harry began his career as a trainee Social Worker in Rutherglen in 1974 before going on to complete his professional training in 1978. He has held posts in various social work facilities, and in his current role is responsible for statutory planning, support to people who use services and carers, children's rights, contracts, management information, and public information.

Dennis Tourish is Professor of Leadership and Management for Aberdeen Business School at the Robert Gordon University. He is the co-author or co-editor of six books on leadership, management and organisational communication, and has consulted with many private and public sector organisations on these issues. Having published over 60 major journal articles, Dennis is also an Associate Editor of *Management Communication Quarterly*.

Dr Siv Vangen is Senior Lecturer at The Open University Business School and Head of the Public Leadership and Social Enterprise Research Unit. Her award winning research focuses on the development of a practice-oriented theory about the management of collaboration – known as the Theory of Collaborative Advantage. She is co-author with Chris Huxham of *Managing to Collaborate: The Theory and Practice of Collaborative Advantage* (Routledge 2005).

Carole Wilkinson is Chief Executive of the Scottish Social Services Council. A registered social worker mainly practising as a child care worker, Carole was Director of Housing and Social Work in Falkirk Council before joining the Scottish Social Services Council. She was a member of the 21st Century Review of Social Work 'Changing Lives' and currently chairs the National Workforce Group.

Subject Index

Author Index